CONTEMPORARY ADOLESCENT LITERATURE AND CULTURE

Ashgate Studies in Childhood, 1700 to the Present

Series Editor: Claudia Nelson, Texas A&M University, USA

This series recognizes and supports innovative work on the child and on literature for children and adolescents that informs teaching and engages with current and emerging debates in the field. Proposals are welcome for interdisciplinary and comparative studies by humanities scholars working in a variety of fields, including literature; book history, periodicals history, and print culture and the sociology of texts; theater, film, musicology, and performance studies; history, including the history of education; gender studies; art history and visual culture; cultural studies; and religion.

Topics might include, among other possibilities, how concepts and representations of the child have changed in response to adult concerns; postcolonial and transnational perspectives; "domestic imperialism" and the acculturation of the young within and across class and ethnic lines; the commercialization of childhood and children's bodies; views of young people as consumers and/or originators of culture; the child and religious discourse; children's and adolescents' self-representations; and adults' recollections of childhood.

Also in the series

Constructing Girlhood through the Periodical Press, 1850–1915
Kristine Moruzi

The Idea of Nature in Disney Animation
From Snow White *to* WALL-E
David Whitley

Genre, Reception, and Adaptation in the "Twilight" Series
Edited by Anne Morey

The Orphan in Eighteenth-Century Law and Literature
Estate, Blood, and Body
Cheryl L. Nixon

History and the Construction of the Child in Early British Children's Literature
Jackie C. Horne

Heroism in the Harry Potter Series
Edited by Katrin Berndt and Lena Steveker

Contemporary Adolescent Literature and Culture

The Emergent Adult

Edited by

MARY HILTON
University of Cambridge, UK

and

MARIA NIKOLAJEVA
University of Cambridge, UK

ASHGATE

Published by
Ashgate Publishing Limited
Wey Court East
Union Road
Farnham
Surrey, GU9 7PT
England

Ashgate Publishing Company
Suite 420
101 Cherry Street
Burlington
VT 05401-4405
USA

www.ashgate.com

British Library Cataloguing in Publication Data
Contemporary adolescent literature and culture: the emergent adult. – (Ashgate studies in childhood, 1700 to the present)
　1. Young adult fiction, English – History and criticism. 2. Young adult fiction, American – History and criticism. 3. Teenagers in literature. 4. Adolescence in literature. I. Series II. Hilton, Mary, 1946– III. Nikolajeva, Maria.
　823.9'2099283-dc23

Library of Congress Cataloging-in-Publication Data
　Contemporary adolescent literature and culture: the emergent adult / edited by Mary Hilton and Maria Nikolajeva.
　　p. cm. — (Ashgate studies in childhood, 1700 to the present)
　Includes bibliographical references and index.
　ISBN 978-1-4094-3988-2 (hardcover: alk. paper) — ISBN 978-1-4094-3989-9 (ebook)
　1. Children's literature—History and criticism. I. Hilton, Mary, 1946– II. Nikolajeva, Maria.
　PN1009.A1C648 2012
　809'.89282—dc23

2012000958

ISBN: 9781409439882 (hbk)
ISBN: 9781409439899 (ebk)

MIX
Paper from
responsible sources
FSC
www.fsc.org
FSC® C018575

Printed and bound in Great Britain by the
MPG Books Group, UK.

Contents

Notes on Contributors

Clémentine Beauvais is a second-year doctoral student at the Faculty of Education, University of Cambridge. Her research focuses on the uses of political theory in understanding politically committed contemporary children's literature.

Nicole Brugger-Dethmers is a graduate student at Hollins University, where she is pursing a Master of Fine Arts in Children's Literature. She received her Bachelor of Arts in English from Hope College. She is the author of several short stories for both young adult and adult audiences.

Karen Coats is a Professor of English at Illinois State University, where she teaches children's and young adult literature. She is the author of *Looking Glasses and Neverlands: Lacan, Desire, and Subjectivity in Children's Literature* (2004) and co-editor (with Roderick McGillis and Anna Jackson) of *The Gothic in Children's Literature: Haunting the Borders* (2007) and (with Shelby A. Wolf, Patricia Enciso, and Christine Jenkins) *The Handbook of Research on Children's and Young Adult Literature* (2010).

Shirley Brice Heath is Margery Bailey Professor of English and Dramatic Literature and Professor of Linguistics Emerita, at Stanford University. Her research interests centre in voluntary learning by children and adolescents. She analyzes features of learning environments that foster creativity, play, linguistic development, and uses of structured symbol systems. Such environments range from children's free play and sociodramatic play to studios, rehearsal zones, and laboratories. She is the author of the classic *Ways with Words: Language, Life, and Work in Communities and Classrooms* (1983/1996) and the sequel to this volume, *Words at Work and Play: Three Decades in Family and Community Life* (2012). With Shelby A. Wolf, she co-authored *The Braid of Literature: Children's Worlds of Reading* (1992). She and Wolf have published two series of research reports: *Visual Learning in the Community School* (2004) and *Dramatic Learning in the Primary School* (2005) for Creative Partnerships, London.

Mary Hilton is a Senior Research Fellow at Homerton College Cambridge. She was previously a University Lecturer in Education at the University of Cambridge where she taught literature for children and young adults, the history of reading and popular culture, and the history of women educationalists, childhood, and schooling. She has recently written and published *Women and the Shaping of the Nation's Young: education and public doctrine in Britain 1750–1850* (2007) and, together with Christine Doddington, *Child Centred Education: Reviving the Creative Tradition* (2007). With Jill Shefrin, she has co-edited *Educating the Child in Enlightenment Britain: Beliefs, Cultures, Practices* (2009).

Georgie Horrell is a Lecturer of English Literature and International Literature at the University of Cambridge and Bye Fellow at Homerton College Cambridge. She was co-organiser of The Letters Home Festival (2003, St John's College; an international conference on South African writers in exile). She has publications and research interests in South African writing and postcolonial children's writing.

Lydia Kokkola is Professor of English and Didactics at Lulea University of Technology, Sweden. She wrote this chapter whilst she was a collegium research fellow at the Turku Institute for Advanced Studies (TIAS) at the University of Turku, Finland. She is also head of a research project *Silence as Voice: Re-empowering the Disempowered in Contemporary English Literatures*, which is financed by the Academy of Finland. Her forthcoming monograph has the working title *Silence & Sexuality: Reticent Responses to Adolescent Sexuality.*

Bettina Kümmerling-Meibauer is a Professor in the German Department at the University of Tübingen, Germany. In 2010 she held the guest professorship in memory of Astrid Lindgren at the Linnaeus University, Växjö, Sweden. She was one of the advisory editors of *The Oxford Encyclopaedia of Children's Literature.* She is author of a two-volume encyclopaedia of international children's classics (1999) and a study on canon formation in children's literature (2003), editor of *Emergent Literacy: Children's Books from 0 to 3* (2011), and co-editor (with Teresa Colomer and Cecilia Silva-Díaz) of *New Directions in Picturebook Research* (2010) and (with Astrid Surmatz) *Beyond Pippi Longstocking: Intermedial and International Aspects of Astrid Lindgren's Works* (2011).

Elia Michelle Lafuente is an educator, writer and editor who holds a Master of Fine Arts in Writing from Spalding University, a Master of Arts in Children's Literature from Hollins University and a Bachelor of Arts in Spanish from the University of Pennsylvania. She is.currently engaged in doctoral research at the George Washington University in Washington, DC. Her research interests include literature of exile and diaspora, Latino children's literature and issues in education.

Maria Nikolajeva is a Professor of Education at the University of Cambridge, previously a Professor of comparative literature at Stockholm University, Sweden, where she taught children's literature and critical theory for twenty-five years. She is the author and editor of several books, among them *Children's Literature Comes of Age: Toward the New Aesthetic* (1996), *How Picturebooks Work*, co-authored with Carole Scott (2000), *From Mythic to Linear: Time in Children's Literature* (2000), *The Rhetoric of Character in Children's Literature* (2002), *Aesthetic Approaches to Children's Literature* (2005), and *Power, Voice and Subjectivity in Literature for Young Readers* (2010). She was one of the senior editors for *The Oxford Encyclopedia of Children's Literature.*

David Whitley is a Lecturer in English at the Faculty of Education, University of Cambridge. His research interests include poetry, film, media education, and children's literature. He is the author of *The Idea of Nature in Disney Animation: from Snow White to WALL-E* (new edition 2012).

Jennifer Lynn Wolf is a lecturer at Stanford University in the School of Education and the Program in Human Biology, having previously taught English and drama in California public high schools. She examines the role of literature and the arts in learning. Her publications include *Acting, Learning & Change: Creating Original Plays with Adolescents* (with co-author Jan Mandel, 2003). Her most widely read article is "Wanting to Look a Thousand Times: Blending Visual and Textual Elements in the Contemporary Young Adult Novel," published in *A Handbook on Teaching Literacy through the Communicative and Visual Arts*.

Introduction
Time of Turmoil

Mary Hilton and Maria Nikolajeva

The terms "adolescent" and "Young Adult fiction" are both cultural constructions that share some of present day society's most painful anxieties and contradictions. Real teenagers are all around us in the everyday world. As society's adolescents, they often present a focus for adult anxiety: lolling in front of televisions, behaving rowdily in public places, sulking in bedrooms, challenging parental and educational authority, appearing difficult, recalcitrant, contradictory, alienated, and troublesome. Fictional young adults likewise are just as often configured by their adult authors as awkward, rebellious, unhappy, presenting loci of suffering, injustice, of unfulfilled longings and deviant sexualities. Both constructions resonate with each other in ways that have succeeded in opening up a powerful literary genre. Young Adult literature and culture, articulating a profound instability and inexperienced sexuality in the emergent adult, targets adolescent readers and consumers, and in doing so evokes a powerful metaphor that this book sets out to explore. Through sympathetically portraying the alienated pains and pleasures of adolescence, through *enacting* adolescence with all its turmoil, writers bring young readers face to face with different forms of cultural alienation itself: the legacy of colonialism, political injustice, environmental desecration, sexual stereotyping, consumerism, madness, and death. As Roberta Trites argues,

> Twenty-first century critics take it as a given that novels for youth often rely on adolescents' growth and imply hope in the future. What we often fail to recognize, however, is how frequently these texts create a parallel between the individual's need to grow and the society's need to improve itself. In focusing on the growth of an individual character, we often miss the metaphorical use to which the individual's growth has been put.[1]

When did adolescence, and then Young Adult fiction, metaphorically linking political and emotional instability to social critique, first come into being? Scholars accept that the psychologist and educationalist Stanley Hall first used the term "adolescence" to describe a separate state of being in his classic work of

---

[1]   Trites, Roberta Seelinger. *Twain, Alcott, and the Birth of the Adolescent Reform Novel*. Iowa City: University of Iowa Press, 2007, 144.

that name of 1904.[2] Although many people were deeply aware of the problems of "youth" throughout the Victorian period, both in Britain and America, it was Hall who yoked the fashionable psychology of normative development to distinguish a separate age between the onset of puberty and mature adulthood. In two weighty volumes Hall set out to describe many aspects of the "physical growth and the mental and moral perversions incident to adolescence," covering "normal genetic psychology, beginning with sensation and proceeding to feelings, will, and intellect."[3] Hall, then, constructed the now taken-for-granted disjuncture between child and adolescent upon which recent writers and artists have elaborated so poignantly, harnessing the emergent adult's apparent insecurities to multiple societal and political anxieties, thereby creating new moral perspectives. Clearly, as Kent Baxter points out, after Hall, adolescence became defined as a process, in contrast to the static concept of "boy" or "girl," a path by which the child becomes an adult. This was not always liberating. In fact, Baxter argues, "the history of the discursive category of adolescence has been a self-perpetuating and never-ending dance between the 'real' and the 'ideal' adolescent, where the constructed image of one has served as cultural repression of the other."[4]

Yet the construction of adolescence in psychology as a time of internal turmoil, of storm and stress, at the turn of the twentieth century did not immediately result in its representation in fiction for the young. The sentimental tradition of writing about children for children simply stretched to include the teenage years. When we turn to the late nineteenth and early twentieth century, realist children's classics of the Anglo-American canon – *Little Women* (1868), *What Katy Did* (1872), *Rebecca of Sunnybrook Farm* (1903), *Anne of Green Gables* (1908), *Daddy Long Legs* (1912)[5], and in Britain *Treasure Island* (1883), *Kim* (1901), *The Railway Children* (1906) – we find a clear sense of integration between child and emerging adult. These pre First World War fictional children grew up and developed into young adults in poignant, yet inevitable and integrated stages of growth and change.

Little Women by its very title suggests that all-important delicate fusion of child into adult. Here, in America's foremost work for children, the sentimental tradition in children's literature is consolidated through aspects of Utopia with its isolated setting allowing for an autonomous, mono-gender micro-society, its absence of serious threat, and a general sense of security, happiness, and harmony. Alcott presents a powerful sentimental ideology of the family as the idyllic locus of peaceful adolescent growth, the novels based on the contrast between "home,

---

[2]   Hall, Granville Stanley. *Adolescence: Its Psychology and its Relations to Physiology, Anthropology, Sociology, Sex, Crime, Religion and Education.* 2 vols. New York: Appleton, 1904.

[3]   Hall, *Adolescence*, vol. 2, 1.

[4]   Baxter, Kent. *The Modern Age: Turn-of-the-century American Culture and the Invention of Adolescence.* Tuscaloosa: The University of Alabama Press, 2008, 13.

[5]   See Griswold, Jerry. *The Classic American Children's Story. Novels of the Golden Age.* New York: Penguin, 1996.

sweet home" and the cruel outside world. Charles Strickland argues that in Alcott's world, "good parents ... seek to protect the innocence of children by shielding them from exposure to the world and its ways, for if children are not precisely saintly, nevertheless they are vulnerable."[6] In this way, Alcott fulfilled the Utopian ideas of her father within her own writing by accentuating the strong family bonds and loyalty between women.[7] Although this domestic Utopia is destroyed, first by death, which claims Beth, and then by Laurie, who "proves to be the insidious if charming serpent in the March Garden of Eden,"[8] this does not happen until later volumes. The first book is a perfect picture of harmony and idyll of home and family, the very essence of the integrated emergence of adulthood from innocent childhood. As Victor Watson writes,

> It is clear, in the story of the March family, that adult life involves the putting away of childish pleasure and a growing awareness of the seriousness and sadness of human experience. But, in spite of the skill with which Alcott suggests this sober progression, the novels do not engage seriously with the changes and challenges of maturation.[9]

In a similar vein, the young adult Anne of Green Gables might feel she has been "pruned" as she acknowledges maturity, but the taming of her childish wildness is an acceptable and integrated part of the story of her journey to adulthood.

The inherent tensions within the sentimental idea of an integrated transition from childhood to adulthood are strikingly articulated, however, in the highly controversial Great American Novel, *Adventures of Huckleberry Finn* (1884), seemingly at first a mere sequel to *The Adventures of Tom Sawyer* (1876), the epitome of carefree childhood. It has perhaps functioned as a sequel in children's reading; yet Huckleberry Finn's quest should rightfully be titled Trials rather than Adventures. Mark Twain sets the parameters of the pseudo-sequel in the much quoted "Conclusion" of *Tom Sawyer*: "So endeth this chronicle. It being strictly a history of a boy, it must stop here; the story could not go much further without becoming the history of a man."[10] *Huckleberry Finn* is arguably the history of a man.

Huck's initial situation, as compared to Tom's, is of lower social status, but greater freedom. When, in the end of *Tom Sawyer*, Huck finds refuge in Widow

---

[6]   Strickland, Charles. *Victorian Domesticity. Families in the Life and Art of Louisa May Alcott*. Tuscaloosa, : University of Alabama Press, 1985, 135.

[7]   See Auerbach, Nina. *Communities of Women: An Idea in Fiction*. Cambridge, Mass.: Harvard University Press, 1978.

[8]   Strickland, *Victorian Domesticity*, 146.

[9]   Meek, Margaret, and Watson, Victor. *Coming of Age in Children's Literature; Growth and Maturity in the Work of Philippa Pearce, Cynthia Voigt and Jan Mark*. London: Continuum, 2003, 10.

[10]   Twain, Mark. *The Adventures of Tom Sawyer* (1876). Harmondsworth: Penguin, 1985, 221.

Douglas's home, he regards it as a prison, because by this time he is ready to go further, as he will in his own book. While Judge Thatcher has great visions for Tom as a lawyer or a military officer, Huck views his riches as a burden and escapes. Although he succumbs to Tom's arguments for a while, he will soon start on a new journey. Tom capitulates and lets himself be socialized; Huck does not. A conflict between "sivilization" and freedom is the eternal theme of children's fiction, but in *Huckleberry Finn* it is resolved in a new and different way. Although the novel has a sort of a "happy ending," it also suggests an aperture, because Huck is not going to stay with Aunt Sally and be "sivilized" once again. Huck has gained his passage into the adult world. Hence *Huckleberry Finn* is perhaps the first Western novel of adolescence in its intensive search for identity. It also introduces one of the most prominent formal traits of the future genre, first person narration, today a repeating convention in Young Adult novels.

Yet despite the new psychological configuration of adolescence as a separate part of human existence, troubled and troubling, the Great War and then the Depression resulted in a continuing absence of adolescent subjectivity in literature for British young people. While in America there was a small efflorescence of the "coming of age" narratives, books such as Sherwood Anderson's *Winesburg Ohio* (1919), Ernest Hemingway's Nick Adams stories, and Katherine Anne Porter's Miranda stories, in Britain real teenagers continued to be offered pre-war children's fiction: domestic stories, school and adventure stories. They continued to immerse themselves in imperial adventure where boyhood and manhood were conflated in stories based on the romance quest in hostile territory. Girls, including adolescent girls, were served school stories, such as those of Angela Brazil and heroic tales of famous brave young women in the story papers such as *The Girl's Own Paper*. In none of this fiction do the teenage characters have inner lives of significant depth and affect. In America, teenage readers were offered more than a thousand novels in different series published by Edward Stratemeyer, which included *The Bobbsey Twins* (1904–), *Tom Swift* (1910–), *The Hardy Boys* (1928–), and *Nancy Drew* (1930–), all with a common moralizing thematic focus on hard work and enterprise. Yet here also, adolescent interiority is largely absent. As Kent Baxter argues, each of the teenaged characters in these books is "taken outside of any real developmental framework, and is, for all intents and purposes, turned into an adult."[11]

Why did teenage subjectivity get left out of inter-war literature for the young? In relating the political structures of the inter-war period in Britain to the literature of trauma and cultural memory, new scholarship offers a more nuanced account of the crucial connection between structures of feeling and political culture. In a number of recent scholarly works, the emotional and mental consequences of unbearable war-related experiences, enormous loss of life, and devastating grief for many Britons, attested to in diaries and letters throughout the war and beyond, was connected to the widespread appeal of conservative politics after the Great

---

[11]   Baxter, *The Modern Age*, 141.

War.[12] New understandings of the ways the shattering of many families by grief, and the death and disability of so many young men, led to an extended period of shock and trauma throughout the twenties and thirties. During these troubled decades, popular writing and film became important signifiers of public mood and escapist need. The Northcliffe press, the cheap edition, and the film had established themselves before 1914, but the twenties saw in their mutation into the mass circulation daily, the best-selling novel, and the popular film.[13] Romance fiction expanded exponentially, and countless magazines published stories, many by women, which had happy endings – often a precondition of publication. In the 1920s and 1930s the British reading public, conservative and in deep grief, was certainly not in a position to accept a radical literature of teenage angst.[14]

Only slowly, throughout the twenties and thirties, did even adult writing in Britain begin to encompass existential alienation after the most horrendous war of its history. In a range of unsentimental writing from T.S. Eliot's *The Wasteland* of 1922 to Evelyn Waugh's *A Handful of Dust* of 1934, a new young generation of writers began to depict the moral and spiritual crises of that disinherited era. Nevertheless, although it was during the inter-war period that the term "adolescence" became widely used in education and therapy, providing a new generation of psychologists a clear sense of disjunction between the innocent child and the sexualised, hormonal semi-adult, this was not reflected in literature for the young. The childlike innocence of pre-war middle-class England, a time that now seemed golden and stable for several significant writers for children, made it impossible for them to articulate for young readers the more anxious, frightening, dreary grown-up world of the post-war aftermath. While the young "flapper" generation engaged in new mindless pleasures in Britain and America, literature for the young remained sacrosanct and relentlessly cheerful. Here the lovable Christopher Robin, Just William, and Billy Bunter amused children alongside such comfortable adult figures as Mary Poppins, Biggles, and Dr Dolittle, all happy characters totally devoid of angst or development that looked neither backwards nor inwards, provided a bulwark against national memory. As Victor Watson observes, "One consequence of the Great War was that for more than half

---

[12]   See, for example, Kingsley Kent, Susan. *Aftershocks: Politics and Trauma in Britain, 1918–1914*. Basingstoke: Palgrave Macmillan, 2009. Conservatives, albeit part of a coalition, were in office for the entire interwar period except for nine months in 1924 and for two and a half years from 1929 to 1931. For an overview of this period, see Pugh, Martin. *We Danced All Night: A Social History of Britain Between the Wars*. London: Vintage Books, 2009; McKibbin, Ross. *Classes and Cultures: England 1918–1951*. Oxford: Oxford University Press, 1998.

[13]   Melman, Billie. *Women and the Popular Imagination in the Twenties: Flappers and Nymphs*. Basingstoke: Macmillan, 1988.

[14]   Hunt, Peter. *Children's Literature*. Oxford: Blackwell, 2001, 195. Hunt describes the period 1914–45 as characterised by "retreatism" – that is, retreat from war, social and intellectual change, and the threat of war.

a century, writers of children's books set their hearts against maturation."[15] Despite the increase in psychological and educational literature about adolescence, and an increasing sense of crisis around the political and social behaviour of "youth," the fictional teenager remained an ambiguous figure, either undeveloped in the American publisher Stratemeyer's two-dimensional fictions or embalmed within British children's outdoor adventure stories. These older children were quite grown up in practical terms: able to set up camp, catch villains, swim, hike, to reef and sail, but like Arthur Ransome's characters, and later Enid Blyton's, always uniting this practical understanding with childlike innocence, total asexuality, and an athletic devotion to the outdoor adventure cum mystery quest.[16] In Britain and America, in inter-war fiction for child and teenage readers adolescent subjectivity was notable only by a silence.

It was the Second World War that forced the change. Writers who had survived the war as children and young adults themselves began to reject the sentimental tradition and the invisibility of teenage interiority in twentieth-century literature for the young. The publication of the real and poignant diary of Anne Frank opened a genuine autobiographical space where the different experiences of blitz, evacuation, and in her case hiding, betrayal, separation, and death, could be articulated within a new, more cynical, young adult sensibility. Nina Bawden, Robert Westall, David Rees, and Jane Gardam in Britain began to produce semi-autobiographical stories for children set in war time while two or three of the few surviving Jewish writers such as Esther Hautzig and Johanna Reiss wrote for young people of their horrific experiences as children in Hitler's war. Despite the remaining sentimental contours of much of children's literature, the harsh realities of these war-time stories began to problematise the inner lives of their older characters, and existential ideology, valorised in such texts as the *The Dolphin Crossing* (1967) and *Fireweed* (1970) by Jill Paton Walsh, began to permeate British writing for the young.

Sociological factors structured new understandings. Despite its absence in children's literature in the inter-war period, in America and Britain the psychological construction of adolescence had been increasingly elaborated within their school systems. In Britain, with Butler's 1944 Education Act bringing secondary education for all, after World War II the period of youth became extended and enshrined in law. In both countries from 1945 the term "teenager"

---

[15]   Meek and Watson, *Coming of Age in Children's Literature*, 25.

[16]   Meek and Watson, *Coming of Age in Children's Literature*. As Watson writes: "The innumerable series of school stories, camping and tramping stories, career stories, one-off adventure stories and fantasies that were produced with such amazing abundance had little to say about maturation ... it was taken for granted throughout the 1920s, 1930s and until some time after World War II that children's books should be predominantly about play" (25–26).

became widely used within the realm of consumption.[17] Post-war prosperity from the early 1950s led to a rise in young people's consumption of goods, and the media – firstly radio, then television and eventually the home video – exended the range of style and self-fashioning possibilities. It was in the context of these new freedoms for youth that J.D. Salinger's *The Catcher in the Rye*, of 1951, founded the Young Adult canon, re-invoking the old relationship of Mark Twain's Huckleberry to "sivilisation," between the subversive adolescent and a critique of wider society, and dazzlingly provided the genre with new psychological depth. As Roberta Trites has pointed out, the adolescent reform novel of the late nineteenth century had contained protagonists, ethical characters who transcend their society by some form of self reliance, providing a hope for society's future change.[18] Now, in Salinger's powerful invocation of this relationship in the Second World War aftermath, the adolescent protagonist appears as vulnerable to breakdown and inner conflict as society itself.

The Catcher in the Rye portrays a young person in a marginal situation, socially and psychologically. Holden Caulfield's childhood is over, and adulthood is looming, an unknown territory with its attractions and anxieties. He looks back at his childhood as a carefree idyll, while he is at the same time curious about the strange, previously forbidden adult life, which he often perceives as threatening. Holden watches with excitement and sorrow his younger sister riding the merry-go-round, while he himself stands aside knowing that he has become too old to participate in the joys of childhood. Yet he is not ready to take the step into adulthood, to start a sexual relationship, or to adjust to the demands of adult society. The adult temptations, typically depicted as alcohol and sex, both attract and disgust. Holden's adored dead brother becomes a powerful symbol of the happiness of not having to grow up. The cruel insight about the inevitability of adulthood leads Holden to a nervous collapse. The open ending of the novel does not give the reader any guidance to the question of whether Holden is now ready for initiation: his time of trials has just started. However, he has definitely stepped off from the circular merry-go-round of childhood into the inexorable linear pathway to adulthood.[19] Hence *The Catcher in the Rye* established in literature for and about the young adult the powerful metaphorical connection between a troubled

---

[17]   Savage, Jon. *Teenage: The Creation of Youth Culture*. London: Chatto and Windus, 2007.

[18]   Trites, *Twain, Alcott, and the Birth of the Adolescent Reform Novel*. Trites argues that Twain and Alcott's novels for youth solidified a reforming genre that became a literary legacy in the United States. "Both authors relied on adolescents as metaphors for reform; that is, for both of them, the young represented the capacity for change that is necessary for a culture itself to change" (xiv).

[19]   See Nikolajeva, Maria. *From Mythic to Linear: Time in Children's Literature*. Lanham, Md.: Scarecrow, 2000. This study argues that while children's literature presents time as circular and reversible, Young Adult novel takes the protagonist out of the circle into a linear movement toward adulthood, ageing and death. Sexuality is an important part of this movement.

inner life of the adolescent and the injustices and cruelties of wider society. Since then this idea has been taken up and developed by a host of writers of Young Adult fiction, Robert Cormier, S.E. Hinton, Aidan Chambers, Katherine Paterson, John Marsden, Cynthia Voigt, Margaret Mahy, David Almond, Philip Pullman, Meg Rosoff, and Siobhan Dowd, to name a few.

Yet, despite its history as a lively post-war literary trend, and its profound relationship to studies of adolescence, Young Adult literature has as yet generated far less critical scholarship than studies of children's literature, and in general surveys, little if any attention is paid to its specific traits, although both genres share some major concerns. With few exceptions, as in all literature for children, Young Adult novels are written by adults, which means that they are in fact not about what it is to be an adolescent but are about what it might or should be, since, perhaps unconsciously, adults want to instruct young people and guide them into adulthood. Here in fiction, representations of adolescence are images of what adults want teenagers to believe about themselves and their lives.[20] Hence it is a very powerful ideological tool, although it is only recently that the critical eye has begun to turn to it.

Some key early works in the critical field emerged in Europe, the chief source of inspiration being a study by the Yugoslav scholar Aleksander Flaker, *Models of Jeans Prose.*[21] The subject of Flaker's investigation was the East German writer Ulrich Plenzdorf's *The New Sufferings of Young W.* (1972), a novel showing close affinity with *The Catcher in the Rye* and in many ways setting a pattern for Young Adult fiction in Europe.[22] The concept of "jeans prose" was quickly adopted by German and Scandinavian criticism, appearing in quite a number of essays and full-length studies devoted to the phenomenon. Departing from Flaker's definitions, scholars identified as the most prominent features of Young Adult fiction the young protagonists' alienation from society and their pronounced search for identity, emphasized by a dress code. Another impact came from Julia Kristeva's insightful essay "The Adolescent Novel," focusing on Carson McCullers's *The Member of the Wedding* (1946) and emphasizing specifically female adolescent experience.[23] Since then a range of British and American scholars have begun to address the complexities of Young Adult fiction.[24]

---

[20] See Nikolajeva, Maria. *Power, Voice and Subjectivity in Literature for Young Readers.* New York: Routledge, 2010.

[21] Flaker, Aleksander. *Modelle der Jeans Prosa.* Kronberg: Scriptor, 1975.

[22] See Hornigk, Therese, and Alexander Stephan, eds. *The New Sufferings of Young W. and Other Stories from the German Democratic Republic.* New York: Continuum, 1997.

[23] Kristeva, Julia. "The Adolescent Novel. In her *Abjection, Melancholia and Love,* 8–23. London: Routledge, 1990.

[24] The first edition of Alleen Pace Nilsen and Kenneth L. Donelson's comprehensive overview *Literature for Today's Young Adults* was published as early as 1980. In addition to works referred to elsewhere in this Introduction, there are some historical surveys, such as Michael Cart's *From Romance to Realism. 50 Years of Growth and Change in Young Adult Literature* (1996); there are books on ideological aspects of the genre, such as Robyn

In this book we stake out some critical territory in this rapidly expanding field through exploring aspects of the powerful metaphor that has been set up around young adult experience. If Young Adult literature and culture can link society's turbulence, its most pressing and disturbing issues, with the adolescent's quest for identity in coming of age, then we consider it crucial to uncover the ways it carries through this purpose and to ask to what extent it erects new structures of feeling for its readers and critics. This volume brings together a variety of critical perspectives that address these central questions. Moving from concerns with the environment, to political and social unrest, to issues to do with identity construction and the body, and finally framing the instability of the adolescent mind, it examines in depth the ideological and emotional contours of different works designed for the teenage reader.

Studies of the Young Adult novel have frequently pointed to its characteristic spatio-temporal construction, the combination of short duration (Holden Caulfield's three eventful days in New York, Frankie's long and lonely day) and urban setting. The compressed time of Young Adult fiction, so radically different both from the cyclical movement in *Little Women* and linear, goal-oriented trajectory in *Huckleberry Finn*, accentuates the depiction of the adolescent protagonist in a moment of crisis. Although recent Young Adult fiction is has incorporated a new rich variety of other places and worlds, many of the founding texts were deliberately located far away from the traditional idyllic countryside of so much children's literature, using the realism of city streets to symbolize the threats and temptations of adult life. The urban realism of contemporary young adult literature was, till very recently, its most distinguishing characteristic.

In the opening chapter, David Whitley turns to this crucial critical idea, that Young Adult fiction has formally decoupled for all time adolescent subjectivity from the natural world. At first it seems that wrenched away from any sustaining imagery of nature or identification with it, the adolescent protagonists of much Young Adult fiction are doubly disinherited: from society and, in a godless world, from nature, that other source of consolation that nourishes the child in so much classic children's literature. Yet, as Whitley argues, this hypothesis is too sweeping to stand investigation. He points to the complex ways recent Young Adult fiction in fact re-engages with the natural world through transforming different archetypal narratives of children's literature. In the twenty-first century there is

McCallum's *Ideologies of Identity in Adolescent Fiction: The Dialogic Construction of Subjectivity* (1999), and there are books written from a gender perspective, such as Hilary Crew's *Is it Really "Mommie Dearest"? Daughter-Mother Narratives in Young Adult Fiction* (2000). There is a large number of books on specific genres, especially popular genres (crime, science fiction, romance), among the most recent being Alison Waller's *Constructing Adolescence in Fantastic Realism* (2009) and Amy S. Pattee, *Reading the Adolescent Romance: Sweet Valley and the Popular Young Adult Romance Novel* (2011). The phenomenon of crossover, books marketed for and read by multiple audiences, has been examined, for instance in Rachel Falconer's *The Crossover Novel* (2009). Many specific Young Adult authors have been subjects for book-length studies.

a new poignancy to the discursive category of nature. The adolescent's troubled journey to adulthood is now coloured by the urgency around ever-increasing life-threatening environmental desecration. The relationship between the "natural" and the "socially constructed" moves to a central position where often the adolescent protagonists carry the burden of renewal and hope from a position of subordination and powerlessness.

It is only very recently that some more profound issues of Young Adult fiction have been investigated, as scholars have been able to draw on feminist, psychoanalytical, and post-structural theories, particularly to consider the ways the genre opens up issues of power and repression.[25] If the early studies mainly investigated the adolescent position toward society, in the more recent works the painful process of liberation from and reconciliation with parental authority has come firmly into the foreground.[26] Further, the examination of the formal aspects of the adolescent novel has found inspiration in contemporary narrative theory, moving on from simple statement about the predominance of first-person perspective to in-depth analysis of the construction of subjectivity, where the discrepancy between the experience of the adult author and the young narrator-protagonist presents the foremost challenge.[27]

It is often questioned, especially by feminist, postcolonial, and queer theorists, whether male writers can successfully depict the internal life of female characters, white writers of black characters, or heterosexual writers of homosexual characters, a scepticism based on the unequal power positions, in which the "empowered" writer has only a limited capacity to understand the mentality of the "oppressed" protagonists and readers. Yet a general consensus about adolescent literature has existed that holds that adult writers can easily penetrate a young character's mind, while logically and sceptically for the above reasons it should be infinitely more difficult than to enter the mind of another adult. Even though all adult writers have been young once, the profound difference in life experience, as well as in linguistic skills, creates an inevitable discrepancy between the (adult) narrative voice and both the focalized young character's and the implied young reader's levels of comprehension. The infamous "double address," where the adult author talks to the adult co-reader over the young reader's head,[28] although primarily referring to

---

[25]   Trites, Roberta Seelinger. *Disturbing the Universe: Power and Repression in Adolescent Literature.* Iowa City: University of Iowa Press, 2000. Complemented by Trites's *Twain, Alcott, and the Birth of the Adolescent Reform Novel*, this is a key study from the point of view of theorising characteristic features of Young Adult fiction.

[26]   See also Crew, *Is it Really "Mommie Dearest"*; Coats, Karen. *Looking Glasses and Neverlands. Lacan, Desire, and Subjectivity in Children's Literature.* Iowa City: Iowa University Press, 2004.

[27]   See McCallum, *Ideologies of Identity*; Wilkie-Stibbs, Christine. *The Feminine Subject in Children's Literature.* New York: Routledge, 2002; Nikolajeva, *Power, Voice and Subjectivity*.

[28]   Wall, Barbara. *The Narrator's Voice: The Dilemma of Children's Fiction.* London: Macmillan, 1992.

the implied audience rather than the textual perspective, nevertheless conveys the essence of the dilemma. Cognitive theories of memory confirm that our long-term memories are fragmentary and unreliable. The adult writers of adolescent fiction who claim that they remember exactly "how it felt to be a teenager" in fact do not hold authentic memories, but articulate an imaginative reconstruction of the past based on their subsequent life experience. This reconstruction can further be affected by the author's ideological, educational, or aesthetic project.[29]

How then do writers represent "adolescence" in ways that seem and feel authentic? Two important foci for authorial projects in relation to young adult writing are the portrayal of the adolescent's struggle for fully adult capability and identity in areas that do in fact mark the teenager off from the child: in firstly *political* and in secondly *sexual* agency and awareness. Often those two real properties of maturation – growing political awareness/agency, a consciousness that is usually born within and then shaped by injustice – is intertwined with sexual coming-of-age. If Anne Frank's diary provided an archetype of the young female protagonist secretly turning into an adult while the horror of an adult's war was played out around her, since then, puberty and adolescence have provided the opportunity for many writers to map the interior turmoil of the newly aware teenager onto the essences of political conflict and injustice in their environing contexts. Elia Michelle Lafuente explores the quality of hope and the sadness of memory in contemporary Caribbean-American fiction for those teenagers who did manage to escape the cruel dictatorships of Dominican Republic and Haiti. Despite their escape, an identity struggle, unresolved and "bicultural," continues to haunt these dislocated and disinherited young adults.

In the next chapter, Georgie Horrell maps the painful transition of adolescence onto the intensity of transition of power and knowledge, this time in "New South Africa." She shows the ways that the coming-of-age narrative archetype is used in two key Young Adult books to map sexual awakening onto political awakening and hence to postcolonial awareness. Horrell reminds us that postcolonial existence is itself analogous to adolescence. If children are viewed colonial subjects, then adolescence is a time of political emergence, coming to more equal terms with adult colonizers. Hence again, written by "oppressors," the postcolonial project can be flawed. Horrell questions whether, despite the transgressive sexual and political practices of the young white protagonists in the two key texts she discusses – love across race and politics – they are in fact constructed at the expense of the black characters, who remain childlike and partially invisible. This means that the lessons enacted for young readers still retain residual racism, exposing the patterns of thought that underlay apartheid.

Clémentine Beauvais also uses postcolonial critical construction, in this case Homi Bhabha's concept of "hybridity," to explore notions of power and contestation in Young Adult fiction. Taking Malorie Blackman's *Noughts and Crosses* (2001–

---

[29]   Cf. Nalbantian, Suzanne. *Memory in Literature from Rousseau to Neuroscience.* Basingstoke: Palgrave Macmillan, 2003.

05) series and Stephenie Meyer's *Twilight* series (2005–08), she shows that the sagas share similarities in their representation of trans-racial (or trans-species) relationships, accidental pregnancy, and the motif of the hybrid child. The hybrid child, Beauvais argues, is not solely a new character but an ideological response to the divided socio-political configurations of the young adult characters' worlds. In both cases, the child's birth is presented as an opportunity for counter-power. In the dystopian or unsatisfactory universes of the sagas, trans-racial parenting is a political act for the teenage heroes. However, Blackman and Meyer differ in their treatments of the hybrid child's power to reconcile the opposite forces of the worlds they describe. These authorial decisions define the very different ideological orientations of their works. The protagonists of *Noughts and Crosses* are on the very edge of adulthood, and by the end of the novel they have encountered the two most profound and interconnected experiences of life, procreation, and death. Roberta Trites identifies death and sexuality as distinctive issues in Young Adult fiction.[30] When the protagonists have been introduced to these aspects, childhood is over, and there is no way back to Arcadia. It is this period of uncertainly, anxiety, and pain that the foremost Young Adult novelists depict.

If political instability in the search for identity can be mapped onto the processes of adolescent maturation, then sexual awakening and hormonal turmoil is also a marker of the disjunction between child and adolescent. For most young people, the quest for fully adult identity becomes, in the first place, an attempt to discover and accept their sexuality. Cross-dressing, examined by Nicole Brugger-Dethmers in this volume, is one way of testing sexuality, of literally trying on different gendered attires and performing – a notion borrowed from Judith Butler[31] – sexuality in a safe mode. Performativity is also a way of dealing with power hierarchies. This chapter expands on Butler's work on gender performativity to propose that identity is similarly constructed in Young Adult literature and to argue that performativity extends beyond gender to include age, class, race, and ethnicity. Brugger-Dethmers explores the ways the act of transgressing traditional, acceptable, and/or "given" roles, allows adolescent protagonists to investigate unfamiliar and perhaps taboo experiences, and the knowledge and understanding derived from the experience helps him or her along the path of self-discovery.

For the character of *Push* (1996), the focus of Lydia Kokkola's chapter, sexuality is something forced upon her. Unlike Sephy's and Callum's baby in the sequel to *Noughts and Crosses*, who is supposed to symbolise hope, the triumph of love, and the continuation of life (even though this idea can be contested), Precious' baby is the result of violation of her body. The sexually abused

---

[30]   Trites, *Disturbing the Universe.* See also Nikolajeva, *From Mythic to Linear.* It is symptomatic that two scholars have independently and simultaneously emphasised these dimensions of Young Adult fiction. See further James, Kathryn. *Death, Gender and Sexuality in Adolescent Literature.* New York: Routledge, 2009.

[31]   Butler, Judith. *Gender Trouble: Feminism and the Subversion of Identity.* 2nd ed. New York: Routledge, 1999.

adolescent body is quintessentially abject. Where voluntary sexual activity is often troped in literature as marking the end of childhood and entry into adulthood, the involuntary sexuality of father-daughter incest places the victim outside the semiotic order. She is no longer a child, yet she is also not an adult. More monstrous than human, the sexually abused adolescent body fills its perceiver with horror, and yet it is endlessly fascinating. Incest is a source of such shame that it is perhaps the greatest of all sexual secrets. And precisely because it is such a closely guarded secret, even amongst adults, it fascinates us even whilst we are disgusted by it. This chapter examines the ways in which *Push* by Sapphire represents the body of an incestuously abused adolescent body. The novel also shows how an adolescent's race, body size, and pregnancy can be perceived as monstrous. By probing the characteristics of the horror Precious's body incites, the chapter aims to expose the power play behind such representations, and show how politically motivated writers like Sapphire may work within the tradition to expose the mind set which supports the maintenance of these views.

Bella's baby in the *Twilight* series is crossbred of human and inhuman. A fictional adolescent's sexuality is always problematic – can it once again be a matter of adult authors' concerns, perhaps even a warning? Young female characters' negative perception of their changing bodies, described in scholarship as abjection, is a distinctive feature of the adolescence novel.[32] The changes in the growing body are much more prominent in literature featuring female characters, presumably because conventional male heroes are too busy with adventures to bother about bodily changes. Female characters, looking inward, perceive the changes in their bodies with fear and anxiety. Here the original adoration of a child body in Romanticism, the image of the child as a-sexual, stems from its difference, different from the corrupt adult body, connected with sexuality and procreation. Now as change occurs, a huge contradiction for the teenager is opened up. The adult body becomes the norm in society, and the child body is re-configured as a deviation, a monster, a grotesque body, an Other body, undeveloped, unfinished, lacking substantial attributes of a mature body, including, but not limited to, its reproductive organs. The multi-layering of these contradictions means that adolescence implies a transition from deviation to norm, yet through still more grotesque states. Cross-dressing may in fact be a strategy to conceal abjection.

Yet if the adolescent body is portrayed as pressured, problematic, often out of control, still more so the adolescent mind. Here the latest findings of neuroscience, the brain imaging of blood flows, shows fascinating concordance with literary intuition. The imaginative representation of the turmoil of the teenage mind, which has grown up alongside its detailed construction in the field of psychology, now seems to be verified by hard experimental evidence. Might this be because, as some scholars suggest, neuroscience itself being socially constructed, it offers

---

[32]   The concept of abjection was introduced into literary and cultural studies in Julia Kristeva's *Powers of Horror: An Essay on Abjection.* New York: Columbia University Press, 1982.

simply another layer of description? Nevertheless, what literature and science seem to agree about is the overall plasticity of the still developing, transitional nature of the adolescent brain. We have seen how writers of Young Adult fiction deploy a felt instability and turbulence of adolescence; recently neuroscience has confirmed a spurt of brain growth at puberty, accompanied by a surge of hormonal expansion and activity.

Karen Coats in this volume approaches this issue from a Lacanian perspective, as she has done before, but expands her field of attention to the recent brain research.[33] Considering brain research and the radical pedagogy of Mark Bracher, Coats argues that whereas in literary criticism it is a commonplace to associate agency nearly exclusively with voice as linguistic competence, most teenagers are in fact more invested in the emotional and perceptual aspects of their identity. She points out that we have tended to neglect the significance of music in adolescent lives and literature. Coats argues that teenagers use music more than any other language or cognition-related activity to regulate and alter their moods, establish and consolidate both core and tribal identities, celebrate the joys of embodiment, sublimate aggressive sexual or violent feelings, mourn relational losses, generate courage for new endeavours, affirm their values and beliefs, and worship their gods. Recent brain research reveals that heightened emotional responses are a result of the particular stages of adolescent brain development. Successful emergence into adulthood is not a singularly cognitive achievement; it requires mature emotional development and a strong sense of attunement to one's embodiment. Attention to the role of music in brain development and identity formation through teen literature can help us strengthen our understanding of what might make that process successful.

Given its high degree of instability, the intuitive imaginative possibilities open to writers who seek to get inside the adolescent mind can extend its framework beyond the range of normality. William Faulkner is frequently given the credit of penetrating the interior world of a mentally disturbed person in *The Sound and the Fury* (1929), as well as John Steinbeck in *Of Mice and Men* (1937). The adolescent novel repeats these literary achievements constantly and consistently and indeed the framing of young adult inner tumult allows within the genre exploration of mental states beyond most authors' experience. Bettina Kümmerling-Meibauer argues that recent research in cognitive psychology and neurobiology moves forward the understanding of the psychological and emotional development of teenagers. The discovery of the mirror neurons by the Italian neuroscientists Giacomo Rizzolatti and Leonardo Fogassi in 2003 is regarded as a milestone in the investigation of human emotions. In this regard, the concept of empathy plays a significant role, since it influences the multi-levelled acquisition of emotional competence. On the basis of these theoretical issues, Kümmerling-Meibauer's chapter discusses how emotions are presented in three young adult novels in which the protagonists present extreme forms of mental deviance from normal competence.

---

[33]   Coats, *Looking Glasses and Neverlands*.

Although this book is primarily concerned with social realism, it would, however, be wrong to claim, as is sometimes done, that Young Adult fiction is always firmly anchored in the here and now. Moving beyond the argument and scope of this book to the historical novel, fantasy, dystopia, and horror for teenagers, each in its own ways offers excellent possibilities for creating situations in which young people's dilemmas can be represented and tested.[34] There is perhaps reason to contemplate whether adolescent fiction is a homogeneous genre or whether it encompasses a variety of genres, as does children's fiction. Nevertheless, although the texts discussed in this volume represent a wide range of genres and modes, and a wider register of themes, they all have something in common. They all offer young people situations, including extreme situations – political injustice, premature sexuality, drugs, suicide, self-harm – which they, in most cases, fortunately will not be exposed to in real life. In the hands of inspired writers, vicarious experience can prove sufficiently strong to grip young readers without exposing them to actual dangers. At the same time, through its profundity and relevance, Young Adult literature can help teenagers to think about, and hopefully to transcend, the rigid and dysfunctional structures of popular culture, stereotyping, oppression, and injustice.

In the final chapter, Shirley Brice Heath and Jennifer Wolf focus on teenage readers themselves. They argue that those who study these Young Adult readers benefit from reading in tandem the findings from cognitive neuroscience and anthropological studies of teenage readers in their everyday lives. Biological changes during adolescence bring about behavioural changes that show up in neuroscientific studies. As teenagers move through periods in which they are often lonely and feel the need to assert their independence, and seek social affirmation from peers, they intensify the social foundational nature of learning management and interpretation of complex symbol systems. These authors argue that adolescents often find in Young Adult novels an interactive, responsive, "listening" audience to which they feel they can and should respond. In this context, the authors argue that adolescents in their behavioural interactions with Young Adult literature put their neuronal capacity for *envisionment* and *embodiment* into play. Here the changing conventions of Young Adult texts draw readers in as the publishing industry responds to how, when, and what their readers want. Of primary importance to adolescent readers is the ability to form social relationships through participating with the characters, plot, and strategies of texts. Heath and Wolf lay out the features of Young Adult literature that make possible the relationship-building that forms the foundation of teenage readers' participation with the texts they read and write. The authors note and integrate the fact that, critical to adolescent development in the twenty-first century is the rapid acceleration of multimedia literacies.

---

[34] See, for example, Latham, Don. *David Almond: Memory and Magic*. Lanham, Md.: Scarecrow, 2006; Waller, *Constructing Adolescence in Fantastic Realism*; Trites, Roberta Seelinger. "The Harry Potter Novels as a Test Case for Adolescent Literature." *Style* 35, no 3 (2001): 472–85.

By encompassing the impending chaos of environmental damage, political injustice, racism, sexual awakening, social alienation, and the turmoil of the adolescent mind, this book addresses anew the poignant relation between cultural anxiety and representations of the emergent adult in fiction for the young. In taking a wide-based arc of critical perspectives on adolescent literature, culture, and response, it sets out to explore anew the moral, ideological, and literary landscapes presented to teenagers on their journey to adulthood.

Chapter 1

Adolescence and the Natural World in Young Adult Fiction

David Whitley

I would like to begin with a disarmingly simple hypothesis – that Young Adult fiction decoupled adolescent self consciousness from its grounding in the natural world. Texts that have come to be seen as seminal in marking off a distinctive territory of Young Adult fiction within the wider domain of writing for children – J.D. Salinger's *The Catcher in the Rye* (1951), S.E. Hinton's *The Outsiders* (1967), Robert Cormier's *The Chocolate War* (1974) – are all resolutely urban in their settings.[1] These seminal novels are all American, of course, but very similar qualities are evident in British novels, such as Colin MacInness's *Absolute Beginners* (1959). The protagonists of these novels embody the malaise of their respective eras by finding it impossible to fit in to the established order. Their search for alternative identities, that would make the uneasy transition towards adulthood authentic and meaningful, render their immediate experience – by turns – confused, painful, alienated, and contradictory. But there is little attempt in these novels to seek either consolation or direction from a natural world that might – in other contexts – be seen as an alternative source of value to a social order that appears so endemically false. Whatever dilemmas these protagonists face, they appear to be largely on their own, and the new face of adolescence seems cut off from imagery and associations that might traditionally have been a sustaining undercurrent through difficult rites of passage.

In subsequent novels about adolescence that these seminal texts have arguably influenced, such characteristics continue to be in evidence. The dominant tendency is towards an urban realism that engages with some of the extremes of contemporary experience, often in compelling and challenging ways. The big themes are of dislocation, exposure and uncertainty – seen variously in relation to war, immigration, drugs, violence and sexuality – and the novels' resolutions tend to rely little on images of reintegration and harmony that are founded, as in many more traditional narratives, on tropes of the natural world. This may be

---

[1]   Evidence of novels where the natural world remains intrinsic to young adults' development can be clearly seen in a range of fiction from earlier or transitional phases, such as: Stella Gibbons *Cold Comfort Farm* (1932); John Steinbeck *The Red Pony* (1937); Maureen Daly *Seventeenth Summer* (1942); Dodie Smith *I Capture the Castle* (1948); William Golding *Lord of the Flies* (1954); Harper Lee *To Kill a Mockingbird* (1960).

in part because many young adult novels limit the scope for development and maturation of their protagonists, and might be more usefully categorised as *entwicklingsroman*, novels of "mere growth, mere physical passage from one age to the other without psychological development."[2] Roberta Seelinger Trites, certainly, has recently developed this notion in persuasive and influential new ways, linking the reluctance of many authors of Young Adult fiction to bring their protagonists to a point of being successfully integrated within adult society (in the manner of earlier exemplars such as Alcott's *Little Women*, 1868, or Montgomery's *Anne of Green Gables*, 1908) to problematic issues of power and identity that are inherent within the new form.[3] This only partially accounts for Young Adult fiction's apparent severing, or reconstituting, of the links with the natural world that were so crucial in the fuller, *bildungsroman* style, novels for young adolescent readers written prior to the 1960s, however.

Already, though, my straightforward hypothesis requires some qualification, and we must also acknowledge a theoretical difficulty about the premises on which it is founded. Qualification is required because the dominant tendency identified above exhibits a number of notable exceptions. A small, but important, number of writers, for instance, have set their adolescent rites of passage firmly and centrally within the natural world, often with the protagonists forging a sense of themselves without human companions, in survival narratives that rework the Robinson Crusoe archetype but with contemporary resonances. Some of these, such as Scott O'Dell's *Island of the Blue Dolphins* (1960) or Jean Craighead George's *Julie of the Wolves* (1972), challenge the assumptions of modern, industrial societies by embodying deep understanding of traditional, non-Western cultures (though perhaps with more ambivalence than the novels' claims for authenticity might initially suggest, as Maria Nikolajeva has recently pointed out[4]). Other novels, such as Michael Morpurgo's recent *Running Wild* (2009), engage with contemporary themes such as the loss of rain forest environments, the threat of species extinction and the relationship between human and animal nature, by recentring the genre of the adventure narrative within exotic, ecologically vulnerable environments in the present day. Other types of narrative, mixing realism with fable or with poetic/fantasy devices (as in David Almond's novels), can also explore central connections between human consciousness and nature in fruitful ways.

Perhaps the most important qualification to my immodest proposal, though, needs to be made within those novels of adolescence where the connection to the natural world does indeed appear most attenuated. For even these, though references to nature may seem very thin on the ground, offer a touchstone or

---

    [2]   Pratt, Annis (with Barbara White, Andrea Loewenstein and Mary Wyer). *Archetypal Patterns in Women's Fiction*. Bloomington: Indiana University Press, 1981, 36.

    [3]   Trites, Roberta Seelinger. *Disturbing the Universe: Power and Repression in Adolescent Literature*. Iowa City: University of Iowa Press, 2000, 1–20.

    [4]   Nikolajeva, Maria. *Power, Voice and Subjectivity in Literature for Young People*. New York: Routledge, 2010.

deeper perspective within which the dominant preoccupations of the novel come into a different kind of focus. Consider, for instance, *The Catcher in the Rye*. Holden Caulfield is so preoccupied in the novel by his own idiosyncrasies, the phoniness of those around him, and his failure to find a place in the world where he can thrive, that he barely seems to notice the natural world at all. Apart from expressing rather whimsical curiosity to a taxi driver about the movement of ducks in Central Park, there is virtually no mention of a tree, plant, animal, or landscape within the entire, first-person-narrated, novel. Yet Salinger is careful to position the novel, via its title, in relation to pastoral traditions of folk song. Holden may misquote Robert Burns' famous song about a young girl's sexual encounter in a field of rye, and twist the song's imagery to a bizarre focus of his own. But there is no doubt about either the poignancy or centrality of the imagery derived from the song; the obscurity of its significance and the instability of its relation to other themes in the novel simply reflect the degree to which the protagonist drifts free of any secure base. The natural world becomes an absent presence in a novel with no sense of anchorage, a kind of abyss on which Caulfield's shifting consciousness – like the children he wants to save before they fall over the edge in the rye field – is founded. Similarly in S.E. Hinton's *The Outsiders*, Ponyboy's profound response to the beauty of sunsets, which he shares with Cherry, keeps alive a sense of connectedness that is set off against the vortex of disintegration and tragedy propelling the teenage gangland world of the central characters. Hence, even within those exemplars of Young Adult fiction in which nature appears to be dismissed as of marginal concern, there remains evidence of continued connection at a deeper level.

Even if we accept these qualifications however, it should be acknowledged at a theoretical level that recent ecocritical writing has tended to resist the kind of binary distinctions on which my initial hypothesis may appear to be founded. This is partly due to suspicion about the idealising functions of traditional pastoral. Pastoral was reformulated within Romanticism as a site on which authentic forms of experience could be founded, often perceived as resistant to the emergent industrial society's project of rationalist, scientific mastery of the world. More recently though, attempts to forge a link between authentic forms of human identity and the virtues of the natural world that can be found in much post-romantic writing have been critiqued by major theorists such as Leo Marx (1964), Raymond Williams (1973), and Laurence Buell (1995) for the degree to which this mystifies the operation of social power.[5] Post-Romantic pastoral has come to be perceived, in adult literature, as frequently naive, even disingenuous, written from positions that unconsciously adopt the assumptions of privilege. As Michael Bennett remarks, sharply, in his study of African American slave writing:

---

[5]   Buell, Laurence. *The Future of Environmental Criticism: Environmental Crisis and Literary Imagination*. Oxford: Blackwell, 1995; Marx. Leo. *The Machine in the Garden: Technology and the Pastoral Ideal in America*. New York: Oxford University Press, 1964; Williams, Raymond. *The Country and the City*. London: Chatto and Windus, 1973.

The kinds of spaces that most mainstream environmentalists and ecocritics validate – the pastoral and the wild – were not likely to be appreciated by ... slaves whose best hopes lay with negotiating an urban terrain. Slavery changed the nature of nature in African American culture, necessitating a break with the pastoral tradition developed within European American literature.[6]

The perception that the very "nature of nature," as Bennett puts it, is imbricated in the radically differentiated experience and values of social groups has led to re-evaluation of the relationship between urban and rural archetypes. Some recent thinkers indeed, such as Timothy Morton in *Ecology Without Nature*, have attempted to move beyond the concept of a separate "nature" altogether, attempting to formulate the basis for what he calls a new "environmental aesthetics."[7] Much recent writing has also been taken up with exploring the way 'nature' operates – in unacknowledged, residual, or incursive forms – both within urban environments and in liminal spaces, that are neither urban nor rural in a traditional sense. Michael Symmons Roberts and Paul Farley's *Edgelands* is characteristic of a different form of nature writing that attempts to move beyond traditional boundaries and categories.[8]

Two points need to be made about the way recent ecocritical theory has shifted our understanding of the relationship between rural and urban experience, however. First, even though the distinction between urban and natural environments is not nearly as straightforward as has sometimes appeared, the excising of referents to natural phenomena from so many of the seminal texts of Young Adult fiction remains a striking feature of this new kind of writing, whose implications still need to be probed and debated. Second, it is by no means clear that tropes of nature within writing with child or adolescent protagonists function in predominantly nostalgic, idealising, or escapist modes that eschew any realistic engagement with the operation of power. Roni Natov's *The Poetics of Childhood* has shown persuasively how complex and varied responses in children's literature have been to the legacy of Romantic conceptions of nature.[9] And, in pre-1950s literature with adolescent protagonists, the natural world often figures as a space within which issues of authority, exclusion, and otherness are contested and may be only partially resolved. In *Anne of Green Gables*, for instance, the heroine's identity as an outsider makes her status within the community unstable, and at times precarious. The emotional intensity of her responses to the natural world around her give dramatic force to a sense of her difference as she grows up – nature

---

[6]   Bennett, Michael. "Jeremiad, Elegy and the Yaak: Rick Bass and the Aesthetics of Anger and Grief." In *The Literary Art and Activism of Rick Bass*, edited by O.A. Weltzein, 205. Salt Lake City: University of Utah Press, 2001.

[7]   Morton, Timothy. *Ecology Without Nature.* Cambridge, Mass.: Harvard University Press, 2007.

[8]   Farley, Paul, and Symmons Roberts, Michael. *Edgelands: Journeys into England's True Wilderness.* London: Jonathan Cape, 2011.

[9]   Natov, Roni. *The Poetics of Childhood.* New York: Routledge, 2006.

becomes almost literally a theatrical space onto which she can project a wilder, more imaginatively indulgent, sense of self than the puritan ethos of her adoptive family's domestic regime would normally allow. While the extremes of Anne's self fashioning Romanticism are generally tolerated, and her connection to the natural world is ultimately an integrative force within the rural community depicted, it also sets off a pattern of confrontations in which Anne is repeatedly subject to adult discipline and attempts at control. It is part of the delicate balance that the novel sets out to achieve however, that it is rendered unclear whether the adults or Anne, in her emergent adolescent phase, learn more from these confrontations. Although negotiations between authority and outsiderness take place in a relatively benign context within *Anne of Green Gables*, it is worth noting that even texts for younger readers whose engagement with the natural world has a predominantly elegiac undertone have the potential to disturb. The autobiographical, child-centred perspective of Laura Ingalls Wilder's *Little House on the Prairie* (1935), for instance, renders the relationship between white settlers and Native Americans in as unsettled and unsettling forms as in any self-consciously postcolonial novel for adults. Jacqueline Rose has argued influentially that it is impossible for the fiction of a child-centred narrative not to be imbued with – often disguised or unconscious – adult agendas.[10] Clearly a book like *Little House on the Prairie*  takes part of its disturbing force from the layering of a child's consciousness of threat with a retrospective adult awareness of the dark histories that have shaped the destiny of the American Indian people. But this surely complicates, rather than erases, perceptions of power and their grounding within images of the natural world.

How then should we consider the significance of such grounding and the changing forms that references to nature take in Young Adult fiction? My contention is that such continued connections can best be understood in relation to a typology of the natural world that is demonstrated most richly and clearly in two classic texts from around the turn of the nineteenth century – *The Secret Garden* (1911) and *Huckleberry Finn* (1885). Two major tendencies are counterpointed in these texts, which are structured around contrasting images of the natural world, construed either as essential in nurturing human development (*The Secret Garden*); or as a form of freedom that is inevitably disjoined from the forces that shape what it means to be civilized (*Huckleberry Finn*). Both these tendencies can be traced back to Romanticism, and the differences between them perhaps reflect, in part, differences in how the Romantic legacy has been interpreted within British and North American traditions. Although the heroine in *The Secret Garden* is pre-adolescent, the novel embodies the tendency I wish to describe in its purest form and, as we shall see, has been an influence on the development of both Young Adult and children's fiction in some ways that are perhaps surprising.

---

[10]   Rose, Jacqueline. *The Case of Peter Pan or The Impossibility of Children's Fiction.* Philadelphia: University of Pennsylvania Press, 1993.

To show how this legacy may operate in practice, I would like to look in detail at two more recent examples of young adult fiction that demonstrate not only continuity, at a deep level, with these founding types but also quite radical revision. The first of these is Meg Rosoff's *How I Live Now*, a novel which, I shall argue, develops the archetype of *The Secret Garden* in quite remarkable new ways.[11] The plot of *How I Live Now* has strong affinities with Frances Hodgson Burnett's classic novel. The heroine, Daisy, is uprooted from her home in another continent and arrives in a large, rambling English country house where she has to adjust to very different cultural expectations. Like Mary Lennox in *The Secret Garden*, Daisy begins the novel emotionally messed up, the combined result of the early loss of her mother, inadequate parenting, and a culture that has made her out of touch with fundamental values. And, as in *The Secret Garden*, Daisy's emotional development and recovery of a more authentic self take place both in response to the relationships she develops with other young people in her new, adoptive family and through the regenerative, healing qualities of the natural world. The quirkily romanticised England that Daisy encounters is characterised by farm animals, rivers, barns, and spring sunshine as much as it is by Daisy's eccentrically individual cousins. Indeed Daisy's English cousins – in a range of different ways – show extraordinary understanding and rapport with the creatures with whom they share this rural landscape. As Susan Anderson puts it:

> Daisy's three younger cousins all seem to have the ability to communicate telepathetically with humans and animals to varying degrees. For Isaac, his telepathic ability is linked to the aspects of his personality that are described as animal-like, to the extent that Daisy comments: "At times I thought he was more animal than human'."[12]

Daisy, like Mary Lennox, is initially wary and defensive in an environment so radically different from that of her metropolitan upbringing. However, the sassy, New Yorker scepticism with which Daisy's first-person voice takes stock of her new surroundings ("It was getting to be like Walt Disney on E outside the house what with squirrels and hedgehogs and deer wandering around with the ducks and dogs and chickens and goats and sheep ...")[13] does not prevent her recognition of profound change taking place at a deeper level. Already, by one-third of the way through the novel, she has come to acknowledge that "The only thing I knew for certain was that all around me was more life than I'd experienced in all my years on earth and as long as no one shut me in the barn away from Edmond at night I was safe."[14]

---

[11]   Rosoff, Meg. *How I Live Now*. Harmondsworth: Penguin, 2004.

[12]   Anderson, Susan. "The Child in the World: Challenges to Traditional Literary Landscapes in the Young Adult Fiction of Meg Rosoff." In *Deep Into Nature: Ecology, Environment and Children's Literature*, edited by Jennifer Harding, Elizabeth Thiel, and Alison Waller, 71. Lichfield: Pied Piper, 2009.

[13]   Rosoff, *How I Live Now*, 58.

[14]   Rosoff, *How I Live Now*, 61.

Yet the thematic parallels between this novel and *The Secret Garden* should not distract from the equally significant differences. The natural world Mary Lennox encounters at Misselthwaite Manor may engender deep change within the characters at a personal level, but, as in the more conservative traditions of English pastoral, the social order that allows renewal to take place has long historical roots and is made to appear relatively stable. In Daisy's England, by contrast, the pastoral idyll, though precious, is rendered supremely vulnerable to the historical forces that surround it. No sooner has the natural magic started to work in the deeper recesses of Daisy's soul, than the whole social order is ripped apart by a war that has been forecast from the novel's inception. Continuity is never a given; it must be struggled for – often against the odds – at each stage of the novel's development. Hence Daisy's wry comment about nature's capacity to poison as well as to provide sustenance, when she and Piper are forced to go on the run – "This is one of the things I most dislike about nature, namely that the rules are not at all precise"[15] – takes on a larger significance within the novel as a whole. The natural world provides images of instability and casual suffering, almost as much as it nurtures spiritual growth and renewal.

In certain respects, this difference perhaps marks a shift in deep structural affinities between the children's novel and the forms of Young Adult fiction. Annis Pratt has demonstrated how, in many adult novels written by women, there appear to be archetypal patterns that underlie, and mesh with, the cultural assumptions of different periods and societies. She argues that –

> The principal archetypes ... recur in women's fiction – the green-world epiphany, the green-world lover, the rape trauma, enclosure, and rebirth – find counterparts in ... three particularly important archetypal systems – the Demeter/Kore and Ishtar/Tammuz rebirth myths, Arthurian grail narratives, and the Craft of the Wise, or witchcraft.[16]

Within the realm of children's fiction, by its very nature, only the first of these archetypal patterns – the green-world epiphany – is likely to be present; and the recurrence of this motif within books, such as *The Wind in the Willows*, that are gendered in exclusively masculine forms, alongside female classics such as *The Secret Garden*, suggests a provenance prior to the more intensive forms of gendered differentiation that take place in adolescence. In *How I Live Now*, in contrast, a case could be made for the presence of all Pratt's archetypes. Edmond could certainly be seen as a "green-world lover" (though perhaps the fact that the green-world affinity is shared equally by the other cousins, representing a kind of collective protagonist, could be seen as retaining some residual links with the pre-sexualised patterns of children's fiction too). Daisy is not literally raped, but she undergoes a traumatic journey through a radically transformed countryside, culminating in her witnessing a scene of mass genocide. This journey, arguably,

---

[15]   Rosoff, *How I Live Now*, 169.

[16]   Pratt, *Archetypal Patterns*, 170.

has some equivalence to Persephone's being seized and taken to the domain of the dead in Hades. Certainly, Daisy then undergoes a period of enforced "enclosure," when she is institutionalised on her return to New York; and then an emotional reawakening, or "rebirth," when she is finally able to get back to England and see Edmond again.

Just as Pratt shows how women's fiction is ultimately unable to resolve the division between "the hero's green-world authenticity and the social world of enclosure,"[17] so Daisy's eventual "rebirth" and return to the site of her green-world awakening in England is also shown to be fraught with ambivalences. The central ambivalence is revealed most strikingly in the closing stages of the story, when Edmond begins work on creating his own "secret garden," as a way of working through the crippling trauma of a war that has psychologically shattered him. This therapeutic garden is the antithesis of Burnett's image of recovering an innocent and integrative psychic space through work on nature in *The Secret Garden*. Edmond's garden expresses rage; rather than the traditional *hortus conclusus*, it is emblematic of a journey through hell, the apple trees trained on espaliers by being "cut into sharp crucifixes," the latent sexuality of tulips rendered gross as they are "spread open too far, splayed, exposing extreme black centres."[18] Yet something more than a straightforward reversal of traditional associations is being offered here, for the garden retains an aspect of its restorative potential when it is viewed once more with courage, commitment and openness to change by Daisy at the end. What is happening here is more complex than the resolution offered by *The Secret Garden* then, even though there are residual elements of optimism and confidence in the ultimately triumphant power of a loving universe that pervade children's fiction here. The ending suggests that Edmond's slow journey towards recovery may only ever be partial however, and it lacks the child's faith in a renewal that is total and unconditional. Again there may be parallels here with underlying mythic structures. Pratt suggests that the "archetype of the green-world lover seems related to the dying god in the stories of Aphrodite and Adonis, Ishtar and Tammuz, Isis and Osiris. These goddesses have lovers who die and whom they restore to life."[19] Adonis and Tammuz are only restored to life for six months of the year, however, the rival claims of the underworld ensuring that they reside half their time in the domain of the dead. The ambiguity displayed in Rosoff's ending, over whether Edmond will ever fully recover from his death–in–life emotional frozenness, strikes obvious parallels.

Beyond this, though, the novel may also embody aspects of Wordsworth's recognition, in 'Tintern Abbey,' that we both perceive and "half-create" the significance of nature.[20] The garden seems to be able to reflect back whatever is in

[17]   Pratt, *Archetypal Patterns*, 25.

[18]   Rosoff, *How I Live Now*, 196.

[19]   Pratt, *Archetypal Patterns,* 171.

[20]   Wordsworth, William. *Lyrical Ballads*. First published 1798. London: Methuen, 1978.

the mind of the beholder, its restorative potential for Edmond limited by his inner state of psychic disintegration. There may even be hints here of the emergence of a shift in the terms within which we can respond to the relationship between what is "natural" and "socially constructed," akin to what Raymond Williams called the development of a new "structure of feeling," an idea which developed to its fullest extent in *The Country and the City*.

The possibility of a new structure of feeling emerging is also evidenced in Geraldine McCaughrean's 2004 novel *Not the End of the World*.[21] Here, though, the archetype that is reworked is closer to Mark Twain's *The Adventures of Huckleberry Finn*. McCaughrean's novel takes a fresh look at the biblical story of Noah's flood; written for a contemporary context in which fundamentalist religion has re-emerged as a potent and largely destructive force, it is highly circumspect about the way faith operates in crisis. As in Twain's classic novel, the narrative is structured around the tensions and bonds emerging within a group travelling in desperate circumstances along a stretch of water, though there are obviously differences between Huck's Mississippi odyssey and Timna's survival narrative on Noah's ark in McCaughrean's revisionist narrative. What they share at the most fundamental level, though, is a scepticism about the belief systems that bind people together in the dominant society and a sense that the natural order is problematically opposed to this, embodying a more open, and vital, freedom.

Timna's consciousness, like Huck's, is founded on a profound contradiction. Just as Huck's growing love and respect for his black slave companion Jim cuts across his moral sense that he should adhere to the segregationist laws that bind the American South as a society, so Timna struggles to align herself with her (literally) patriarchal father's salvationist narrative of their family's unique destiny, despite the contradictory evidence of other survivors and her brother's inhuman fanaticism. As Noah's youngest daughter, Timna has not been assigned a sexual partner in the brave new world that is envisaged after the flood, and her undefined female role teeters dangerously between celibate slave-servant to the families designated to repopulate the earth and scapegoat, who must be sacrificed when the male belief system defining the new order encounters incompatible realities.

The role the natural world plays in orchestrating and giving significance to this crisis is fascinating. McCaughrean presents the animals in an utterly unsentimental way that paradoxically highlights their central importance. Early in the narrative Timna questions why they have had to fill the ark with so many different animal species, when they could have saved hundreds more fellow humans in the space this requires. Her naïve but wholly understandable doubt raises a myriad of further questions about human dominance, dependence on other life forms, and the long-term necessity of biodiversity that are left implicit but provide a rich underlying philosophical texture to the narrative. More immediately pressing are the practical issues raised by living on a primitive floating zoo for several months.

---

[21]   McCaughrean, Geraldine. *Not the End of the World*. Oxford: Oxford University Press, 2004.

Within Timna's divided consciousness this provokes disgust at times, seeing the animals instrumentally as "nothing but vats for turning food into dung! I hate them with a vengeance!"[22] But the animals are a fundamental part of the process of ethical questioning whereby she eventually breaks free of her family's restrictive modes of thinking too. In this latter sense, the increasingly foul, putrefying, and dangerous floating zoo that is the ark becomes symbolic of the repressed inner life of the human inhabitants, as they try to accommodate themselves to the simplistic dogma of their male spiritual leaders. Timna's decision to start a new life away from the ark at the end marks her alignment with the more open flux of the natural world's development. She comes to see the flood in more ecological terms, as a localised disaster within Africa that will regenerate species variety in its own ways within time, rather than as an absolutist process of ethnic cleansing, designed to produce rigid lines of racial and spiritual purity. Like Huckleberry Finn, who strikes out for undeveloped territory beyond the Western Frontier at the end of the novel, because he cannot stand the idea of returning to the aunt who will "sivilize" him, Timna also opts for an open space beyond the reach of her family. Yet the image of preserving other life forms by incarcerating them in a narrow space, that forms the symbolic centre of McCaughrean's novel, is very different from anything that can be found in *Huckleberry Finn*. McCaughrean's imaginative re-engagement with an archetypal narrative enacting the human desire both to dominate and be responsible for the natural world raises profoundly problematic issues that speak to the particular historical conjuncture of our own time in new, complex, and challenging ways.

Perhaps the most significant challenge offered by McCaughrean's novel, in the present context, lies in its probing of the concept of mastery. Mastery, indeed, has been one of the central themes preoccupying ecocritical theory generally, where critique has often been underpinned by the notion that the technological revolution begun in the West harnessed a desire for the exploitation and control of nature to serve human needs to an unprecedented – and dangerous – degree. Contesting the largely unquestioned assumptions underlying this process has involved attempts to construct an alternative ethics – based on an ecological perception of complex interdependencies between all living organisms, rather than human mastery and control – as well as an alternative politics. The variant forms of this alternative politics have shared a common focus in charting a very different route for human survival of the imminent environmental crisis than that prescribed by mainstream politics; and in questioning dominant assumptions of what 'progress' means.

McCaughrean's novel clearly develops an oblique perspective on both these core issues; the microcosmic world of the ark, distanced in historical, mythic time, enables the kind of sharp, reductive focus that parables use to shake up our ethical sensibilities. At the same time, the novelistic technique – realistic, detailed, and multiply focalized on a variety of human and animal protagonists' perspectives – ensures complexity of viewpoint. At the level of the parable, then, the story can

---

[22]   McCaughrean, *Not the End of the World*, 93.

be read as reclaiming an archetypal salvationist narrative, predicated on powerful masculine notions of racial, spiritual, and gendered hierarchy, for an alternative feminist viewpoint. Timna, like Huck, begins by accepting the patriarchal view of a racially segregated society implicit in her father, Noah's, master narrative of the flood. All the women in the story, indeed, operate within the aegis of patriarchal assumptions articulated with utter clarity by Timna's mother, Ama:

> A man should obey God, and his wife should obey man. That was the shape
> of the cradle my mother laid me in. That was the lesson she drilled home time
> and time again – taught me by her own example ... Noah would obey God and
> I would obey Noah.[23]

The stark absoluteness of this image of patriarchal culture provides a vivid dramatic structure for the novel's multifaceted processes of questioning to pitch against. At first, the questioning of male authority is located exclusively within Timna's consciousness, in her increasing awareness that her brother Shem's pathological zeal expresses the dark side of Noah's apparently more benign, unshakeable faith in his version of destiny. But in a rather brilliant chapter two-thirds of the way through the novel – which overturns the perception of unthinking female complicity in patriarchal rule that has been built up previously – all the significant female figures are revealed as having been operating in secretly subversive modes. Whilst publically supporting the male leaders' absolute certainty in their increasingly oppressive spiritual roles, the adult females have privately been plotting their own course of closet dissent, eventually enabling Timna to break free from the claustrophobic tyranny of the ark community. Thus the feminist parable emerges through subterranean passages within a collective female consciousness.

Two elements of the way this feminist parable is performed are especially striking and relevant here. First, it is clear by the end that Timna's journey is towards a community founded on an ethics of dissent and that there are energies present within the apparently oppressive mainstream community of the ark that nurture and support this development. This is significant because it is sometimes argued that the apparent rebelliousness of much Young Adult fiction is actually contained within an ethics of individualism and consumerism that is ultimately either conformist or solipsistically inward-looking. As Anne Scott McLeod rather starkly put it, Young Adult fiction from the 1960s onwards:

> ... shifted the focus of adolescent development from adaptation to the larger world
> to contemplation of the inner self, a contemplation that was neither spiritual nor
> intellectual, but psychological. The task for adolescents in these books had less
> to do with finding a place in society than with achieving a tolerable level of
> emotional comfort.[24]

---

[23] McCaughrean, *Not the End of the World*, 154.

[24] McLeod, Anne Scott. "The Journey Inward: Adolescent Literature in America, 1945–1995." In *Considering Children's Literature: A Reader*, edited by Andrea Schwenke Wyile and Teya Rosenberg, 206. Peterborough, ON: Broadview Press, 2008.

Even more recent Young Adult fiction, she goes on to argue, which tends to accept "non-traditional models of the family, concedes sexual knowingness of the young, and acknowledges a more equal standing of adolescents with adults," still depicts maturity in rather inchoate forms that are "personal rather than social."[25] McCaughrean's novel suggests the possibility, however, that, at least where the trope connecting adolescent development with nature is retained in substantial, though radically revised modes, the social dimension of growth to maturity may remain strong.

This brings me to the second striking element of *Not the End of the World* in terms of its engagement with the theme of mastery. For both the feminist parable and the questioning growth towards maturity of the central character are embedded within an interconnected narrative of the fate of the natural world that is much more than simply a metaphor for human development. The ark itself may well, ultimately, dramatise in microcosm irreconcilable tensions between humanity's self appointed roles as both guardians and consumers of nature. But there are persistent attempts to show animal nature within the ark in and of itself, rather than as an adjunct of human need or consciousness. "It is never sensible to credit animals with human qualities," reflects Ama, at a critical moment in the plot; "... there is not much room in a bird for anything other than hunger, fright and the occasional egg."[26] Moreover the survival of living organisms is revealed at the end of the novel to have taken place independently of the hubris-ridden human project to preserve breeding pairs of each species by incarcerating them within the ark. The catastrophe of the flood is confined, in the novel, to a region within the African continent. It is cataclysmic for terrestrial life forms and human civilization within its reach, but of local significance from the perspective of a global ecology: hence the colloquial pun of the title. It is literally "not the end of the world," and this framing perspective effectively decentres the narrative from the viewpoint of its main human protagonists and forces the reader to engage with a larger, ecological vision.

Moreover, the processes of questioning human authority and of envisaging a society with an alternative ethics are both linked, at a profound level, to perceptions of the natural world. In part this has to do with the novel's examination of the social basis upon which knowledge is founded. The biblical incident of a raven being released from the ark to bring back evidence of emergent land formations is reconstrued in the novel, for instance, to exemplify the complacency of male authority and the ignorance upon which this may be based. Instructed by Shem to release a raven, Ham mistakenly selects a Mynah bird instead, and lets the bird go off, uncorrected by a group in thrall to the incontestable truth of male pronouncements. When the bird returns with no vegetation in its beak, this is interpreted as a sign that the floods have not yet receded; it is only Ama who becomes aware that the bird's gullet contains the remnants of undigested, hard

---

[25]   McLeod, "The Journey Inward," 209.

[26]   McCaughrean, *Not the End of the World*, 153.

grapes, and draws her own conclusions. Women notice details that are occluded in the goal-oriented, prophetic vision that defines the male leaders' consciousness, and the significance of these details ultimately to require a realignment of human destiny with the endless flux and change that characterise the natural world.

The novel, indeed, charts the emergence of a reconfigured consciousness of natural processes that is expansive in terms of awareness of space, as well as tolerant of difference – both of human groups and of non-human life forms. The paradigm of the ark suggests a nature dependent on human care and control that must be, literally, herded and corralled if it is to survive. The chaotic, slurry filled, disease ridden pit that this creates could perhaps itself be read as a rather sly conceit – a hyperbolic image projecting the parallel consequences of narrow adherence to functionalist versions of sustainable growth and progress in the modern world. The failure of the anti-pastoral ark image gives way, by the end of the novel, however, to an alternative paradigm offered by migrating finches that inhabit the freedom of the air. Not only do the finches immediately restock the land that emerges from inundation, completely independently of the human agency of the ark, but they also serve as a touchstone for the ethics of two contrastive versions of human society that re-establish themselves, initially, in different niches of the post-flood environment. While the closed world of the nascent community of the ark is projected as discordant with nature – its rituals are of "dead-animal sacrifice," the site chosen to recommence farming "much too high for the vines to thrive"[27] – the community within which Timna finds herself, after her escape is both more open and depicted as more in tune with the environment. Noah's sons hurl rocks into the sky "to dissuade the hungry finches from landing,"[28] while in Timna's emergent community "people don't even try to drive off the ravenous finches, delighting instead in their vivid colours and hopping busyness."[29] No doubt there is more than a touch of overt didacticism in the contrastive images of this ending, but the astute observation of multiple levels at which culture and nature intersect that have preceded this perhaps justify the contrivance. Certainly the simplification, in the mode of the best parables, challenges the reader to consider further lines of connection, rather than closing down thought. Ultimately the contrast operates probingly within the domain of what Val Plumwood has identified as a central trait of modern society – "a weakened sense of the reality of our embeddedness within nature" which "is seen in the cultural phenomenon of ecological denial."[30]

In a sense then, *Not the End of the World* could be seen as refocusing some of the core features of the *Huckleberry Finn* archetype, to engage with central dilemmas of our own time. In *Huckleberry Finn*, the openness and resistance of natural processes to the oppressive dimensions of what "sivilize" means ultimately

---

[27] McCaughrean, *Not the End of the World*, 172–73.

[28] McCaughrean, *Not the End of the World*, 173.

[29] McCaughrean, *Not the End of the World*, 174.

[30] Plumwood, Val. *Environmental Culture: The Ecological Crisis of Reason*. London: Routledge, 2002, 97.

orientate the reader's consciousness westward, towards the freedom implicit in an image of America as boundless, the limit of its frontier as yet undefined. By contrast, *Not the End of the World* works with a central image of nature as controlled and hemmed in by the human order. If McCaughrean's novel, like Twain's masterpiece, undermines the premises on which this closed in human order is founded, then it also recognises a world that appears smaller and more tightly interconnected than Twain's. The role of the adolescent protagonist in coming to terms with this more circumscribed world is necessarily a complex one, but it includes – indeed, arguably, is centred on – a challenging ecological vision of the multiple levels at which "the reality of our embeddedness within nature" operates. The strategy of decentring the prerogatives of human agency and control that this involves is shared with a number of other significant recent Young Adult novels, particularly those which feature intimate relationships between adolescents and animals (such as Michelle Paver's *Chronicles of Ancient Darkness* series) or even humans becoming animals (as in Melvyn Burgess's *Lady: My Life as a Bitch*).[31] Although it is beyond the scope of this chapter to consider this in detail, it is interesting to speculate whether, in general, novels such as this, that re-engage with the natural world as a significant dimension of adolescent development, also give more weight to the position their protagonists take up in society than is common in Young Adult fiction. Certainly the end of *Not the End of the World* is more concerned with the kind of society Timna will grow into as an adult than it is with the subjective status of her inner self. It is perhaps significant though, that this emphasis is so strong in a mythic-realist novel that concludes with a choice between alternative historical versions of pastoral, rather than a more direct engagement with contemporary urban society. Even in Burgess's *Lady: My Life as a Bitch*, which is determinedly urban in setting and where the female protagonist prefers her life as a dog at the end to the repressive strictures of her human society, the move towards alignment with wildness is perceived as an escape from the existing, imaginable human society rather than attempting a reconfiguration of it. Perhaps, as in Pratt's assessment of how impossible it is in women's novels to incorporate the wildness of the natural energies that constitute female protagonists authentic selves into a viable social identity, so Young Adult fiction can only ultimately envisage some form of divided consciousness in its re-engagement with the natural world, if it is to remain true to itself.

What both these recent Young Adult books demonstrate, then, is continued engagement in depth with questions of how the natural world may affect the transition towards adult identity within adolescence. It seems the terms of reference have undergone some quite radical transformations however. If the dialectical shape of my argument – a thesis that novelists depicting adolescence have disengaged from the natural world countered by the notion that this may still take place in altered forms – does not yield a neat Hegelian synthesis as its

---

    [31]   Paver, Michelle. *Chronicles of Ancient Darkness*. London: Orion, 2004; Burgess, Melvyn. *Lady: My Life as a Bitch*. Harmondsworth: Penguin, 2003.

conclusion, then this is hardly surprising. For we are at a stage of urgent and unsettled questioning of where we stand in relation to the whole domain of nature at the moment, and we should not expect literature, whose role is to open us up to different possibilities, to relieve us of this burden. Nevertheless these novels demonstrate an imaginative reach that suggests they may be moving beyond depictions of human consciousness where animals function as adjuncts, or even – as Lévi-Strauss described their function in traditional societies – as vital tools that humans can use to think and feel.[32] The questioning of human centred perspectives in recent fiction can clearly explore the possibilities of new kinds of environmental philosophy and may also break away from the solipsistic concern with the inner life of protagonists that has arguably limited the scope of the dominant tradition within Young Adult fiction – even in its most groundbreaking forms.

---

[32] Lévi-Strauss, Claude. *Tristes Tropiques*. Translated from the French by John and Doreen Weightman. London: Jonathan Cape, 1974.

Chapter 2
Nationhood, Struggle, and Identity

Elia Michelle Lafuente

Many Young Adult novels focus on a disruption in the life of the protagonist and the subsequent personal growth that the character experiences. These disruptions often propel the main character forth on a journey – literal, metaphorical, or both – that leads to self-discovery, a higher level of emotional maturity, and, in general, a greater awareness of her identity. These disruptions serve to catalyse the emergence of a young adult from adolescence. Contemporary Caribbean-American coming-of-age literature shares this characteristic. But, whereas in most novels for young adults, the disruption is caused by personal circumstances such as death, divorce, and abuse, works by Caribbean-American authors in this genre also typically focus on the turmoil that occurs outside of the immediate environment of the protagonists and impels migration. Often, their works, while dealing with many of the same themes commonly examined in Young Adult literature, centre around the social and political problems that have affected the countries in the Caribbean and the impact these conflicts have on the narrator's lives and their transformation as emergent adults.[1]

In these texts, the setting of political turmoil serves various purposes. On one level, it shines a light on twentieth-century history in these countries that, because of the repressive nature of those governments, has not been widely publicised. It also gives a voice to the millions of people who have been silenced under political tyranny. On another level, the backdrop of political unrest functions to intensify the conflict in the life of the adolescent protagonist. In addition, the national tension parallels and serves as a metaphor for the inner struggle that the main character feels while growing up. Conversely, the personal change that the protagonist experiences serves as a metaphor for the turmoil occurring within her country.

While social and political turmoil trigger the passage into adulthood for the protagonists in these novels, like the revolutions and upheavals themselves, this process is not necessarily orderly or expeditious. On the contrary, personal transformation – emergence from childhood to adulthood – can be protracted and

---

[1] See Smith, Katherine Capshaw. "Trauma and National Identity in Haitian-American Young Adult Literature." In *Ethnic Literary Traditions in American Children's Literature*, edited by Michelle Pagni Stewart and Yvonne Atkinson, 83–97. New York: Palgrave Macmillan, 2009. Smith writes of recent Caribbean literature as depicting "an experience of migrancy, with characters motivated by economic or political circumstances to leave the Caribbean for the United States or Canada" (84).

gradual. For the protagonists in these texts, the result is a prolonged liminality, a marginal state. As a consequence of the problems that plague the homelands of the main characters in contemporary Caribbean-American coming-of-age fiction, the protagonists often flee from their countries, choosing exile over oppression. Thus, while the main characters are experiencing the personal journey of maturing from children to adults, they also undergo a literal journey in which they immigrate to the United States, where they develop hybrid identities as bicultural young adults. The unsettled political and social context of these novels enhances the central theme of personal growth and discovery, culminating in the development of an identity on the border of two cultures.

This theme is not limited to Caribbean-American texts but, rather, is a common focus of many contemporary multicultural works.[2] In "Children on the Edge," Rocío Davis affirms:

> [E]thnic narratives in the United States today tend to center on themes such as the awareness of difference and the struggle to understand cultural uniqueness, the recognition and affirmation of a hybrid identity, the need to escape, the role of the past, the question of home, the drama of language, and, often, the creation and establishment of the new self in a new setting.[3]

Nonetheless, the diasporic history and even the geographic layout of Caribbean nations naturally lend themselves to the development of identities characterised by multiplicity, as Julia Alvarez expresses when she states, "We are islands, permeable countries. It's in our genes to be a world made of many worlds"[4]

Before We Were Free[5] by Julia Alvarez, *Flight to Freedom*[6] by Ana Veciana-Suarez, and *Behind the Mountains*[7] and *Breath, Eyes, Memory*[8] by Edwidge Danticat articulately capture the coming of age of specific characters and of other young adults while recording the experiences of their countrymen in their narratives. Not only do the narrators undergo a personal coming of age in the texts, but this transformation also represents the parallel experiences of the citizens of the countries in which they live. The authors are telling two stories in each case: One is the familiar Young Adult scenario that involves personal conflict and ultimate growth, and the other uses the main character as a prototype for her people and their larger political and social struggles. The personal changes that the characters

---

2   See Davis, Rocío G. "Children on the Edge: Leaving Home in Sandra Cisneros's *The House on Mango Street* and Lois-Ann Yamanaka's *Blu's Hanging.*" In *Literature on the Move: Comparing Diasporic Ethnicities in Europe and the Americas*, edited by Dominique Marçais et al., 37–47. Heidelberg: Universitätsverlag Winter, 2002.

3   Davis, "Children on the Edge," 37.

4   Alvarez, Julia. *Something to Declare*. Chapel Hill: Algonquin Books, 1998, 175.

5   Alvarez, Julia. *Before We Were Free*. New York: Random House, 2002.

6   Veciana-Suarez, Ana. *Flight to Freedom*. New York: Orchard Books, 2002.

7   Danticat, Edwidge. *Behind the Mountains*. New York: Orchard Books, 2002.

8   Danticat, Edwidge. *Breath, Eyes, Memory*. New York: Soho Press, 1994.

of these books experience also serve as a metaphor for the turmoil occurring in the countries at the time and vice versa. This is not to say that as the protagonists grow from girls to young women, their nations are liberated – merely that this turbulence mirrors the internal struggles of the protagonists and provides them with the impetus to go forth on their journeys into adolescence.

Due to the brutal dictatorships in the Caribbean region, much of the contemporary literature produced by exile writers from the area is of a political nature. Authors such as Alvarez, Veciana-Suarez, and Danticat document their own experiences and the experiences of others through their works of fiction. They chronicle the living conditions, injustices, and oppression that the citizens of their countries were subjected to in what is known as *testimonio* (testimony). *Testimonio* speaks for the individuals in a community as well as the community as a whole. Kelli Lyon Johnson writes that testimonies themselves are collective, as Latin American *testimonio* speaks for all those oppressed, disappeared, and imprisoned.[9] Johnson goes on to state that testimony is based on an oral tradition of witnessing.[10] Through their *testimonio*, the authors break the silences imposed by the dictatorships that stripped them and their countries of origin of their freedom of expression and other basic liberties.

In the Author's Note at the end of *Before We Were Free*, Alvarez writes of her motivations for writing the book as well as the tradition of *testimonio*. She speaks of the horrors of the Trujillo dictatorship in her native Dominican Republic and tells the story of her family's exile. Alvarez suggests that all those in exile must tell their stories: "It is the responsibility of those who survive the struggle for freedom to give testimony. To tell the story in order to keep alive the memory of those who died."[11] While Alvarez's *testimonio* depicts Dominican society under the reign of Trujillo, in a sense it is representative of life under any oppressive regime. On this subject, the author states, "This story could have taken place in any of the many dictatorships in Nicaragua, Cuba, Chile, Haiti, Argentina, Guatemala, El Salvador, or Honduras – a sad but not uncommon occurrence in the southern half of our America not too long ago."[12] Similarly, other writers, such as Edwidge Danticat from Haiti, and Ana Veciana-Suarez from Cuba, share their *testimonio* through their coming-of-age novels, simultaneously expressing the stories of their young protagonists, of their people, and of oppressed societies in general.

The works by Alvarez, Danticat, Veciana-Suarez, and other exile authors publicise the experiences of the people living in repressive regimes, which intentionally suppress literature of this nature. Dictatorships never chronicle the rampant human rights abuses and injustices inflicted upon a country. Through

---

[9]   Johnson, Kelli Lyon. "Both Sides of the Massacre: Collective Memory and Narrative on Hispaniola." *Mosaic: A Journal for the Interdisciplinary Study of Literature* 36 no. 2 (2003): 75–92.

[10]   Johnson, "Both Sides of the Massacre," 82.

[11]   Alvarez, *Before We Were Free*, 166.

[12]   Alvarez, *Before We Were Free*, 166.

these works of historical fiction, the accounts of authors such as Alvarez, Veciana-Suarez, and Danticat expose the true experiences of themselves and their fellow people. Johnson echoes this sentiment when she states that Alvarez seeks to "fill the absences left from the silences of the trujillato,"[13] or the Trujillo regime. About Danticat's works, Johnson expresses a similar idea that "Danticat breaks that official silence, creating from her own research and the collective memory of those to whom she spoke a narrative of the history of the victims."[14] The sanctuary of exile allows these authors the freedom of expression that they were denied in their native countries.

Dictatorships and other repressive governments, of varying degrees, have long been a characteristic of Latin American societies and have resulted in the dehumanization, imprisonment, and murder of countless victims. While the Dominican, Haitian, and Cuban societies were far from egalitarian and democratic before these leaders took power, when they assumed their positions as Heads of their respective countries, any semblances of democracy and freedom were obliterated. The twentieth-century dictatorships in the Dominican Republic, Cuba, and Haiti were long-lasting, and their effects still resonate.

In the Dominican Republic, Rafael Trujillo's reign, or the *trujillato*, lasted from 1930 – to 1961. Trujillo was a fascist dictator who ruled for more than thirty years, either directly as President or through puppet presidents like his brother.[15] Trujillo depended on the military as his main support, and he maintained an elaborate secret police force that closely monitored and sometimes assassinated his opponents. His human rights violations were not isolated to his own country: when Trujillo discovered that the Haitian government had killed some of his undercover agents in Haiti, he commanded the massacre of 20,000 mostly unarmed men, women, and children.[16] With time, the Trujillo regime became increasingly isolated, and on 30 May 1961, Trujillo was assassinated.[17] After Trujillo was assassinated, his son, Rafael Jr., briefly assumed control, and the Dominican Republic underwent a civil war and several other authoritarian leaders until democracy was achieved toward the end of the twentieth century. The plot of *Before We Were Free*, by Julia Alvarez, focuses on life during the end of Trujillo's reign, in 1960.

In *Before We Were Free*, the journey of the main character, Anita de la Torre, begins with the realisation that "El Jefe," the leader of the Dominican Republic whom she has always revered and adored, is actually a brutal dictator that Anita's family is conspiring against. Throughout the course of the novel, Anita is transformed from a sheltered girl to a mature, more thoughtful teen one year later.

---

[13]   Johnson, "Both Sides of the Massacre," 89.

[14]   Johnson, "Both Sides of the Massacre," 90.

[15]   Haggerty, Richard. *Dominican Republic and Haiti: Country Studies*, 28. Washington D.C.: Library of Congress, 1989.

[16]   Haggerty, *Dominican Republic and Haiti*, 29–30.

[17]   Haggerty, *Dominican Republic and Haiti*, 30–31.

Before We Were Free is a coming-of-age journey about adolescence, family, and discovering what it means to be free.

Slowly, as the novel unfolds Anita becomes more aware of the harsh realities of her society.. She pieces together the disappearance of her uncle Toni while collecting mysterious clues about the terrifying regime and her family's plot to displace the dictator. Meanwhile, the SIM, or secret police, raid the de la Torre house regularly. As Anita gains knowledge that her family is leading the resistance group against El Jefe, she is also experiencing the changes of typical pubescent girls, such as taking an interest in boys. Once loquacious, she ceases to speak as she copes with the terror of the government and begins to write all of her observations and feelings in her diary and then to erase her words daily so as not to incriminate her family. Her older sister, Lucinda, must flee the country for the United States to escape the sexual advances of El Jefe. Anita's life is dramatically changed when her father and uncle are arrested for killing the dictator, her brother, Mundín, must flee the country, and she and her mother must hide in the bedroom closet of benevolent friends for several months. Eventually, they are extracted in a daring operation by friends involved in anti-regime intelligence and operations, and they flee to New York. The story ends as Anita begins to adapt to life in the United States with her relatives, except for her father and her uncle Toni, who are murdered by the regime of Trujillo's son.

Anita's personal growth is evident in *Before We Were Free*. In the beginning of the text, Anita is a chatty, naïve young girl. At one point Papi, Anita's father, speaks with his daughter, telling her, "I want my children to be free, no matter what. Promise me you'll spread your wings and fly."[18] In response, Anita thinks, *"What on earth are you talking about, Papi?"*[19] As the book ends, after Anita has matured tremendously, she reflects, "I think about Papi and Tío Toni and their friends who died to make us all free. The emptiness inside starts filling with a strong love and a brave pride. Okay, Papi, I promise I'll try."[20] Rather than allowing her loss and grief to weaken her, Anita uses her knowledge and experiences to become a stronger person. While Anita is maturing, the society of the Dominican Republic is also changing. As the repression escalates, so does the resistance against Trujillo's government, until, finally, the dictator is eliminated. On the night El Jefe is assassinated, Anita receives her first kiss from a boy, and in this climactic passage, the parallel between Anita's coming of age and the country's political upheaval is most vividly exemplified. The triumph is short-lived, however, as El Jefe's son assumes power soon after his father dies, and Anita and her mother go into hiding. Nonetheless, Anita and her family are ultimately liberated when they flee to the United States, where they regain the ability to express themselves.

The theme of silence serves to illustrate the idea that the changes in Anita's life symbolise the greater changes happening in Dominican society. As surveillance of

---

[18] Alvarez, *Before We Were Free*, 80.

[19] Alvarez, *Before We Were Free*, 80.

[20] Alvarez, *Before We Were Free*, 163.

Anita's house intensifies, her family must be increasingly secretive, speaking in whispers. Anita stops talking and often cannot find words to express herself. She states:

> I want to tell Mami the truth, how I've gotten my period, how I'm already lonely for Lucinda, how I feel just awful that my father has to kill someone for us to be free, how I'm scared about what's going to happen to us, but all the words seem to have emptied out of my head.[21]

Anita's lack of words conveys the silence imposed by the Trujillo regime on Dominican society. They have lost all hope, and, living in terror, they keep quiet. This idea is further exemplified throughout the book, specifically during another instance where Anita is at a loss for words, and to solve this problem, Anita says, "I put my crucifix in my mouth. Sometimes, doing so helps me remember the words for what I want to say."[22] In this statement, Alvarez is expressing that hope allows individuals to find their voices. Without hope, Anita, like her country, remains silent.

This theme of silence, symbolic of oppression, is magnified and complemented by a lack of imagery relating to nature. The majority of the novel takes place on the family compound, an enclosed and secluded area containing a group of homes belonging to Anita's family. When Anita and her mother must spend almost two months in hiding, they live in solitude indoors, completely isolated from nature. In contrast, the author uses imagery of butterflies throughout the book to express the theme of freedom. The opposition group led by Anita's father is called Las Mariposas, or the Butterflies. The family's clairvoyant maid, Chucha, also refers to Anita and her family as butterflies who will take flight on a journey to freedom, according to a dream she has had. As the book concludes and Anita has been reunited with her family in New York, she experiences her first snowfall. She marvels at its beauty and purity, and she and her cousins play in the snow, making snow angels. Later that night, looking out the window, Anita sees the snow angels, but instead thinks of them as butterflies, "reminding me to fly."[23] Whereas Anita's time in isolation is marked by stark solitude completely devoid of any connection to the natural world, freedom is embodied by this image of the butterfly.

Like the Dominican Republic, Anita does not remain unscathed from the transformation. Once in the United States, she mourns quietly for her father, her uncle, and her homeland. Anita admits this when she says, "I walk around and pretend everything's okay. Meanwhile, inside, I'm all numb, as if I had been buried in sadness and my body got free, but the rest of me is still in captivity."[24] Anita's feelings mirror the sentiments of many immigrants who have escaped oppression. While technically she is free, she will always be haunted by the events that led to

---

[21] Alvarez, *Before We Were Free*, 79.
[22] Alvarez, *Before We Were Free*, 84.
[23] Alvarez, *Before We Were Free*, 163.
[24] Alvarez, *Before We Were Free*, 159.

her liberation. What Anita has experienced in her home nation has affected her so profoundly that, although time has passed, she remains in an in-between state, in which she is inextricably tied to her past.

Edwidge Danticat echoes this sentiment in *Breath, Eyes, Memory*, in which the narrator states, "I come from a place where breath, eyes, and memory are one, a place from which you carry your past like the hair on your head."[25] Although the narrator of the novel, Sophie Caco, has escaped Haiti and settled into her adult life in the United States, she is trapped in her past experiences and will never escape. In a sense, she is living amid the past and the present, her old self and her new self. However, living between two worlds does not necessarily imply having an equal foothold in each. Katherine Capshaw Smith argues that a balance between two cultures is impossible, "because the home culture bears with it the palpable weight of trauma."[26]

Like the Dominican Republic, Haiti underwent political unrest throughout the twentieth century. After decades of instability and various dictatorships in Haiti at the beginning of the twentieth century, François Duvalier was elected in 1957. Duvalier's rule was repressive and authoritarian: he violated the constitution repeatedly and terrorised his people, having more than thirty thousand Haitians killed for political reasons during his presidency.[27] When Duvalier died in 1971, his legacy passed on to his son, Jean-Claude "Baby Doc" Duvalier, who was nineteen at the time. Duvalier Jr.'s regime was basically an extension of his father's, only he was much less of an active leader than his father had been. Throughout his corrupt rule, poverty, hunger, and malnutrition spread, causing discontent and much unrest and prompting a revolt in the provinces. Meanwhile, the international community became alarmed at the deteriorating state of the nation, and the U.S. distanced itself from the Duvalier regime by cutting back aid to Haiti. Duvalier Jr. was left with no support base and ultimately fled Haiti. While Haitians rejoiced to be rid of such a callous dictator, their standard of living did not improve, as the country was left in shambles.[28]

Since the Duvaliers, several leaders have governed in Haiti; however, the country is still characterised by political, economic, and social instability. The political backdrop of *Breath, Eyes, Memory*, by Edwidge Danticat, is the tumultuous Haitian society under Duvalier, and in *Behind the Mountains*, by Danticat, the protagonist is a Haitian refugee who has immigrated to New York during the year 2000, as society after Duvalier proves to be just as repressive after President Aristide is forced out in a coup d'état by the army.

In *Breath, Eyes, Memory*, Sophie Caco lives in a Haitian society beset by physical violence and civil unrest. She is the product of her young mother's rape. Her mother moves to the United States when Sophie is born, leaving Sophie to be raised by her aunt, Tante Atie, in Haiti. To Sophie, Tante Atie has always been

---

[25]   Danticat, *Breath, Eyes, Memory*, 234.

[26]   Smith, "Trauma and National Identity," 85.

[27]   Haggerty, *Dominican Republic and Haiti*, 234.

[28]   Haggerty, *Dominican Republic and Haiti*, 238.

her mother, so when her birth mother, Martine, sends for her, she is devastated at the thought of travelling to a foreign country and living with a mother she does not know. However, it is considered her obligation to comply with her mother's wishes rather than do as she pleases. Eventually, Sophie adapts to living in New York with Martine. They have a tumultuous relationship but do not stop loving each other. Sophie marries a musician named Joseph and has a child, Brigitte, whom she adores. She finally has some stability in her life, when her mother, who has been plagued by night terrors for years, commits suicide. The book ends in Haiti, where Sophie has returned to bury her mother.

Whereas in *Before We Were Free*, Anita flees to the United States toward the end of the novel and the majority of the book illustrates her life in the Dominican Republic and the sequence of events that leads to her escape, *Breath, Eyes, Memory* is written from a different perspective. Sophie moves to New York shortly after the book begins. In the opening chapter, the setting is rural Haiti, and scenes of police violence toward citizens depict the reality of everyday life there. When Sophie is fourteen and her mother sends for her, she leaves Haiti but returns several times, each time witnessing that while those in power might have changed, the violence has not stopped. This setting, characterised by turmoil and brutality, mirrors Sophie's life – from her turbulent relationship with her mother, including the fact that she was born a product of rape, to her rocky relationship with her husband. Her state of flux, back and forth between the United States and Haiti, represents the liminal state of her identity, not quite belonging and not stably rooted in either country.

In *Before We Were Free*, the story ends with the sense that Anita's problems have been resolved to a certain extent, as she has fled from oppression. A resolution in *Breath, Eyes, Memory* is not so easily tied to physical exile but, rather, occurs when the protagonist is truly able to break free of the repression and silence that her life events have wrought on her psyche. Sophie has returned to Haiti for her mother's funeral after she commits suicide, and while, despite her state of mourning, she is somewhat at peace, she is still troubled by her past – the violence, the loneliness, and the isolation. There is no suggestion that she is any less tormented now than in the beginning of the book, however; at Martine's funeral, Sophie's pain reaches a boiling point, and she unleashes her aggression, releasing years of repression. As she watches the dirt being shovelled atop her mother's grave, Sophie cannot stand it any longer and runs away from the funeral. In an emotional account, the narrator tells of her inner liberation, in which she runs through a sugar-cane field and attacks a cane stalk, beating it and uprooting it, hurting herself in the process. The funeral crowd follows Sophie to the cane fields and watches her, and her grandmother shouts, asking her "Ou libére?"[29] Are you free? Her aunt, Tante Atie echoes these words, proclaiming, "Ou libére!"[30] You are free! By releasing years of pent up pain and emotion, Sophie is truly liberated and finally able to cross the threshold that she had remained on since the beginning of

---

[29]   Danticat, *Breath, Eyes, Memory*, 233.

[30]   Danticat, *Breath, Eyes, Memory*, 233.

her journey into adulthood. Through this passage, Danticat could be imparting a message to all Haitians, and, more generally, to all oppressed peoples, showing them that they, like Sophie, will be free once they break their silence.

Behind the Mountains, also by Edwidge Danticat, takes place in a more contemporary Haiti, in the year 2000. But while *Behind the Mountains* is set years after *Breath, Eyes, Memory*, the same violence still plagues Haiti. Celiane Espérance lives in the country with her mother, her grandparents, and her brother Moy. Her father has moved to New York to make a better life for his family. He saves money to establish a home and to bring his family to the United States. His sister, who is a nurse and lives in the city of Port-au-Prince, uses her connections to try and obtain permission for Celiane and her family to be reunited with her father in Brooklyn. Celiane's life in rural Haiti is fairly stable, save for the absence of her father. Her childhood in Beau Jour is even somewhat idyllic. The very name of her hometown, Beau Jour, or Beautiful Day, evokes beauty, serenity, and happiness. The narrative is rich with sensual imagery of the Haitian countryside. In sharp contrast to the vivid description of the natural beauty of Beau Jour is a distinct lack of presence of nature in the more urban environments of Port-au-Prince, and her new life in New York, as Celiane moves away from home, as well as away from childhood. When she leaves her isolated town of Beau Jour to visit her aunt, Tante Rose, in the city, Celiane witnesses bombings, beatings, and other brutality and is nearly killed herself in a bombing while in transit. Celiane begins to see her country in a different light as she broadens her experiences at the same time as she embarks upon adolescence.

After Celiane is injured in the bus bombing, she is hospitalised before her brother and mother find her alive. She has awakened to the fact that her father left Haiti for reasons much greater than financial gain, and, although she is sad to leave her grandparents, her best friend, and her home, she also fears staying in Haiti. In the United States, Celiane's family struggles financially while adapting to a very different society. She and her family are homesick for Haiti despite the perilous conditions of life there. But although they must endure hardships, the family is now reunited and adjusting to a new life. Nonetheless, while the Espérance family is together again, Celiane does not quite feel as if she is home. However, because of the unrest in her native Haiti, it is impossible for her to return to the home she remembers. So, just as her place as an adolescent is neither in girlhood nor in womanhood, her place as an immigrant is now neither in Haiti nor in the United States.

The political pattern in the Dominican Republic and Haiti indicates the nature of leadership in many Caribbean societies – it is a constant struggle for power. Although Cuba began the twentieth century with a democratic society, tyranny ultimately prevailed and has taken various forms throughout the century. In 1959, Fidel Castro rose to power by a force of arms and easily took power under the guise of espousing democratic ideals, before slowly revealing his true agenda.[31]

---

[31] Vázquez, Ana María B., and Rosa E. Casas. *Cuba*. Chicago: Children's Press, 1994, 73.

Castro ordered the execution by firing squad of masses of citizens and soldiers accused of political crimes and implemented various reforms, through which he seized private properties and businesses and nationalized schools and other private institutions. It took only a few years for many Cubans to realise that Castro's Cuba was far from the Democratic society that they had originally envisioned. Hundreds of thousands of people went into exile in Spain, the United States, and other countries.[32] Castro's government has remained in power for more than fifty years and has repeatedly been named by Amnesty International and other prominent organisations as one of the world's most repressive regimes. In *Flight to Freedom*, by Ana Veciana-Suarez, the protagonist, Yara Garcia, flees Cuba as a result of the reality of life under Castro's oppression Yara Garcia and her family live in Havana, Cuba, in the 1960s. In 1967, about eight years after Castro's coup d'état, many Cubans are awakening to the reality that the Revolution bears no resemblance to the one Castro initially described would occur. Reality in Cuba is bleak: citizens must now stand in line to get their food rations, children are obligated to participate in forced labour camps, and those considered to be traitors face imprisonment or the firing squad. In order to obtain permission to emigrate, Yara's father must work in a forced labour camp. Because Yara's family is against Castro's government, they are called *gusanos* (worms), as dissidents of the Revolution were labelled. Due to the political repression they experience, Yara and her family go into exile.

While Cuba is experiencing dramatic political, social, and economic changes, Yara is coming of age, experiencing personal change. As she begins the process of maturation, Yara is propelled on a physical journey to the United States, where she will find her new home. Once in Miami, Yara feels out of place. She knows little English and is not accustomed to U.S. society. After her first day of school, Yara writes in her diary, "I hate it! I hate it! I hate it! I know I will never get used to this, and I know I will never ever ever like this school. How am I to understand anything the teacher says? English sounds like popcorn popping fast and hard on the stove."[33] Eventually Yara and her family adjust to life in Miami, free from Castro's oppression but nonetheless yearning for their homeland. At the end of the novel, Yara is still nostalgic for Cuba, albeit a free Cuba, rid of Castro. When her father says, "Next year, we'll be in Cuba,"[34] a common statement and sentiment among Cuban exiles in the first years after the Revolution, Yara thinks, "I wish I could believe him,"[35] and with this statement of longing, the book is concluded. Anita echoes Yara's nostalgia in *Before We Were Free* when she is asked on her first day of school in the United States to speak about the Dominican Republic. Anita feels like an outsider and knows that she wouldn't be able to effectively describe her country of origin to her classmates. She asks herself, "Where do I begin telling strangers about a place whose smell is on my skin and whose memory

---

32   Vázquez, *Cuba*, 73.

33   Veciana-Suarez. *Flight to Freedom*, 46.

34   Veciana-Suarez, *Flight to Freedom*, 205.

35   Veciana-Suarez, *Flight to Freedom*, 205.

is always in my head? To them, it's just a geography lesson; to me, it's home."[36] When Anita first arrives in the U.S., like Yara, she has not yet adjusted to life in her new country, and while, with time, she embraces her new home, her homeland will always remain an important part of her.

Like all immigrants, when the protagonists of all of these texts go into exile, they develop an identity characterized by duality or hybridity. Whether they are Dominican-American, Haitian-American, or Cuban-American, these characters are part of both of their cultures but not completely part of either. Alvarez and other exiled writers refer to this as "living on the hyphen." Pauline Newton resists the notion of hyphenation, however, stating that immigrants "cannot perfectly homogenize or hybridize their old and new lands."[37] Newton observes, "These migrants do not emerge as perfectly acculturated U.S. Americans, but as women of multiple, shifting cultures and identities."[38] Alvarez's writing, like Danticat's and Veciana-Suarez's, expresses the assimilation as well as the conflicts that arise from being part of two cultures. The authors' works are a reflection of the multiple identities they have assumed as Americans, Latin Americans, and women. The novels deal with the duality of the immigrant experience, or life within the realm of the hyphen, as Alvarez puts it. Through their texts, the authors depict the clashing, as well as the coming together, of two cultures. Their homes are simultaneously in both countries and neither country.[39]

Smith writes that literature dealing with migrancy "emphasizes the migrant's unsettled identity in relationship to both sites."[40] This state is at once one of connectedness and disconnectedness, belonging and not belonging. África Vidal describes this concept of living on the border as being "inextricably linked to this double allegiance."[41] It is an inherent part of the immigrant experience.

In *Flight to Freedom*, Yara grapples with the dilemma stemming from her dual identity as Cuban and American. She questions whether she can have allegiance to both countries, and if accepting the traditions of the United States will come at the expense of losing her Cuban identity. Yara asks, "Do you stop loving your homeland if you live somewhere else and fly that country's flag? Must you surrender your memories to adapt to all the new demands of another life?"[42] These poignant questions are ones that many immigrants ask themselves, and they show that the

---

[36]   Alvarez, *Before We Were Free*, 144.

[37]   Newton, Pauline T. *Transcultural Women of Late-Twentieth-Century U.S. American Literature: First-Generation Migrants from Islands and Peninsulas*, 9. Aldershot: Ashgate, 2005.

[38]   Newton. *Transcultural Women*, 10.

[39]   See Vidal, África. "Resisting Through Hyphenation: The Ethics of Translating (Im) pure Texts." In *Border Transits: Literature and Culture Across the Line*, edited by Ana Maria Manzanas, 225–41. Amsterdam: Rodopi, 2007.

[40]   Smith, "Trauma and National Identity," 84.

[41]   Vidal, "Resisting Through Hyphenation," 228.

[42]   Veciana-Suarez, *Flight to Freedom*, 185.

dual identities that Yara and the characters in the other texts form as foreigners in the United States are often not without emotional crisis. In other words, striking a balance between assimilation and preservation of one's heritage is not always a smooth process. In fact, Smith proposes that, in the case of Haitian narratives, a balance cannot be achieved because "Haiti is too powerful to be fused with the American experience."[43] Perhaps the experiences one has and identity she forms in her homeland render it impossible for her to achieve a true sense of synthesis.

Danticat expresses the idea of living on the hyphen throughout *Behind the Mountains*. In New York, Celiane attends classes that are conducted in Creole and are made up of other Haitian students. Despite the fact that they are now living in the States, she and her family maintain their connection to Haiti by listening to a Haitian radio station and cooking Haitian dishes. The Espérance family is a part of both cultures, yet not completely part of either. At the same time, their essence is Haitian. Smith asserts:

> [I]n her young adult novel, *Behind the Mountains,* Danticat redefines the term hybridity: instead of emphasizing Haitian-American migrant hybridity, Danticat imagines *Haitian* identity as syncretic ... For Haitian characters in America, any experience of multiplicity, possibility, or incompletion points toward a core Haitian identity, rather than a fusion of America with Haiti.[44]

While Celiane is adjusting to life in America, her identity is still intrinsically Haitian. Smith theorizes that Danticat characterizes migration as the foundation of the Haitian identity, and that her characters adopt a hybridity anchored in their Haitian identity.

Danticat's use of French shows the dual nature of the protagonist's identity, in *Behind the Mountains* and in *Breath, Eyes, Memory*. Both books are written in English, yet Danticat sprinkles Creole French throughout the two texts. Although *Behind the Mountains* is an English language text, Danticat clearly infuses Haitian culture into the book, not only through Creole words and names, but also through the language she uses, which has a distinctive, lyrical voice. Also, Danticat makes it explicit that English is a foreign language to Celiane. One day when she and her brother, Moy, are practicing their English, she states they are "still the same people we have always been, the same people living in a different language."[45] Here, Danticat illustrates the theme of liminality: Celiane and the rest of the Espérance family are living in the United States, but Haiti is still a significant part of who they are. Just as Danticat uses French, Alvarez and Veciana-Suarez use Spanish to exemplify the duality of the main characters in their books. The authors sprinkle Spanish throughout the works to illustrate the presence of two cultures in the lives of the young women. In addition, native languages enhance the authenticity of the texts and increase the sense of alienation the protagonists feel in their new cultures.

---

[43] Smith, "Trauma and National Identity," 86.
[44] Smith, "Trauma and National Identity," 86.
[45] Danticat, *Behind the Mountains*, 126.

Anita's experience during her first day of classes in the United States demonstrates the importance of language, as well as the marginalization she experiences in her new home. When Anita is asked to share a few words or thoughts with her classmates, and she is at a loss for words, she thinks, "At the very least I should show them that I can speak their language, so they don't think I'm a complete moron who is almost thirteen and still in the second grade."[46] Anita thanks her class for accepting her into their country. By speaking English, she shows her desire to be accepted and to assimilate somewhat to the culture of her new home. This passage shows Anita as an outsider looking into and attempting to enter U.S. society. However, she fled from her country because, as *gusanos*, she and her family are now considered outsiders. Therefore, as her homeland is undergoing major changes, and as she is experiencing significant personal maturation, her cultural identity is also transformed. She is now on the border of two cultures, as well as two phases in life.

Like other coming-of-age novels, the works examined here explore the theme of young adults as being emergent, or in a transitive state from childhood to adulthood. One such manifestation of this particular emergence is a prolonged existence at a threshold. For the protagonists in these and other Caribbean-American novels, this threshold spans two countries and cultures – at times, literally, and at times, figuratively. From speaking in two different languages to feeling alienated in both their countries of origin and their new homes, the protagonists are, to a certain extent, living in the margins of society, due to this duality. In addition to telling the journeys of self-discovery of protagonists set during a turbulent period, the authors use these narratives to explore the transitional states of their homelands and the mixed cultural identities that have arisen because of political circumstances.

These stories serve as particularly effective coming-of-age novels because, in each case, the conflict within the native country parallels, reinforces, and even intensifies the adolescent narrator's internal struggle. For everyone, self-discovery during adolescence is a challenging process. But the hardships in the journey to find one's identity are magnified when coupled with the dangers of living under an oppressive political system and the trauma of displacement to a new country whose customs and language are foreign.[47] Through the authors' *testimonio*, these works construct an analogy between individual struggle and national tension. In writing these powerful coming-of-age novels, Danticat, Alvarez, and Veciana-Suarez also reveal the similar experiences of others and the stories of their nations of origin, so that their struggles, and that of their countries, are shared with the world.

---

[46]   Alvarez, *Before We Were Free*, 144.

[47]   For additional examples of external factors exacerbating the emergence into adulthood, see Kaywell, Joan F., et al. "Growing Up Female Around the Globe with Young Adult Literature." *The ALAN Review* (Summer 2006): 62–69. For specifically Caribbean examples, see Gregory, Lucille H. "Children of the Diaspora: Four Novels About the African-Caribbean Journey." In *African-American Voices in Young Adult Literature: Tradition, Transition, Transformation*, edited by Karen Patricia Smith. Metuchen, 277–92. N.J.: Scarecrow Press, 1994.

Chapter 3
Transgression and Transition

Georgie Horrell

Literature has the tremendous quality of allowing us to engage imaginatively in the lives of others. It enables us to move beyond ourselves and our own experiences. If we allow ourselves to respond to it fully, it can be a great educator. For those of us brought up monoculturally, literature which springs from outside our own boundaries can be a life-line.

—Beverley Naidoo[1]

Adolescence is, of course, a time of transition. Young Adult fiction at its most potent engages with this notion of change and transformation: protagonists move – often painfully – from dependent, highly managed and regulated childhood to a more fluid, uncertain and yet more agential (young) adulthood. The process of maturation becomes in multiple ways the very substance of the novel; thus the text connects with the target reader in a manner which is provocative and enabling – perhaps even empowering. Although the experiences of the primary characters are more often than not intensified, dangerous, and magnified versions of the average teen reader's life, there is nonetheless a sense in which the knowledge acquired by the reader's vicarious experience becomes the source for transgressive and transformative possibilities. Postcolonial Young Adult fiction is particularly significant in this regard.

As other critics (notably Perry Nodelman and Roderick McGillis[2]) have pointed out, the notion of the colonial in relation to children – and, as I shall argue, *adolescents* most particularly in terms of the *transition* to *postcolonial* – is metaphorically apt. If, as McGillis suggests, "children are colonial subjects" and "adults are the colonizers"[3] then the adolescent is precisely located at that point at which the requirement for a liberatory, transgressive narrative is most apposite. Quayson's concept of the postcolonial as the text's participation in a "process"

---

[1]   Naidoo, Beverley. *Through Whose Eyes? Exploring Racism: Reader, Text and Context*. London: Trentham Books, 1992, 16.

[2]   McGillis, Roderick. *Voices of the Other. Children's Literature and the Postcolonial Context*. New York: Garland, 2000; Nodelman, Perry. "The Other: Orientalism, Colonialism, and Children's Literature." *Children's Literature Association Quarterly* 17, no 1 (1992): 29–35 and *The Hidden Adult. Defining Children's Literature*. Baltimore: The John Hopkins University Press, 2008, 163–69.

[3]   McGillis, *Voices of the Other*, xxvii.

of "coming-into-being and of struggle against colonialism and its after-effects"[4] connects meaningfully with the notion of adolescence as a "process" of change. Whilst I agree with Clare Bradford's observation that the relationship of child to adult differs in a number of crucial ways from the relationship of "Orientals" to "Orientalists,"[5] there is nonetheless an interesting meshing of power structures that comes into play when one considers Young Adult novels through a postcolonial lens. Furthermore, the notion of the adult as "colonizer" produces a complex set of power dynamics for the writer (and indeed the postcolonial adult critic) of Young Adult fiction. Nodelman's productive consideration of Edward Said's theory – whilst it might "sidestep the question of race"[6] – pushes the adult critic of writing for children towards a position of acute and critical self-awareness and self-reflectivity.[7] I would like to suggest that the *postcolonial* writer (or critic of children's literature), is thus in a doubly delicate position which requires a highly critical and yet fluid self-reflectivity.

South Africa is in many senses an adolescent state: the country moves painfully from being the "New South Africa" towards a time when the intensity of transition, of unstable and shifting relations of power and knowledge, might give way to something apparently more settled, more "adult." Whilst trying to leave behind a history of oppression under apartheid, in which the majority of the population were without agency and without voice, the fledgling state progresses in the direction of a more distinct sense of independent identity. With this in mind, a consideration of South African Young Adult fiction acquires a particular poignancy. In this chapter I shall consider how recently published novels for adolescents written by two "ex-South African" white women enact transition and explore liberatory and transgressive possibilities. Written post-apartheid and in the aftermath of the Truth and Reconciliation Commission, in each case their novel enacts a negotiation with the past under apartheid. In fact, in each case the text performs multiple functions – rather than simply an expression or representation of adolescent experience, it is also a (somewhat overt) hi-jacking of the coming-of-age narrative in order to perform a postcolonial function. By postcolonial here I refer to an impulse in the text towards freedom, an impulse which is also intended to critique and dismantle the structures which constitute ongoing discourses of domination and repression. This impulse has, furthermore, a didactic edge: the teenage reader is supplied with information about apartheid, historical South Africa, and institutionalised racism, as well as the effects of these on the lives of young people. Postcolonial in this sense is, as McGillis suggests,

---

[4]   Quayson, Ato. *Postcolonialism. Theory, Practice or Politics?* Cambridge: Polity Press, 2000, 9.

[5]   Bradford, Clare. *Unsettling Narratives: Postcolonial Readings of Children's Literature.* Waterloo: Wilfred Laurier University Press, 2007, 7.

[6]   Bradford, *Unsettling Narratives*, 7.

[7]   Nodelman, "The Other," xxiii. Nodelman, *The Hidden Adult*, 163–69.

Postcolonialism as an activity of the mind is quite simply intent on both acknowledging the history of oppression and liberating the study of literature from traditional and Eurocentric ways of seeing ... The postcolonial writer confronts directly the forces of cultural domination and racial intolerance.[8]

In her book, *Radical Children's Literature: Future Visions and Aesthetic Transformations in Juvenile Fiction*, Kimberley Reynolds considers how children's literature contributes to the "social and aesthetic transformation of culture by ... encouraging readers to approach ideas, issues and objects from new perspectives and so prepare the way for change," thus viewing "writing for the young as replete with radical potential."[9] It is this "radical potential" – the power of the fictional text to confront "domination" and "intolerance" and to transform "ways of seeing" that I shall consider in relation to Linzi Glass's *Ruby Red*[10] and Gaby Halberslam's *Blue Sky Freedom*.[11]

In each of these novels, the principal character is a teenage girl who is enabled to understand – to empathise – with those crushed by a racist political tyranny. Political awakening, an awareness of the Other, is mapped onto sexual awakening or romantic love – a key modality in Young Adult fiction. Thus the divides between "black" and "white," rendered impassable by apartheid's strictures, are crossed: the transition from ignorance/naivety to experience/knowing is a journey in which the adolescent protagonist (and indeed, the adolescent reader) is escorted into a place of political – "postcolonial" – awareness. Furthermore, this transition is marked by intensely ambivalent interaction with – and ultimately independence from – key black parental figures: nanny figures. Adolescent issues: "experience of physical sexual maturity, experience of withdrawal from adult benevolent protection, consciousness of self in interaction, re-evaluation of values"[12] are woven tightly into the fabric of the novels in a manner which is significantly marked by the historical, geographical, social and political setting of these texts.

In the interests of illuminating the delicate position of both writer and critic of postcolonial Young Adult fiction, I shall begin by considering the autobiographical inflections in the two novels. Like many other contemporary writers of South African fiction publishing in the UK and USA, Linzi Glass and Gaby Halberslam both left South Africa when they were young adults. Their comments on this life experience make clear the role that their early years played in their framing of

---

[8] Nodelman "The Other," xxiii.

[9] Reynolds, Kimberley. *Radical Children's Literature. Future Visions and Aesthetic Transformations in Juvenile Fiction*. Basingstoke: Palgrave, 2007, 1.

[10] Glass, Linzi. *Ruby Red*. London: Macmillan, 2007.

[11] Halberslam, Gaby. *Blue Sky Freedom*. London: Penguin, 2008

[12] Russell, D.A. "The Common Experience of Adolescence: A Requisite for the Development of Young Adult Literature." *Journal of Youth Services in Libraries* 2 (1988), cited in John Stephens. "Linguistics and Stylistics." In *Understanding Children's Literature*, edited by Peter Hunt, 79. Abingdon: Routledge, 2009.

the narrative. The young white girls in their novels to a certain extent express the political coming-of-age of these writers themselves.

> My parents, being liberal white South Africans, decided that they no longer wanted to live in a country where there was no democracy and where the country was literally a "police state." The riots occurred in June, 1976 and by the following year we had left and were living in America.[13]

> I lived in South Africa until the age of fifteen ... *Blue Sky Freedom* is not really autobiographical but the setting and plot does draw heavily on what I remember from my childhood and learned afterwards about the apartheid system.[14]

In this sense the novels are rooted in personal history as much as in a particular nation's past. The novels are set in South Africa around the time of the 1976 Soweto uprising – in itself a young people's cause, as it was a series of school children's protests against the Afrikaans government who wished to impose Afrikaans as the official language in all black schools. During these riots, teenagers lost their lives, gunned down by policemen. However, the novels represent more than a narrativisation of this period in South African history: they also represent a negotiation with the past. They enact a consideration of the somewhat problematic place of a middle class white girl within the apartheid system and the means by which this character's developing agency and political awareness is brought about. Generally speaking, white girls in South Africa would have been largely oblivious of the traumatic events occurring in the Townships. They would certainly not have been involved in the riots in any way. Apartheid was highly effective in its pathological separation of the races. White high school girls would not have dared enter black townships. The protagonists in these novels are privileged and initially protected, but both Halberslam and Glass place their primary characters in positions which both endanger them and which simultaneously transgressively threaten the dominant culture. There is, perhaps, a sense in which the protagonists enact a politicised agency unavailable to the writers' younger selves.

Written from a geographical distance, as much as from the distance created by time (and adulthood), there is a distinct and observable attempt to locate the narratives within a credible and informed context. Apart from the historical details revealed in the story, each writer provides extra information in "Author's notes" at the end of the book. This is of course as much a reflection of the target readership (these books were both published outside South Africa, ostensibly for young adults who would be largely uninformed about South Africa's past), as it is indicative of authorial diligence. Jenkins and Mather quite rightly warn against the impassioned but insufficiently informed "trans-cultural engagement"

---

[13]   Glass, Linzi. Interview. http://www.linziglass.com/interview_004.html Accessed 1 Jan 2011.

[14]   Halberslam, Gaby. Biography. http://gabyhalberstam.co.uk/biography.php Accessed 1 Jan 2011.

which produces "distort[ed]" representations of both society and (via critics) of its literature.[15] However, Glass and Halberslam work hard to reveal their credentials in narrative detail as well as in extra material – both (auto) biographical and historical.

> "A story of love, loss and courage set against the backdrop of apartheid-torn South Africa."[16]

> "Ruby Red. The colour of passion. The colour of danger."[17]

Of course, a political narrative does not in itself make gripping reading for the average teenager, no matter how well researched. Significantly, what these writers are able to tap into in a particularly interesting way is the excitement of the transgression that lies at the heart of interest for most adolescents: sexual awakening. Mapping political education onto romantic interest, both Glass and Halberslam make use of the particular pathologies and rifts created by South African politics in order to create a heightened sense of drama, danger, and rebellion for their respective protagonists. Under apartheid, sexual relationships between races were illegal.[18] White girls would certainly not have considered black boys appropriate as boyfriends or objects of legitimate desire. The discourses of apartheid rendered such an alliance abject. Thus Victoria's first kiss (*Blue Sky*) – with Maswe, the black servant's teenaged son – is transgressive on a variety of levels.

> I nodded. Then a shudder rose up from my chest and I had to stop myself from crying all over again. I reached up. It felt like forever before my hands touched the sides of his face. He looked at me. Then he bent and pressed his lips to mine.[19]

This romantic moment is not only the culmination of a number of days of Victoria's hiding Maswe from the Security Police (and indeed from her family), but it also represents a breach of the law in itself – and furthermore transgresses all that white culture sought to preserve in South Africa at the time. Victoria's being called a "Kaffir lover" by her peers (they are not aware of the full implication of their taunts) is appropriate in a number of ways; the derogatory nomenclature applies

---

[15] Jenkins and Muther critique Donnerae MacCann and Yulisa Amadu Maddy's *Apartheid and Racism* (MacCann, Donnerae, and Yulisa Amadu Maddy. *Apartheid and Racism in South Africa Children's Literature, 1985–1995*. London: Routledge, 2001) by outlining the critics' failure to grasp the nuances of South African fiction for Young Adults – largely as a result of their cultural ignorance. See Jenkins, Elwyn, and Elizabeth Muther, "Cross-Cultural Misreadings: MacCann and Maddy's *Apartheid and Racism* Revisited." *The Lion and The Unicorn* 32, no 3 (2008).

[16] Dust jacket of *Blue Sky*.

[17] Dust Jacket of *Ruby Red*.

[18] The Immorality Act (1950–85) was one of the first laws of apartheid.

[19] Halberslam, *Blue Sky*, 159.

both to her political sensibilities and to the desired romantic attachment – both would be considered repulsive by her classmates, as well as by her family.

The enormously precarious (and, perhaps, ultimately unconvincing) romantic alliance between Victoria and Maswe is short lived, as Maswe is brutally beaten and murdered whilst detained in a police station. It is this event, however, which is the catalyst for Victoria's family's hasty departure from South Africa – and the turning point for Victoria's own political coming of age as well as the establishment of her agency as an independent political activist.

Glass's novel complicates this political/sexual awakening by means of a further point of transgression: Ruby falls in love with an Afrikaans boy, a member of the oppressive ruling elite.[20] Although Johann himself does not support apartheid, Ruby's romantic alliance with this son of a staunch racist serves to create a more complex questioning of the power structures and rigidly defined racial groupings within South African society. Her liberal parents do not initially approve of her relationship with the blue-eyed, blond-haired Johann. English-speaking South Africans enjoyed the privileges which were accorded to them as a result of their whiteness under apartheid (and did – and to a degree still do – enjoy economic dominance), but in many instances they could simultaneously take the moral high ground with reference to the plight of the "non-whites" of South Africa. Liberal white South Africans saw themselves as somewhat absolved from responsibility for the horrors of apartheid, as it was the National Party government – and the Afrikaners – who were considered culpable.[21] Indeed, in Glass' story, Ruby parents actively oppose apartheid: her mother attempts to support young black artists and breaks a variety of laws in order to do so. Although Ruby seeks to emulate her anti-apartheid parents in terms of their undermining of the dominant culture, she further challenges *their* perceptions and prejudices concerning the Afrikaans community, forcing them to adopt a more discriminating and less monolithic – less racist – perspective. In this manner, the protagonist demonstrates the (compulsory) rebellion against parental authority characteristic of adolescent fiction and at the same time challenges a simplistic approach to racism. Ultimately, the book argues for a deeply individual, humanist understanding of identity:

> We flew that night, Johann and I, higher and higher, to a place where there were
> no longer boundaries that kept us separate, English and Afrikaans, boy and girl.
> We were, in those moments, or perhaps they were hours, in the darkness, as one.[22]

---

[20]   The National Party, which introduced Apartheid and which ruled South Africa from 1948 to 1994, was largely representative of white, Afrikaans-speaking South Africans – mostly descendants of the Dutch settlers.

[21]   This oppositional stance between Afrikaans- and English-speakers in many respects originates in the period of British colonial rule in southern Africa and the antagonisms and loyalties which found explicit expression in the Anglo-Boer War (1899–1902). Many of the policies put in place by the National Party after 1948 were attempts to address the extreme poverty and disinvestment suffered by Afrikaners after the Boer War.

[22]   Glass, *Ruby Red*, 132.

Significantly, it is of course romantic love that dissolves boundaries and enhances enlightenment in both these novels. Whilst this is pertinent in the light of apartheid – and fitting in terms of the expectations of the teenage reader, it is also perhaps no more than an authorial sleight of hand. Ruby's blonde-haired, blue-eyed Afrikaner love may expose her to harsh criticism and anger; Victoria's illicit passion across the race barrier may endanger both her and her lover, but neither alliance suggests for the reader a realistic anti-racist discourse, or a viable means for overcoming political oppression. Rather, the narrative engages with the teenage reader at a point of awakening (sexual) with which they will already have engaged in order to facilitate the political (or postcolonial) imperative in the text.

In both these novels language differences underline the manner by which the protagonists are hampered in their attempt to overcome racial divides. English-speaking Ruby stumbles when trying to hold telephone conversations with Afrikaans Johann and his sister in *Ruby Red*; Victoria knows very little Xhosa, despite having been brought up, largely, by Maswe's mother. These gaps and linguistic barriers underline the success of racial divisions in South Africa. However, it would seem that the language of love is deemed sufficient to cross boundaries.

> "'*Nidiya kuthanda.*'"

> *Nidiya kuthanda.* I knew what that meant. Seraphina said those words every day to Charlie, just as she had to Maswe and me when we were little. I love you.[23]

This interchange is interesting in that the narrative seeks to explain commonality and understanding: Victoria has learned these words from Maswe's mother, has heard them every day and thus has a shared basis of experience with Maswe. However, what is equally telling is the manner by which the politics of material difference – class – are elided in this moment. Seraphina is the family's maid, who lives in a small "room" in the family garden. The narrative glosses over what is in effect a complex set of claims relating to "surrogate" mothers, and indeed raises some interesting issues concerning the complex construction of identity for young white South Africans.

Juvenile identity in (white) apartheid narratives is often framed and nurtured by the figure of the maid, servant, or nanny: at once comfortingly strong and yet ultimately vulnerable. In Halberslam's *Blue Sky Freedom*, Seraphina, Maswe's mother, certainly fulfils this role. Her "room" is "trashed" by the security police in the search for Maswe, she has to be taken in and protected by Granny when the protagonist's family flee South Africa, but it is also Seraphina who comforts Victoria and whose room reflects her surrogate mother's position in the white household:

---

[23] Halberslam, *Blue Sky*, 162.

> I'd always loved visiting Seraphina in her room ... I could trace my life in the
> things she had arranged around the room. A doll I'd loved until it became bald
> had been saved from the bin by Seraphina. It now sat on a shelf next to my first
> pair of shoes.[24]

It is, of course, telling that the black servant lives in a space filled by (albeit
cherished) cast-offs from the family. In the notes section that Halberslam provides
at the back of the novel, she says that "the relationship between Victoria and
Seraphina is ... the most tender in the book." The black nanny character is, she
says, "all the nannies we ever loved bundled into one."[25] However, the description
of Seraphina's room points to a problematic ambivalence in this carefully recorded
relationship – an ambivalence pertinent to a consideration of adolescence and the
emergent adult within these texts.

Anne McClintock's important consideration of maids and nannies, and the
abjection of black women, refers to South Africa at the turn of the nineteenth
century:

> the invisible strength of black women presses everywhere on white life so
> that the energy required to deny it takes the shape of neurosis ... the furtive
> intimacies between black women and their white charges ... the fraught relations
> of acrimony, strained intimacy, mistrust, condescension, occasional friendships
> and coerced subservience that shape relations between African women and
> their white mistresses ensure that the colonial home is a contest zone of acute
> ambivalence.[26]

Whilst this describes an earlier era, there is no doubt that McClintock's assessment
has distinct resonance with similar narratives from apartheid, not least with that
of *Blue Sky Freedom*. The nanny/maid is also the figure in the home most closely
associated with patrolling the borders between dangerous defilement and the self.
As nanny *and cleaner* she is not only responsible for taking care of the child's
physical needs but she is also the figure found scrubbing the floor, scouring the
toilet. Most white households marked this identification with signs of abjection, in
that the black servant was not entitled to eat from the same plates or drink from the
same cups as her white employers. Whites commonly expressed revulsion at the
thought of sharing crockery with a black person (whilst expecting their maids to
hand-wash their underwear).[27] Seraphina certainly has her own, separate "enamel
plate": Halberslam presents an authentic description of her living conditions.

---

[24]   Halberslam, *Blue Sky*, 22.

[25]   Halberslam, *Blue Sky*, 261.

[26]   McClintock, Anne. *Imperial Leather. Race, Gender and Sexuality in the Colonial
Context.* London: Routledge, 1995, 271.

[27]   This has resonance with stories told of black women working in white American
homes. Kathryn Stockett's recently published novel *The Help* is illustrative. Stockett,
Kathryn. *The Help*. New York: Penguin, 2010. See also Pope, Mary. "'I am NOT just like
one of the family ...': The Black Domestic Servant and White Family Dynamics in 20th

Melissa Steyn refers to the situation for black maids and nannies under apartheid in her introduction to *Whiteness Just Isn't What It Used To Be*:

> Our maids would prepare our food (except in some homes where the worthy woman of the house would not have black hands work with the food, although such hands could wash the dishes after the meal); they would sleep in a room at the back of the house.[28]

Many white homes were built with separate maid's quarters but if a house lacked a "khaya" or room, it would be unambiguously equipped with servant's (outside, separate) ablution facilities. As Steyn notes, these things were common practice in white homes, "even working-class homes, English and Afrikaans, give or take a few differences in cultural nuances."[29] The black woman marked the boundary of the intimate, the home, and was simultaneously inscribed outside this space. From the perspective of the child, the servant was thus embraced (and embracing), physically and intimately nurtured by her; and yet repelled, forbidden, abjected – both as (surrogate) mother figure and as a black woman. Within many of the texts which consider apartheid's relations, the figure of the nurturing black woman (or man) becomes a cipher for perceived and acknowledged injustice but is also a source of privileged information, a "native informant" who contributes significantly to the white child or adolescent's political awareness.[30] It is interesting that it is to this metonymic, black, feminine figure that Halberslam's postcolonial, post-apartheid narrator returns in order to construct a moment of transition and knowledge.

Read with South African children and adolescents in mind – and a history of subservience and surrogate mothering under apartheid – Nancy Chodorow's theories of mothering and identity formation assist in an understanding of particular implications for the structuring of white identities in apartheid discourses. Given that the white home during apartheid was indeed a "contest zone of acute

---

Century American and South African Literature. *Safundi: The Journal of South African and American Comparative Studies* 7 (2001).

[28] Steyn, Melissa. *"Whiteness Just Isn't What It Used To Be": White Identity in a Changing South Africa*. Albany: State University of New York Press, 2001, xi. See also Cock, Jacklyn. *Maids and Madams: A Study in the Politics of Exploitation*. Johannesburg: Raven Press, 1980.

[29] Steyn, *Whiteness*, xi.

[30] Gayatri Spivak theorises the potency of the Native Informant – largely in the context of the difficulty concerning making a "Third World" perspective available or at least partially accessible to a "First World" audience. Spivak, Gayatri. *A Critique of Postcolonial Reason: Towards a History of the Vanishing Present*. Cambridge, Mass.: Harvard University Press, 1999. I use Spivak's term to refer to the use of the black characters in the text in order to provide an inside view – a privileged access to knowledge inaccessible to a white society.

ambivalence,"[31] with maids and their white madams sharing care for the children, Chodorow's words gain resonance.

> Conflict and ambivalence [in the young child] develop in situations where caretakers [carers] feel conflict and ambivalence, and not solely as a result of an innate anxiety threshold ... Thus, society constitutes itself psychologically in the individual not only in the moral strictures of the superego. All aspects of psychic structure, character and emotional and erotic life are social, constituted through a "history of object-choices." This history, dependent on the individual personalities and behavior of those who happen to interact with a child, is also socially patterned according to the family structure and prevalent psychological modes of a society.[32]

Read against the childhood and adolescent narratives of white writers, Chodorow's conclusions illuminate the intensely conflictual mode of self-development with which white South African identity was (and to some extent still is) constituted. Furthermore, as she insists, these initial, early socially inflected family structures and conflicts are deeply encoded within identities – particularly in terms of the self in relationship with others.

> Elements of social structure, especially as transmitted through the organisation of parenting as well as through the features of individual families, are appropriated and transformed internally through unconscious processes and come to influence affective life and psychic structure. A child both takes into itself conflictual relationships as it experiences them, and organises these experiences of self-in-relationship internally ...[33]

I would therefore argue that the generations of white men and women who grew up in homes with black servants, particularly with black women as nannies, developed identities in which the ambivalent and violent realities of apartheid society were enacted in intimate intensity. This intensity is represented in the young adults' texts I am considering in this chapter: as the adolescent characters make the transition from child to adult, it is precisely the black caregiver who becomes key to this move to "knowing" adulthood. Whilst this is clearly a particular consideration of a particular set of power dynamics located in a highly articulated mesh of domination and control, I would like to suggest that there is nonetheless something to be taken from these reflections which carries implications for the analysis of racism – and its pathologies – in other social frameworks.

Ruby Red takes a different tack to that of *Blue Sky Freedom*: a number of black figures in the novel are welcomed into the family home as friends and protégés of Ruby's mother. Whilst carefully describing the danger associated with such alliances Glass sets up a home which has similarities with that described in the

---

[31]   McClintock, *Imperial Leather*, 271.

[32]   Chodorow, Nancy. *The Reproduction of Mothering. Psychoanalysis and the Sociology of Gender*. Berkeley: University of California Press, 1978, 50.

[33]   Chodorow, *The Reproduction of Mothering*, 50.

autobiographies of key anti-apartheid figures like the Slovos.[34] Ruby's family is presented as a model for anti-racist behaviour within the context of apartheid, so that Ruby's own bid for independence is, as I suggested earlier, of necessity a step beyond this, in the form of a challenge to her parents' political assumptions. However, Glass also draws upon the figure of a gardener, both to evoke the notion of the wise and yet vulnerable black servant, as well as to critique the social conventions that inscribed this figure within discourses of colonial dominance. Whereas adult black men were often referred to as "boys" under apartheid, Glass' narrator, Ruby, pointedly addresses the school gardener as "sir" and makes a further point of using his full name later in the narrative:

> Benjamin Mpatha stood among all that he tended, the majestic trees, the lush green lawn, the rich variety of seasonal flowers ... He must have felt my gaze for he looked up and raised his hand slowly to wave at me.[35]

In her earlier novel, *The Year the Gypsies Came*,[36] Glass similarly uses the figure of a gardener or watchman who, in the absence of mature and responsible white adult figures, takes on the role of wise advisor and nurturer. Indeed here this character fills a parental surrogacy similar to that described in Halberslam's *Blue Sky Freedom*. Avoiding a significant reference to maids or nannies, Glass nonetheless references the importance of the "native informant" in her novels – a figure placed at the crux of the power-knowledge nexus for adolescent characters.

The novels I have considered in this chapter conclude in strikingly different ways. In *Blue Sky Freedom*, a militant, radical Victoria has returned to South Africa to act as political activist and to confront the racist torturers who took Maswe's life.

> 'You are going down *meisie*. You're going – '
>
> 'Hou jou bek, Mr Kloete.' I knew I was being extremely rude but I didn't care. 'I may end up in prison, but on my way I am going to expose you and all the other murderers like you ... You killed Maswe. I will make sure that he did not die in vain.'
>
> I put the phone down.
>
> 'Granny!' I called. 'Let's go. I'm ready.'[37]

---

34   See Gillian Slovo's autobiography, *Every Secret Thing: My Family, My Country*, for a nuanced, powerful description of an anti-apartheid activist family. Slovo's account is revealing in its analysis of the intensely difficult dynamics alive in such a politically transgressive home. Slovo, Gillian. *Every Secret Thing: My Family, My Country*. London: Abacus, 1998.

35   Glass, *Ruby Red*, 192.

36   Glass, Linzi. *The Year the Gypsies Came*. London: H. Holt, 2006.

37   Halberslam, *Blue Sky*, 258.

Halberslam's adolescent protagonist has become an informed, agential young woman. Victoria acts outside of her parent's influence and authority, bravely transgressing norms and conventions in her politically inspired life choices. Thus the novel traces the dangerous path of Victoria's coming-of-age, ultimately producing a fiercely independent, postcolonial character who endorses notions of transgression and radical potential.

At the conclusion of *Ruby Red*, Ruby stands in New York's Times Square on the fourth of July with her father (her mother has remained in South Africa, to support her protégé black artists), clutching a picture painted by a young black artist involved in the Soweto riots.

> We were thousands of miles away from home, but I held the picture of the hopeful young boy from the shanty towns of Soweto, his tattered clothes two sizes too big, up towards the light, the purple crayon glowing ever brighter in his little hand.
>
> 'Look Julian,' I whispered, 'I have brought you with me to freedom.'[38]

Ruby is in many senses more experienced at the end of the novel – she describes her farewell letter to Johann as "mushy" and knowingly faces a life exiled from South Africa as a result of the political stance that she and her family have taken against apartheid. Unlike Halberslam's Victoria, however, Ruby must leave the fighting to someone else (interestingly, her mother).[39]

Once account has been taken of the developing agency and identity of the central white characters, though, it is pertinent to consider the manner in which the black characters are ultimately represented. Whilst it is certainly true that Halberslam and Glass attempt to present their black characters as agential, and indeed, use some small amounts of Xhosa and Zulu to indicate voice, I would like to suggest that the conclusions of the novels are telling: the development and experience of the central characters is somewhat at the cost of key black characters. Maswe is finally a victim, his (meagrely represented) voice removed from the text by his death two thirds of the way through the novel. Victoria's agency as strong, white – potentially powerful – young woman is established precisely in terms of her avenging his death. Similarly, Ruby's coming-of-age is established to some degree at the expense of the vulnerable black characters represented in the text. Julian's painting may have made it to New York, but the reader has no idea of what he is doing whilst Ruby is in Times Square. Furthermore, the painting she holds is sentimental in its description rather than powerful. It speaks of poverty and a child-like state rather than maturity and agency.

---

[38]   Glass, *Ruby Red*, 214.

[39]   This has some resonance with the history of anti-apartheid activists – and the role of strong women in this history. For example, Ruth First (Gillian Slovo's mother) remained to continue the struggle against apartheid in southern Africa, sending her children to safety in England.

The Young Adult postcolonial novel holds a key position in the canon of fiction written for adolescents. The distinct relevance of the liberatory text for readers whose own path is one of progress from a position of submission to (adult) authority towards one of attainment of enhanced agency and independence is clear. I would argue that the novels I have considered in this chapter certainly use key ingredients of adolescent fiction in order to inform their young readers of events and issues in late 1970s South Africa. Each novel is thorough in its attempt to create accurate and historically sound narratives. In both *Blue Sky Freedom* and *Ruby Red*, the main protagonists gain independence and agency, their experiences and coming-of-age enacting and enabling an education in liberation and political awareness for adolescent readers. Furthermore, although the novels are, of course, geographically and historically specific, the text serves to expose the patterns of thought that underpinned apartheid – and which, in multiple forms and guises, linger in racism today. Whilst the stock ingredient in adolescent fiction, sexual awakening, performs a means to overcome racial – and class – barriers, however, these alliances are eventually sacrificed, their significance dissolved within the writers' larger concerns: "confront[ing] directly the forces of cultural domination and racial intolerance."[40] The degree to which these texts hold "radical potential" and are able to transform "ways of seeing" is perhaps limited by the perspective from which the stories are told. The complex web of power structures mentioned earlier in my argument come into play in interesting and observable ways, thwarting to a certain extent the apparent postcolonial purpose of the writer in each case. Ultimately, I suggest, the novels create a sense of identity and agency for the young, white, women primary characters, but the young black characters (Maswe and Julian) are not – contra Ruby – "brought with [them] to freedom."[41]

---

[40] McGillis, *Voices of the Other*, xxiii.
[41] Glass, *Ruby Red*, 214.

Chapter 4
Romance, Dystopia, and the Hybrid Child

Clémentine Beauvais

Romance across the bounds of a divided world is a leitmotif of literature, particularly Young Adult fiction, where the adolescent's universe-disturbing, transgressive feelings respond to the dialectical socio-political order of the parents. In *Romeo and Juliet* fashion, teenagers' ultimate political contestation in these works stems from an emotional accident: falling in love with the offspring of their parents' enemies. The scandal is worsened when it leads to the conception of a "hybrid" child, who cannot be categorised, who exists outside his or her grandparents' restricted terminology – outside established social labels. The hybrid child of a teenager union is a visible crack in the segregating walls of society. Born of very young parents, the child subverts cultural expectations, pointing at a form of nascent sexuality that the adult authority struggles to accept. Born astride socio-political divides, it is also a seditious entity, which forces both the adult world and the young adult reader to recentre their attention onto this threatening bearer of social change.

This chapter analyses the significance of the motif of the hybrid child in two Young Adult series, Malorie Blackman's critically acclaimed *Noughts and Crosses* books (2001–08)[1] and Stephenie Meyer's bestselling *Twilight* tetralogy (2005–08).[2] Both series are generic hybrids themselves, mixing romance and dystopia for *Noughts and Crosses*, and romance and fantasy for *Twilight*. They share many similarities in their treatment of relationships, featuring an irresistible love story between two members of different classes, races, or "species," whose liaison is hindered by socio-political and/or physical imbalance in power. Both couples accidentally conceive a child in one first sexual encounter. The "hybrid" offspring (a girl, in both cases) is then willingly brought to term, the young mother's staunch refusal of abortion bringing about the death of the father in *Noughts and Crosses*, and the end of the mother's human life in *Breaking Dawn*. The narrative then focuses greatly on the hybrid, exploring her efforts and ability to modify the polarised configuration of the world she was born in.

---

[1]   Blackman, Malorie. *Noughts and Crosses*, and others. London: Random House, 2001–08.

[2]   Meyer, Stephenie. *Twilight*, and others. London: Atom, 2005–08.

I argue that trans-racial romance and hybridity in these two examples of highly popular, arguably female-oriented Young Adult sagas, are connected to issues of political and social awareness. They address the young reader's appraisal of his or her own political power. In the dystopian or unsatisfactory societies presented, trans-racial parenting is an opportunity for counter-power; the hybrid child becomes a form of political upheaval against coercive social configurations. But Blackman and Meyer differ in their visions of the hybrid child's power to reconcile the opposite forces of the worlds they describe, and their decisions define the ideological orientations of their works. Analysing their diverging treatments of this motif, I will draw wider conclusions on the politics of Young Adult literature and its sometimes ambiguous representations of adolescent empowerment in an unsatisfactory society.

"You have to live in a world divided":[3] Politics of adolescent romance

The first characteristic of romance, according to Pamela Regis, is that it contains "a *definition of society*, always corrupt, that the romance novel will reform."[4] To the emotional awakening which the Young Adult novel generically enacts – romance being, arguably, one of its most frequent ingredients – responds, in perhaps equal measure, a form of political awakening. This is especially the case in the traditional *Romeo and Juliet* plot (a play which both *Twilight* and *Noughts and Crosses* regularly evoke) where romance strikes teenagers belonging to enemy castes in a divided world. Political awareness and erotic love follow a similar ascent in the life of the enamoured teenagers: the *romantic* transgressive focus on the loved object coincides with a *political* combat: breaking away from the conflicting groups. In other words, the increasing erotic tension between the two teenage bodies is the physical manifestation of a political desire to modify the configurations of their dialectical world.

The dystopian universe of *Noughts and Crosses* features trans-racial and upstairs/downstairs romance between the black, upper-class "Cross" Sephy and the white, working-class "Nought" Callum. The unequal status of their parents relative to each other – Sephy's parents are Callum's parents' masters – is reinforced by the social weight of this difference within the essentialistic political system of the dystopia. Sephy's father, a politician, is a doubly authoritative entity, being both a parental and a governmental figure. From the onset of the saga, the children's relationship, slowly but surely evolving towards erotic love, is transgressive on a personal and on a social level. The teenagers' romantic feelings for the racial and socio-political *other* come to embody the adolescent struggle out of parental authority and into alternative options for community life and social order.

---

   [3]   Blackman, Malorie. *Knife Edge*. London: Random House, 2004, 37.

   [4]   Regis, Pamela. *A Natural History of the Romance Novel*. Philadelphia: University of Pennsylvania Press, 2003, 14.

Twilight, as Anna Silver highlights, is as concerned with questions of communitarian belonging as it is with romance.[5] All tribulations coming in the way of the star-crossed lovers stem from a battle of underground communities within the established human society, with each book uncovering more and more hidden dividing lines between groups. Bella's emotional awakening within what she thinks is the only social order in place ("human," modern America) gradually leads to a discovery of the many conflicting suborders that underscore the establishment. Her attraction to Edward reveals underlying clashes between clans and power imbalance beneath the neat surface of mainstream American culture. The fantasy element of trans-species relationships metaphorically recapitulates the reciprocal attraction of the mainstream for the counter-culture, their coexistence, and their interdependency.

The construction by Young Adult literature of this politico-romantic adolescent impulse to break away from the norm of birth is fraught with ideological ambiguity. Christine Wilkie-Stibbs, in her analysis of *Noughts and Crosses*, notes the non-essentialistic dimension of the romantic aspect of Blackman's saga within the dystopia.[6] Drawing from Slavoj Žižek's Marxist/Lacanian examination of socio-political hegemony, Wilkie-Stibbs notes that Blackman's ideology, whilst critiquing the absolutist discourse and manoeuvres of capitalist imperialism, places itself in a paradoxical position – it becomes an expression of the underlying counter-ideology which capitalist imperialism precisely *needs* in order to subsist. The apparent pluralism of the democratic mainstream allows it to exert, potentially tyrannically, its own conception of social order – *with and against* plural counter-cultural subpowers. *Twilight* enacts a similar kind of paradox. Seen from this angle, the 'monstrous' attraction-repulsion dialectic between the two lovers is not only a symptom of underlying political tensions within the established social norm; it also justifies the very existence of the norm. It is as if the adults' essentialistic social order was *waiting for* the children's disruption of it, existing through it – potentially using it to its advantage, incorporating its disorder into their order. An issue germane to all children's literature, and which here appears to its full extent in the politics of young adult romance, is the extent to which it exalts youth as a territory for social change, or only pretexts it in order to legitimise what is essentially an adult political agenda. Interpretative boundaries in this context are blurred: while Wilkie-Stibbs concludes that Blackman's approach leads to a "hybridized reading experience"[7] in which the vocabulary of the global, imperialistic order loses its power, Pat Pinsent draws attention to Blackman's resulting "middle-class" and

---

[5]   Silver, Anna. "Twilight is Not Good for Maidens: Gender, Sexuality and the Family in Stephenie Meyer's Twilight Series." *Studies in the Novel* 42, nos 1&2 (2010): 121–38.

[6]   Wilkie-Stibbs, Christine. "The 'Other' Country: Memory, Voices, and Experiences of Colonized Childhoods." *Children's Literature Association Quarterly* 31, no 3 (2006): 237–59.

[7]   Wilkie-Stibbs, "The 'Other' Country," 242.

"humanitarian" approach to social conflict, politically branded values which, under Žižek's definition, would contribute to the endorsement of the hegemony.[8]

Adolescent romance in dystopia – or romance in a divided, plural world – is at the crossroads of adult authoritarianism and teenage emotional growth. In the fictional unsatisfactory worlds of the romance novel, adolescent love is a gut reaction against hegemonic discourse, but its contestatory power is relative to the extent to which it is actually *expected* and *utilised* by the adult intelligentsia. The emotional transgression of the counter-culture, stretching towards alternative values, takes full part in the sustenance of hegemonic power. It is manipulated by it, defining it by contrast. The disturbing negotiation which ends *Noughts and Crosses* between Sephy and her parents, after which she is forced to condemn either her unborn baby or her lover to death, constructs the enamoured adolescent as dramatically vulnerable to familial and political pressure. Sephy's choice – very much a Sophie's Choice – to sacrifice Callum in order to save their baby allows the theme of hybridity to deploy itself fully beyond her own transgressive feelings and into the reality of a living being. But in so doing, she is also condemning herself to parenthood – to the very position of authority that she rebelled against – and half-disappears as a lead character, giving way to her daughter as a prominent focus of the subsequent narratives. In *Twilight* the impact of hegemonic discourse on the young heroine despite the apparently transgressive romance is perhaps even more insidious, as Bella eventually finds herself – through almost forced choices of marriage and child-bearing – in a blissful state of youth, matrimonial and maternal eternity, endless riches easily spent on designer clothes and car, and communitarian obligation – a fictional exaggeration of hegemonic capitalist discourse with its accompanying female self-help and magazine industry. Adolescent romance may pave the way to contestation in a segregating society, but the extent to which the hybridised life the adolescent gains is actually contestatory depends on how much it is manipulated, at the core, by the adult values it seeks to subvert.

"Not a choice – a necessity":[9] The political pregnant body

The ambivalence and potential danger of the adolescent's position in this dystopian universe is adequately translated in the representation of sexual intercourse, pregnancy, and delivery displayed in both series. Cross-species pregnancy is deeply rooted into collective imagination, and particularly associated with violence and rape. One of the most famous hybrid "children" in Greek mythology, the Minotaur, is the result of Queen Pasiphae's impregnation by Poseidon's bull, in retaliation for her husband King Minos's greediness. Female erotic love in the form of Pasiphae's passion for the godly bull – and inventiveness in the form of

---

[8]   Pinsent, Pat. "Language, Genres and Issues: The Socially Committed Novel." In *Modern Children's Literature: An Introduction*, edited by Kimberley Reynolds, 191–208. New York: Macmillan, 2005.

[9]   Meyer, Stephenie. *Breaking Dawn*. London: Atom, 2008, 132.

Daedalus's contraption in order to fulfil her sexual desire – leaves no space for free will. The female womb is a displaced locus of revenge, the ultimate humiliation for Minos. It is therefore a political space, in the etymological sense of political: that which refers to the *polis*, the nation-state: it is an attack on Minos's political power. Pasiphae's impregnation is a mythic form of war rape, the hybrid offspring a living monstrosity metonymic of this boundary-breaking relationship.

Twilight and *Noughts and Crosses* present trans-racial and trans-species sexual intercourse as equally violent, equally ambiguous, and equally political. In a Pasiphae fashion, Bella is ready and even happy to endure the seemingly horrifying pain of sexual intercourse with the demi-godly, stone-cold, supernaturally strong Edward.[10] The corresponding scene in *Noughts and Crosses*, although not physically violent, takes place as Sephy is subdued, having been kidnapped and maltreated by a Nought terrorist group to which Callum belongs. Sexual intercourse in these conditions – which her parents mistakenly, but perhaps understandably, believe to be a manifestation of war rape – interrogates the notion of consent and preparation implicit to adolescent sexual awakening. The fact that both events lead to the unwanted conception of a child, and the subsequent restless pregnancy of the mother, further questions the validity of adolescent romance as an ideological liberation from the norm. Who is colonising who? Sexual brutality in both sagas enacts, at the level of adolescent libido, the social struggles of the adult-orchestrated world, writing the underlying class issues of adult society into the bodies of the children – and leaving the latter with only limited control of their own impulses. Like Pasiphae, whose pregnant body becomes a political battleground between king and god, Bella's and Sephy's pregnant bodies are, beyond romance and erotic love, physically colonised by ongoing communitarian tensions.

But Bella and Sephy, unlike Pasiphae, are barely women – they are teenagers. The abused pregnant teenage body, as Lydia Kokkola argues below, is a monstrous body, an aberration of cultural perceptions of natural order.[11] In the case of a "hybrid" pregnancy, it is also a political – or rather a suddenly politicised – body. This is, firstly, because it contains the hybrid baby, who represents potential socio-political change and will be a visible embodiment of transgressive love. The pregnant body bears the mark of the mingling of a divided world, going against the wishes of the hegemonic power in place and the family. The body pregnant with a hybrid child is doubly subversive: the baby, once born, will be doubly "cursed" – socially stigmatised as the daughter of a teenage mother, and ideologically endowed with the identity of a "universe-disturbing" child, in the world of Roberta Seelinger

---

[10] See Silver, "Twilight is Not Good for Maidens," 125–26, for an analysis of Edward's godliness.

[11] Kokkola, Lydia. "Monstrous Bodies: Writing the Incestuously Abused Adolescent Body," in this volume.

Trites,[12] that which enables and embodies adolescent contestation against the power in place. Following on from Trites, however, there is a second and more ambiguous political dimension to the adolescent pregnant body. Trites argues that although Young Adult literature presents (breaking away from the *Bildungsroman* pattern) a portrayal of the growing individual negotiating his or her place within society, this negotiation involves rebellion on a primary level, followed by a gradual process of taming, at the end of which the contestatory adolescent is moulded back into social acceptance. Once again, we must ask whether the hybrid pregnancy, though scandalous on an episodic level, can actually be seen to turn to the advantage of the political power of the divided adult world. This is particularly ambiguous if we consider that the pregnancy dramatically modifies the status of the four teenage parents. By definition, it forces each of them into *parenthood*, certainly hinting at the possibility of generational change but also, in perhaps equal measure, at the possibility of generational replication. The adolescent-parent is not quite an adolescent anymore, but his or her authority is not yet established as that of an adult. Floating in an uncanny limbo between subservience to the grandparents and authority towards their children, the uncertainty of their position is reinforced by the new narrative emphasis on the hybrid baby, which in both *Twilight* and *Noughts and Crosses* (though more so in the latter) forces readers to displace their hopes and expectations onto the hybrid and away from the parents. The body pregnant with the hybrid child is ideologically and narratively disempowered.

The pregnant body is also dramatically vulnerable. Death surrounds the hybrid pregnancy, asking further questions about the legitimacy of the political struggle that subsumes it. Both mothers-to-be are urged to consider abortion, but reject it forcefully. Sephy's refusal leads to Callum's death, powerfully symbolising the sacrifice of the intermediate generation in the struggle for social change. Sephy's decision to let Callum die instead of having an abortion relocates what is at stake in the series within the third generation, forcing the reader to accept that the transgressive couple's power has reached its limits in the creation of a hybrid child, who will now pick it up from there. Bella's staunch rejection of abortion in *Breaking Dawn* is more clearly infused with religious politics. Edward's wishes to give Bella an abortion are justified by the very prominent risk that the baby poses, as it literally sucks her blood. But despite a gory, life-threatening pregnancy, in which the full vision of the "monstrous body" is visible, she sticks to a pro-life ethic which signals, arguably, her ultimate disappearance. During delivery, Bella as the reader knew her dies, giving rise to a super-Bella of the vampire kind. Bella and Sephy, in different ways, leave their state of hybrid pregnancy de-characterised, narratively and ideologically metamorphosed, their now empty bodies having endured a very deathly manifestation of political activism. To justify the pregnancy and to legitimise the change, both writers appeal to the same *deus ex machina* – the expectant mothers' maternal feelings for the foetus. The refusal of

---

[12] Trites, Roberta Seelinger. *Disturbing the Universe: Power and Repression in Adolescent Literature*. Iowa City: University of Iowa Press, 2000.

abortion is "not a choice – a necessity," as Bella puts it, paraphrasing anti-abortion campaigns.[13] The hybrid pregnant body, though politically transgressive with its symbolic potentialities, does not liberate the pregnant adolescent mother. It forces her into a new role, passing on the duty of socio-political change to the third generation, in the person of the hybrid baby.

But is the hybrid baby, who now crystallises all expectations, up to the task, and how does she deal with it? This is where we reach a major divergence between the two sagas, perhaps due, quite simply, to a difference in quality. Blackman adopts a postcolonial outlook on the power of hybridity, which I will now analyse as linked to Homi Bhabha's theory of hybridity in *The Location of Culture*.[14] Meyer, in contrast, conforming to the religious ethics of her saga, presents the hybrid child as a Christic figure. Blackman and Meyer thus differ in their treatments of the hybrid child's power to reconcile the opposite forces of the worlds they describe, and these decisions define the ideological orientations of their works and of their presentations of social change.

Hybridity and disruption: Postcolonial inflexions in *Noughts and Crosses*

Not losing sight of the fact that Malorie Blackman's tale is one of racial discord, it is perhaps unsurprising that we should find postcolonial thought at the core of her ideological message. Her presentation of hybridity, more precisely, localises itself within Homi Bhabha's complex reflection on the subject, betraying a cultural and literary background perhaps less essentialistic than Meyer's. Bhabha's vision of hybridity is not a reconciliatory one: it recognises the hybrid as an agent of disruption:

> Hybridity has no such perspective of depth or truth to provide: it is not a third term that resolves the tension between two cultures, or the two scenes of a book, in a dialectical play of "recognition." The displacement from symbol to sign creates a crisis for any concept of authority based on a system of recognition.[15]

Hybridity in Bhabha's theory represents an anti-essentialistic space where contestation is made possible. Its existence disturbs the established authority, allowing for a liminal counter-power to be set up in linguistic, political, social, and cultural terms. It does not, as Deborah Kapchan and Pauline Turner Strong put it, "[threaten] to dissolve difference into a pool of homogenization," as would more superficial visions of multiculturalism.[16] The hybrid exists in itself and for itself, not as a synthesis of the two opposite forces of the colonised and the coloniser.

---

[13] Meyer, *Breaking Dawn*, 132.

[14] Bhabha, Homi. *The Location of Culture*. New York: Routledge, 2005.

[15] Bhabha, *The Location of Culture*, 161.

[16] Kapchan, Deborah, and Pauline Turner Strong. "Theorising the Hybrid." *The Journal of American Folklore* 112, no 445 (1999): 239–53.

Callie's birth in Blackman's *Knife Edge* allows for a paraphrased reflection on the baby's hybrid status by her mother, Sephy:

> You're new and unique and original. You're a lighter brown than me. Much lighter. But you're not a Nought, not white like your dad. You're a trailblazer. Setting your own colour, your own look. Maybe you're the hope for the future. Something new and different and special ... Find your own identity. I hope and pray you find your own place and space and time.[17]

In a highly romanticised way, Sephy reformulates Bhabha's theory of hybridity. She acknowledges the opening up of a new space of identity and power which Callie inhabits. This space, Bhabha's "third space," is political. Her identity as a human being is superseded by the transgressive fact of her birth, and the multiple tensions that underscore it. Like Bhabha's hybrid, she is a transient, flexible being, both a receptacle for other people's hopes and dreams and an active agent in her own right. Her untouched future – the simple fact of *having not lived yet* – suffices to crystallise onto her both the weight of her grandparents' social order and of her parents' political and erotic desire for an alternative life. She does not *negotiate*, but *initiates*, change. And this change, if Bhabha's theory is to be followed through, will be paved with conflict and perturbations.

The subtlety and slowness of Callie's growing power helps the reader understand it all the better. As a character, Callie is unremarkable physically (apart from her skin colour) and intellectually. Blackman does not idealise her in any stage of her growth other than through the ambiguous opinion of her mother, who both loves and hates her for what she represents. It is ideologically, as a symbol, that Callie inhabits Bhabha's third space of hybrid power. Callie's power as a hybrid is constantly developing, following a trial-and-error process. Her growth as a member of the third, hybrid identity gives rise to a triangular power relationship between herself, her black mother Sephy, and her white uncle Jude. In this personal but also political struggle, each of the three characters schematically represents one social category of colonialism: Sephy belongs to the colonising caste, Jude to the colonised, and Callie to the hybridised. In virtue of their status, each possesses a different type of claim to power and various, manipulative ways of asserting their authority on each other. It is through this struggle, which lasts for two whole books, that Callie's potent hybrid status will gradually develop. She only obtains a narrative voice within the text in *Checkmate*, when maturity allows her to assert herself as an equally authorial character as the other two forces.[18] This new voice begins as strong, but youthful in its excessiveness: having not yet defined a space for her hybridised status, Callie has temporarily given in to her uncle's power; she has been instrumentalised by him to become a suicide bomber. Her opinion very much belongs to someone else, as does her approach to power:

---

[17]   Blackman, *Knife Edge*, 37–38.

[18]   Blackman, Malorie. *Checkmate*. London: Random House, 2005.

My mum is Persephone Hadley, daughter of Kamal Hadley.
Kamal Hadley is the leader of the Opposition – and a complete bastard.
My mum is a Cross – one of the so-called ruling elite …
My dad was a murderer.
My dad was a rapist …
My dad burns in hell.[19]

In this book which takes the form of a collection of flashbacks, Callie reflects on her heritage and gradually constructs her own hybrid third space, whilst developing her political awareness as she finds her own power in her mixed-race background. By the end of the novel, the two castes of the old power structures, embodied by her uncle Jude and her grandmother Jasmine, literally and symbolically destroy each other, while she is forced to adopt a reflective position and understand the political dynamics at work in what constitutes her own identity. She is left transformed by this reflection. On a personal level, she has found in her own genesis evidence of "love, not hatred,"[20] which legitimises emotional affection for her third space of hybridity. On an ideological level, this symbolises the potency of her hybrid identity to modify the political configuration of her divided world. The transgressive fact of her birth has been turned into hope for the future:

A weird and wonderful feeling flooded through me … It took me more than a few seconds to recognize what it was.

Hope.

For the first time in, oh, so long, I had hope for the future.[21]

Reflectivity has been turned into ambition for a productive modification of the world: Callie's position within the complex, fluid third space of colonial hybridity has subverted the norm, that is to say the unchangeable division between Noughts and Crosses. In that, she has fulfilled Bhabha's interpretation of hybridity, placing herself within a threatening, constantly evolving space. She has also become the politically potent hybrid not because she was born as such, but because she has made the choice to transform her hybrid identity into both an identity and a political strength, superior to what either of her parents could ever hope to achieve.

Twilight and the messianic hybrid

Stephenie Meyer adopts towards Bella and Edward's hybrid child a radically different approach. Rather than welcoming the ambivalence and the potent uncertainty of the hybrid's socio-political power, the *Twilight* series present the

---

[19] Blackman, *Checkmate*, 19.

[20] Blackman, *Checkmate*, 507.

[21] Blackman, *Checkmate*, 501.

hybrid child, Renesmee, as little less than a messianic figure. Renesmee's birth in *Breaking Dawn* makes an ideological statement which is linked to the religious ethics which subsume the books. This makes sense if the saga is reinterpreted as an (eroticised) assertion of religious ideals of abstinence and restraint. The vampire/human hybrid could only be conceived as a result of intense physical attraction between members of the two species, but also of superior physical restraint on Edward's part, who had to refrain from quite literally eating his human partner. Renesmee, as a hybrid, belongs to a transgressive space, because within the books' ethics she represents the ultimate achievement, ironically perhaps, of Meyer's religious ascetics: the supremacy of mind control over bodily instincts. For Aro, a member of the ruling caste of vampires who drink human blood, Renesmee is a source of wonder for representing this power, which affirms the possibility for "vegetarianism," that is to say, resistance to natural impulses:

> And so much to learn, so much to learn! ... We came expecting only justice and the sadness of false friends, but look what we have gained instead! A new, bright knowledge of ourselves, our possibilities.[22]

Renesmee, through her hybrid status, indirectly redefines vampirism and the possibility for "morality" within it. This makes her hybridity quasi divine. As Lydia Kokkola notes, the reaction both vampires and humans display when they meet Renesmee is characteristic of "agapic love," similar to the compelling adoration felt for the infant Jesus – arguably the most famous hybrid in Western collective imagination.[23] Renesmee is perceived as a transgressive, potentially threatening force because she legitimises the Cullen's ascetic "diet" and localises it as the source of such agapic love. She is, like Callie, defined primarily by the ethical configurations surrounding her conception, rather than as a sentient being.

Renesmee's power as a hybrid is uncontroversial, contrary to Callie's, both on the level of the story and as a narrative construct. As a character, she is immortal and cognitively superior to all newborns, displays high supernatural powers, accelerated development, and she is devoid of all infant demands on her parents. She has also inherited the very best characteristics from both her parents, aesthetically as well as physiologically. As Edward tells Bella: "She has exactly your color eyes ... they're beautiful ... Her skin seems about as impenetrable as ours [the vampires]."[24] But this makes Renesmee an absolutely idealised child, meant to elicit an easy response in the reader. Her status as a hybrid, not only between vampire and human but also as a both babyish and mature character, does not leave any space for anything other than pure wonder on the reader's part. Her behaviour alternates between mentions of cuteness, which trigger feelings

[22]   Meyer, *Breaking Dawn*, 648.
[23]   Kokkola, Lydia. "Virtuous Vampires and Voluptuous Vamps: Romance Conventions Reconsidered in Stephenie Meyer's 'Twilight' Series." *Children's Literature in Education* 42, no 2 (2011): 165–79.
[24]   Meyer, *Breaking Dawn*, 397.

of attachment in the reader, and descriptions of her precocious communication skills, which elicit admiration. Positive readerly responses are thus targeted, and arguably achieved, in a wide-ranging manner. The third space of hybridity she inhabits may be transgressive on an ideological level, but as a character she is constructed to be completely overpowering, an evidence of absolute perfection. Although she is a hybrid, she is an imperialistic (and thus unrealistic) example of the concept – she does not delineate the "articulation of the ambivalent space" which Bhabha defines as a side-product of hybridity.[25] She does not belong to a fluid, evolving identitary sphere, but to a ready-made domain of perfection. She is an idealised vision of hybridity, a biblical example of the sort, bringing about change, though not explicitly so, in a religious way.

Two settings of hybridity

The gap between Meyer's and Blackman's perceptions of the hybrid is reinforced by diverging presentations of the child's direct environment, which contribute to mapping out, in almost geographical terms, their visions of socio-political change. Anchoring her hybrid into the changing, threatening, human-made urban landscape, Blackman ensures that her non-essentialistic vision of hybridity is propped up against adequate sceneries. A problematic, disruptive concept, hybridity is incorporated within the equally multi-layered cityscape. Being the postcolonial hybrid, Callie inhabits a fluid and boundary-subverting environment which moulds the construction of her sense of self. Conversely, Meyer opts for an overwhelmingly natural setting, which at the end of *Breaking Dawn*, with the appearance of a cottage in the woods in which Bella, Edward, and Renesmee live "happily ever after," even shifts towards the fairytale tradition.[26] The pastoral backdrop of her saga helps the reader perceive Renesmee as both a herald and an embodiment of eternal nature, establishing divine order where chaos was. The ancient trees and the mountains, the height of which is probably exaggerated in the film versions of the novels, are the Corinthian columns to Renesmee's temple, playing on traditional religious imagery of earth-to-sky connections. Even outside the bubble of Forks, WA, Meyer's geographical choices in the fourth book are markedly infused with religious imagery. Edward and Bella's honeymoon on Isle Esme, a temporary slip into a Robinsonnade, adds to the sanctity of their relationship and of the conception of Renesmee, presenting the island as an idyllic mini-garden of Eden.

These different geographical settings are paralleled by diverging temporal settings. Blackman's modern narrative style, characterised by shifting viewpoints, frequent uses of the present tense, and the occasional newspaper clipping, decidedly inscribes her story in immediate, "live" development, throwing her characters and

---

[25] Bhabha, *The Location of Culture*, 160.

[26] Meyer, *Breaking Dawn*, 742.

the reader directly into the action. Meyer's more traditional narrative decisions (though she does, in *Breaking Dawn,* make use of two rather than just one intra-diagetic narrators) lead to the reader's perception of the action as past, Bella's recounting of the events as retrospective. The conservative stance of the *Twilight* series, against the postmodern, postcolonial undertones of *Noughts and Crosses,* contributes to the reader's perception of the hybrid child in each series. Renesmee belongs to an archetypal golden age, Callie to the corrupt streets of a modern city. Renesmee is the *puer aeternus,* Callie the de-romanticised, troubled child. Renesmee is a Christic instigator of perfection, Callie the receptacle of conflicting feelings. Renesmee is constructed as immediately powerful, Callie constructs herself over the duration of three novels. Renesmee is the new centre of gravity of the books, re-focalising narrative and ideological attention; Callie is the roaming child in search of a centre of gravity, contributing a distressed voice to the multiple perspectives of the saga.

Each of the two hybrids gets her idiosyncrasies and constructs her identity from these specific spatio-temporal settings, narrative decisions, strategies of characterisations. Literary bricolages of multiple, ideologically charged mythic and semantic references, Renesmee and Callie present to the young adult reader two very different facets of socio-cultural mobility and political change.

From hybrid child to hybrid reader: Constructions of readerly responses

Two diverging conceptions of hybridity, two diverging presentations of identity construction, two diverging responses from the young adult reader: the motif of the hybrid child epitomises two diverging inclinations of Young Adult literature. Although both Meyer and Blackman display similarities in their treatment of the hybrid baby and of her conception, the former uses it to open up a multifarious sphere of both personal and political experience, knowledge and contestation, whilst the latter creates an ideologically problematic, idealised vision of hybridity which does not leave any possibility for either the hybrid or the reader to evaluate the situation critically. Callie's hybridity gives rise to a perfectible sense of identity, geared towards a modification of the world, and oscillating between different influences and representations of power. She elevates herself beyond the divided world she was born in by learning to decrypt the complexity of its social and political configuration, and thus asserts herself as a resolutely different, flexible, and contestatory power within it. Renesmee, in contrast, represents the absolute victory of the saga's religious ideals of abstinence and the bliss of married life. She does not contest, but sublimates, these ideals. Her birth may be temporarily transgressive, but she is soon perceived as absolutely good and divine. This is only made clearer, of course, by the fact that her birth gives way to her mother's symbolic death as an earth-bound human being, and conversion to "vegetarian vampirism," that is to say, to her father's way of life. Her existence reinforces, justifies, and idealises the power of one of her parents. She does not fit Homi Bhabha's conception of hybridity, where, as Robert C. J. Young explains:

hybridity begins to become the form of cultural difference itself, the jarrings of a differentiated culture whose "hybrid counter-energies," in Said's phrase, challenge the centred, dominant cultural norms with their unsettling perplexities generated out of their "disjunctive, liminal space."[27]

Callie Rose, as for her, belongs to this "disjunctive, liminal space," and the construction of her different identity threatens both the division of her world and its permanence.

The result of this difference in the construction of the hybrid is a difference in its reception. The reader of *Twilight* will be forced by the glorious, idealised and textually seductive vision of hybridity embodied by Renesmee to adopt a conservatory stance, as the religious morality of the books finds itself perpetuated to perfection in the creation of a hybrid being. The complete absence of flaw in the character of Renesmee, and Bella's conversion, will lead the reader to envisage Edward's heritage as dominant; in other words, the reader will yield to one colonising influence: perhaps unsurprisingly, that of the self-controlled, older, puritanical male. In contrast, the *Noughts and Crosses* saga offers a motif of hybridity which unsettles the reader, deliberately placing Callie in an uncertain realm of identity where conflicting forces are at work, and where imperfection reigns. The narrative strategy deployed by the use of several homodiegetic narrators helps perceive Callie's identity in relation to other members of the separate castes. The reader is gradually led to understand the full subversive power of Callie's character, both within her family and on a political level. This power does not negotiate: taking full advantage of its hybridity, it suggests the gradual instalment of a territory of contestation. The reader is thus encouraged to adopt a similar stance, positioning themselves within a critical, ideologically flexible frame of thought.

The success of these two sagas within Young Adult literature, and their arguable appeal to female readers primarily, may point at the appeal for young women of two opposite types of social and political positioning: one which highlights the perfect result of traditional religious values reified into marriage, and one which begs to question and evaluate the many polarisations of the society they were born into. These two visions of hybridity, it can be argued, are two faces of a same coin: adult reactions to the increasing globalisation and civilisation clashes in the modern world. Both series, despite their divergences, impose on the young adult reader a similar reading of hybridity both as a prominent symptom of modern world issues and as their potential solution. They problematise hybridity, pushing it at the front of the action to the detriment of the adolescent parents' transgressive relationship that it emerged from. In so doing they operate a narrative shift, forcing the implied young adult reader to consider not only her own generation but also her future children's generation as the locus of social and political improvement. This is, in fact, more than a narrative shift – it is a paradigm shift, which inscribes the young adult reader's political awareness and wishes for a more satisfactory society

---

[27] Young, Robert J.C. *The Colonial Desire*. London: Routledge, 1995, 23.

into a process of change involving a consequential amount of time. The young adult reader is thus led to consider her own identity-construction as deriving from past communal efforts and prolonging itself into the future. Narrating and reading the hybrid transforms the usually episodic and individualistic efforts of young adult protagonists into a spark, the initiation of a dynamic movement destined to lengthen itself out and away in space and time. The hybrid child introduces a new dimension to the development of conventional political awareness: whilst ensuring that the young reader is fully conscious of her ability to modify the world, she is also reminded that her power to do so is limited in scope. There is no such thing as individual approaches to dystopian or unsatisfactory socio-political situations: rather, the young adult reader is invited, like the adolescent protagonists, to relocate herself within an arguably lukewarm, intermediary generation, and to perceive her own potency within its bounds. Half-erased by the unexpected arrival of a child more powerful than themselves, the adolescent parents are imposed to the young adult reader as a projection of her own eventual disappearance.

As a result – as always – it is worth interrogating to what extent this construction of adolescent socio-political awareness constitutes an oppressive message for the young adult reader, especially if we see the implied reader of both texts – perhaps more obviously *Twilight* – as strongly gender-specific. By rushing their protagonists into parenthood and eclipsing their former lives in the process, the texts construct adolescents whose socio-political development is incredibly short-lived, fused with the emotional growth of adolescence, and ending at the doorstep of adulthood: sexual awakening, and procreation. Leaving little space for maturation, the adolescents' blitzkrieg against the divided world they were born into is in itself a conflicting potion of romantic excessiveness, sexual attraction, rebellion against the parents, and socio-political conscience. The arrival of the hybrid child is as much a culmination of this flash of inspiration as it signals its brutal transformation into something so radically different that it can appear as a narrative and ideological betrayal. Here again, however, there are differences between Meyer and Blackman in their treatment of the adolescent parent after the birth of the hybrid. Sephy in *Noughts and Crosses* arguably becomes, after the death of Callum and the arrival of Callie, only a shadow of the strong character she was before, but her life continues alongside – and often in discordance with – that of her daughter, negotiating the construction and reconstruction of her own identity in the unstable urban backdrop they share. Meyer sends a much more radical message by freezing Bella into the blissful role of a young mother, an authorial and authoritative decision which has interestingly been met with a large amount of disbelief and disapproval from the real-life teenage fans of the series. Rachel Hendershot Parkin has exhaustively documented what can be called the *Breaking Dawn* upheaval, following the publication of the last volume in the series.[28] Feeling cheated by what they perceived to be an oppressive presentation

---

[28]   Hendershot Parkin, Rachel. "Breaking Faith: Disrupted Expectations and Ownership in Stephenie Meyer's Twilight Saga." *Jeunesse: Young People, Texts, Cultures* 2, no 2 (2010): 61–85.

of idyllic female empowerment through maternity, a large number of "Twilighters" complained directly to Meyer in the form of a petition or indirectly in blogs and forums, accusing the author of anti-feminist ideology and of betraying her own canon.[29] In particular, they criticised her portrayal of parenthood, her irresponsible anti-abortion ethos, and rejected the idealistic character of Renesmee. The resistance of even the most committed teenage fans to the conclusion of the saga brings into focus the potentially authoritarian introduction of the hybrid child of adolescent parents within young adult literature. Meyer's arguable failure to provide a satisfactory, modern answer to her own divided fictional world could be read as the failure of the concept of hybridity to convince young readers fully of its potency and significance in the modern world.

Concluding thoughts: Hybridising the reader?

> It is striking that many novelists not only of today but also of the past write almost obsessively about the uncertain crossing and invasion of identities ... So much so, indeed, that we could go so far as to claim it as *the* dominant motif of much English fiction ... This transmigration is the form taken by colonial desire, whose attractions and fantasies were no doubt complicit with colonialism itself. The many colonial novels in English betray themselves as driven by desire for the cultural other, for forsaking their own culture.[30]

Young's analysis of fiction as driven by and infused with "the colonial desire" strikes a chord with much of my previous analysis on the hybrid in Meyer's and Blackman's series. Seen from this angle, the age-old literary tradition of projecting the English-speaking reader out of her cultural sphere and into the postcolonial, shifting empire of identity construction of the postmodern world is powerfully reflected within the Young Adult literature discussed, in all its ambiguity, all its flaws, and perhaps all its oppressiveness. Can we find, distilled within both series, a subsisting Orientalist bias? Signalling the attraction of the hegemonic for the counter-cultural and vice-versa, based on little more than the otherness of the figure described, this *otherness* might be a more potent locus of erotic desire than any significant personality trait. Fuelling romance and rushing the young protagonists towards the procreation of a hybrid, the common strand between both sagas questions the degree to which Young Adult literature can answer real-world preoccupations of globalisations and multiculturalism by appealing to the value-ridden genre of romance.

Working to hybridise the young adult reader, such dystopian tales of romance in Young Adult literature may work towards constructing socio-political awareness, but they may also indirectly reiterate more ancient, and more problematic, literary

---

[29]   The Undersigned. "Petition: Legitimate Concerns About Breaking Dawn." http://www.petitiononline.com/BDFailed/petition.html. Accessed 10/08/2011.

[30]   Young, *The Colonial Desire*, 2–3.

depictions of hybridity. To what extent are young readers prepared to envisage themselves as part of a process of hybridisation? Are they ready to be are part of a dynamic of generational transmission, or will they perceive this very adult insistence on child-bearing as anachronistic and oppressive? Will they incorporate into their identity-constructions these teleological representations of transgressive romance? The arrival of the hybrid child may alienate the young adult reader from any position of true power, substituting the radical and sublime assertion of independence of *Romeo and Juliet* with a lukewarm relegation to the thankless role of adolescent parenting.

The current profusion and success of young adult novels that feature trans-racial or trans-species hybrids calls for further in-depth examinations of their ideological assumptions and narrative power. From Percy Jackson the demigod[31] to Willow the half-angel[32] through to Darren Shan's pseudo-vampirism,[33] Young Adult fiction apparently dodges essentialism, placing its protagonists in undecided spheres of identity. The fates of these hybrid children may delineate, albeit cryptically, the hopes and fears invested in them by the adult inhabitants of an unsatisfactory world.

---

[31]   Riordan, Rick. *Percy Jackson & The Olympians*. New York: Hyperion, 2005.

[32]   Weatherly, L.A. *Angel*. London: Usborne, 2010.

[33]   Shan, Darren. *The Saga of Darren Shan*. London: HarperCollins, 2006.

Chapter 5
Cross-Dressing and Performativity

Nicole Brugger-Dethmers

Who am I? How am I different from everyone else? What if I don't fit in or meet expectations? These are the kinds of questions that arise from the internal turmoil of adolescence. Teenagers occupy the stage of life when one moves from the comfortable familiarity of childhood friends and family to the unfamiliar differentness of the Other: other genders, races, religions, sexual orientations, abilities, and so on, as well as the expectations of society at large. Ultimately, this transition necessitates a re-evaluation of selfhood. The discovery of a unique identity amidst personal uncertainty and during the testing of socially established mores is a difficult yet important task faced by all teenagers. This journey is reflected in Young Adult literature in characters who cross a variety of categorical boundaries and grapple with the resulting physical, mental, and social issues.

Based on Judith Butler's work on gender performativity – that "there is no gender identity behind the expressions of gender; that identity is performatively constituted by the very 'expressions' that are said to be its results"[1] – I propose that identity is similarly constructed in Young Adult literature, and performativity extends beyond gender and applies to age, class, and ethnicity. Furthermore, I wish to argue that *cross-dressing* – here referring to individuals crossing not just gender but also age, class, and ethnic lines – is a trope employed in Young Adult literature to assist in the construction of identity. Together, the performance of a particular aspect of identity like gender or class and the transgressive act of dressing in roles contrary to one's own allow literary characters, and the real-life teenagers they represent, the opportunity to explore and experiment with their notions of selfhood.

From an early age, children are socialised, by parents, school, and the media, into accepting certain gender roles as normal or appropriate, and distinguishing those that are different as deviant or inappropriate. Butler views gender as "the repeated stylization of the body, a set of repeated acts within a highly rigid regulatory frame that congeal over time to produce the appearance of substance, of a natural sort of being."[2] This idea invites us to look at gender roles – and, by extension, age, class, and ethnicity – as a product of society. Certain acts, such as

---

[1] Butler, Judith. *Gender Trouble: Feminism and the Subversion of Identity*. 2nd ed. New York: Routledge, 1990, 25.

[2] Butler, *Gender Trouble*, 33.

playing with dolls or roughhousing, have been labelled as either acceptable female or male behaviour, and the continuation over time of girls playing with dolls or boys roughhousing perpetuates the idea of acceptability, that these actions stem from the natural way of being female or male. This excludes people who do not fit neatly into either category from the imposed view of normality. So, too, are certain attributes associated with elderly or young people, upper class or lower, and even various ethnicities. When an individual does not live up to these expectations, he or she is branded as abnormal, strange, and potentially socially dangerous. The cross-dressed figure, in an attempt to explore the "Other" and construct an identity, is at risk of being denied the opportunity necessary for growth and development, particularly if the exploration is at the expense of social norms.

Cross-dressing, even in the sense of non-gendered cross-dressing, is not a new phenomenon, and possesses a rich historical and folkloric background, even outside of theatrical cross-dressing from the well-known stages of Shakespeare's England to the kabuki theatre of Japan.[3] Marjorie Garber's research on sumptuary laws – laws intending to curb exorbitant expenditures and "to regulate who wore what, and on what occasion"[4] – in medieval through early modern Europe indicates that societies have attempted to control the dressing habits of its members for a very long time. By passing these kinds of laws, people in power intend to limit the performance of individuals to the socially constructed, appropriate binary roles: male or female, upper class or lower class, rich or poor. Men are commanded to dress in what is commonly accepted as male fashion, and women are similarly limited. There can be no aspiring to or pretending to belong to a position to which one was not born, so anyone below the rank of earl in Elizabethan England, for example, was not allowed to wear purple silk except the Knights of the Garter.[5] The issue with cross-dressing at the time was that one could not be certain of a person's sex or social standing from his or her outward appearance. The laws were meant to establish "the sartorial encoding of visible markers for rank and degree,"[6] so that clothes and physical appearance tell everything one needs to know about someone. Thus, "[t]he ideal scenario ... was one in which a person's social station, social role, gender and other indicators of identity in the world could be *read*, without ambiguity or uncertainty."[7] From this government-sanctioned treatment of personal expression comes the inference that identity is inextricably

---

[3]   For a more thorough picture of cross-dressing and its historical context, refer to Bullough, Vern L., and Bonnie Bullough, "Part 1. Cultural and Historical Background." In their *Cross Dressing, Sex, and Gender*, 3–199. Philadelphia: University of Pennsylvania Press, 1993.

[4]   Garber, Marjorie. *Vested Interests: Cross-dressing and Cultural Anxiety*. New York: Routledge, 1997, 21.

[5]   Garber, *Vested Interests*, 26.

[6]   Garber, *Vested Interests*, 23.

[7]   Garber, *Vested Interests*, 26 (Garber's italics).

linked to appearance, which affects the relationship between an individual and the community in which he or she lives.

Image and appearance are also very important aspects of folkloric narratives. Countless tales are filled with illusions, disguises, deceptions, and transformations. For the relatively two-dimensional characters of folktales and fairytales, identity is almost wholly comprised of outward appearances and basic temperaments supplied by the storyteller, which results in cases of mistaken identity and missed connections. Voluntarily undertaken or not, transformations of all kinds often lead to better circumstances for heroes and heroines alike. The heroines of the "A King Tries to Marry His Daughter"-type folktales,[8] such as the titular character from Charles Perrault's "Donkeyskin," must wear grotesque disguises and perform menial labour to escape persecution. Wearing a donkey hide and dirtying her body conceals Donkeyskin's royal identity as she goes out into the world looking for work, and the disguise is "so hideous that no one will ever believe it covers anything beautiful."[9] This ensures that no one will discover the truth without her explicit consent, and ultimately, she is restored to her rightful royal place when she reveals herself. Without this cross-dressing event, however, she would not have found her happily ever after.

Fairytales, Max Lüthi posits, represent "processes of development and maturation."[10] The possibility exists within such stories that the hero can overcome the difficulties set before him and attain the higher realm or truer existence to which he aspires. The end result of the transformations and personal revolutions of fairytales is exactly that: an affirmation of the self. If we can infer that folktales and fairytales inform the children's and Young Adult literature of today, which the countless retellings, adaptations, and works inspired by them seem to indicate, then we can correlate this phenomena of metamorphosis to the changes occurring in the self-identification process of adolescents. Gendered cross-dressing appears in diverse folktales, legends, and mythologies from around the world, ostensibly for a variety of reasons but largely as a response to the social restrictions on what women are allowed to do or where they can go. Many stories of women cross-dressing as men feature a female who does so to further her education, seek a fortune, or become a soldier and fight for family, king, or country – all things expected of sons but usually not daughters. The suggestion seems to be that these

---

[8]   This is Aarne-Thompson folktale type 510B and is similar to other folktales of clothing-related deception. Ashliman, D.L. *A Guide to Folktales in the English Language: Based on the Aarne-Thompson Classification System*, no 11, *Bibliographies and Indexes in World Literature*. New York: Greenwood Press, 1987, 107–108.

[9]   Perrault, Charles. "Donkeyskin," 112. In *The Classic Fairytales*, edited and translated by Maria Tatar. New York: Norton, 1999.

[10]   Lüthi, Max. "The Fairy-Tale Hero: The Image of Man in the Fairy Tale." In *Folk & Fairy Tales*, edited by Martin Hallett and Barbara Karasek, 298. 2nd ed. Peterborough, ON: Broadview Press, 1996.

heroines feel unfulfilled, that the roles prescribed to them by society and culture leave them wanting something more.

Lisa Brocklebank's examination of three French fairy tales featuring gendered cross-dressing establishes the cross-dressed figure as "a touchstone to contest official order and socially constructed representations of power," contending that clothing and other outward indicators of self-identification are the means by which the cross-dressed characters subvert the status quo.[11] This is not to say that all these cross-dressed women are conscious proto-feminists who actively rebel against a patriarchy to assert their rights, particularly because notions of gender equality vary from place to place throughout history. Instead, we can look at the heroines' actions as they correlate with the desire to fulfil a personal need and establish a sense of identity, rather than an overt desire to overthrow a cultural hierarchy. Cross-dressing, in these examples, "effectively demonstrates the need for individuals to be judged for who they actually are, and by the unique qualities each possesses, rather than their ability to fulfil a prescribed social and/or gendered role into which they have had the ill fortune to be born."[12]

In the famous Chinese legend of Hua Mulan, recounted in the "Ballad of Mulan," the young heroine cross-dresses as a male warrior in order to go to war in the place of her ill father, abandoning her traditional duties at home in pursuit of a higher filial duty. At first glance, it may appear that Mulan is not seeking to create an identity for herself, as her cross-dressing is done only to save her father. However, it is worth considering that Mulan has an elder sister, who shows no similar propensity for setting aside customs. The younger brother (and by some accounts, multiple younger brothers) likewise does not exhibit any inclination to take part, though, depending on his age, he could have lied about his age to join the army, a phenomenon known to happen during times of war. Mulan's willingness to cross-dress and enter into battle may suggest something distinctive about her personality and her sense of self.

The last four lines of "The Ballad of Mulan" in John Frodsham's translation read:

> For the male hare tucks its feet in when it sits,
> And the female hare is known by her bleary eye.
> But when two hares are bounding side by side,
> How can you then tell female from the male?[13]

---

[11]   Brocklebank, Lisa. "Rebellious Voices: The Unofficial Discourse of Cross-Dressing in d'Aulnoy, de Murat, and Perrault." *Children's Literature Association Quarterly* 25, no 3 (Fall 2000), paragraph 3, Literature Resource Center (H1420082200).

[12]   Flanagan, Victoria. *Into the Closet: Cross-Dressing and the Gendered Body in Children's Literature and Film.* New York: Routledge, 2008, 48.

[13]   Frodsham, John, trans. "The Ballad of Mulan." In *Classical Chinese Literature*, vol. 1, *From Antiquity to the Tang Dynasty*, edited by John Minford and Joseph S.M. Lau, p. 411, lines 60–63. New York: Columbia University Press / Hong Kong: The Chinese University Press, 2002.

In other words, although male and female hares can be distinguished by certain physical characteristics while standing still, they are indistinguishable while in action. Mulan, who must continually perform masculinity in dress, actions, and attitude, transcends her previously defined feminine identity to create a masculine identity that is indistinguishable from the men beside whom she fights. Not only does Mulan fight, she does so well enough to suggest that she outperforms at least some the men.[14] The fact that she survives a decade of war and receives approbation and rewards from the emperor himself indicates her remarkable level of success.

Alanna of Trebond, the heroine of Tamora Pierce's *The Song of the Lioness* quartet, wants nothing to do with being a proper lady. After mimicking the things she has been told she must do like "walk slowly" and "sit still," she proclaims, "As if that's all I can do with myself!"[15] Her idea of selfhood does not match what has been consistently established over time as the cultural norm. The traditional domestic path of girls from noble families is an anathema to her; she dreams of the glorious, adventure-filled life of a knight. She fights, hunts, and rides horses better than her twin brother Thom, and so, when her father decides to send her off to a convent to become a lady and Thom to the palace to become a knight, Alanna initiates the switch that will allow her to achieve her dream and also fulfil her brother's desire to learn sorcery from the Masters at the convent. When Alanna cross-dresses and presents herself as Thom's twin brother "Alan," she is asserting her right to become the person she wants to be, not who society, or her father, dictates she should be.

For months, Alanna labours under the impression that she must prove her physical prowess to fit in with the other boys, all the while lamenting her small stature and lack of muscle strength. Although one particular boy bullies her and takes advantage of her weakness, Alanna appears to be oblivious of the fact that the other boys like her and almost immediately accept her as a friend. Nobody ever doubts her sex; the simple fact that she is in their midst reinforces the assumption that she is male. If "Alan" is perceived as weak, "Alan" is a weak boy, not under suspicion of being a girl. Yet Alanna continues to equate maleness with physical strength. After the bully Ralon beats her up, she thinks, "This wouldn't have happened to a *real* boy."[16] Her performance continually revolves around trying to live up to a physical ideal of manliness.

Alanna's rejection of femininity is reflected in her aversion to her magical abilities. She shuns the Gift, a capacity for magic that both men and women can possess but originates from the decidedly female Great Mother Goddess. Even the female warriors who guard the Temple of the Great Mother Goddess are not good enough for Alanna, and she flippantly disregards them: "Someday she would wear

---

[14] For further discussion of gender as outperformance, refer to Flanagan, "Chapter 2: Three Models of Gender Disguise," 36–42, in *Into the Closet*.

[15] Pierce, Tamora. *Alanna: The First Adventure*. New York: Atheneum, 1983, 1.

[16] Pierce, *Alanna*, 62. Pierce's italics.

armor too, but she wouldn't be confined to temple grounds!"[17] Perhaps Alanna sees in the duty-bound guards the same lack of freedom that was so reprehensible to her in the expected lives of young noble ladies. When a friend dies of a magical illness, however, and Alanna is consumed with guilt that she could have prevented his passing, she realises the truth of the King's pronouncement that "[a] knight must develop *all* his abilities, to the fullest."[18] She learns to accept her Gift and the duties and challenges that come with it, combining her feminine magic with her proficiency as a masculine warrior to create an arguably stronger identity. Gendered cross-dressers are able to synthesise these disparate parts of themselves; as Victoria Flanagan says of the female cross-dresser in particular, she "draws on elements of both masculinity and femininity, alternating between the two and benefiting from her knowledge of each."[19]

The protagonist of David Walliams' book *The Boy in the Dress*, in contrast to the two previous characters discussed, cross-dresses not out of necessity or as a means to an end but simply because it is enjoyable and makes him happy. Dennis develops an interest in beautiful clothes after seeing a *Vogue* magazine, the cover of which features a girl in a dress very like the one his mother wore in an old photograph of happier times. Dennis' mother left the family prior to the beginning of the novel, and to some extent, the passion for fashion that consumes Dennis could be his way of trying to connect with his missing parental figure. He hides his interest in clothes from his emotionally distant father and brother, fearing even further ostracism from a household that already forbids crying and hugging. Unable to connect in any meaningful way with his heartbroken family other than short-lived football euphoria, Dennis finds escape in fashion magazines: he "pored over every page, mesmerised by the dresses – their colour, their length, their cut. He could lose himself in the pages forever. The glamour. The beauty. The perfection."[20] Dennis soon befriends Lisa, the girl on whom he has a crush and who coincidentally designs dresses. At Lisa's insistence, Dennis tries on a dress, and with this act he finds liberation: "Dressing up had made him feel like he didn't have to be boring Dennis living his boring life anymore."[21] Cross-dressing allows him to be open with his long-suppressed feelings and about the things he loves. It is perhaps telling that Dennis likens his fashion magazine to his own personal Narnia; the magazine, and by extension cross-dressing, is a place of escape, change, and growth for him. In the end, Dennis is able to reconcile the two halves of his persona, the boy who loves football and the boy who loves wearing dresses, and forge a more confident identity.[22]

---

[17] Pierce, *Alanna*, 19.
[18] Pierce, *Alanna*, 97. Pierce's italics.
[19] Flanagan, *Into the Closet*, 36.
[20] Walliams, David. *The Boy in the Dress*. New York: Razorbill, 2009, 49.
[21] Walliams, *The Boy in the Dress*, 107.
[22] Walliams, *The Boy in the Dress*, 50.

Male-to-female cross-dressing often appears in a very different light than female-to-male cross-dressing, with *The Boy in the Dress* being an exception. Consider the protagonist of Mark Twain's *The Adventures of Huckleberry Finn*. Huck disguises himself as a girl but is amusingly found out by Mrs. Judith Loftus, who admonishes him for his unfeminine behaviour: "[W]hen you throw at a rat or anything, hitch yourself up a tip-toe, and fetch your hand up over your head as awkard as you can, and miss your rat about six or seven foot."[23] In context, Huck's inability to pass as a girl is treated as a jest, even while a joke is being made about supposedly typical female behaviour. Treating male-to-female cross-dressing as a source of amusement is often the common approach, particularly in comparison to female-to-male cross-dressing. The discrepancy therein implies an inequality in the direction of cross-dressing. Historically, women performing as men were more acceptable; "a woman who somehow broke through the barriers found herself praised for having a masculine mind or in other ways following the masculine model. In contrast, men who expressed a feminine side were regarded as somehow weak, since femininity was socially defined that way."[24] Society could understand why a woman would want to be like a man, whose sex traditionally held almost all the power in government, religion, and the home, but it was less clear what could be gained from a man dressing like a woman, and thus, such men were looked at with suspicion.[25] Parodic portrayals were admissible because the men were still clearly men and did not threaten any power structure. However, this comedic view gives more credence to Dennis' story and the sincerity of his performance. His is not for cheap laughs or even friendly ridicule but a devotion to his search for his identity.

Performance in regards to identity is not, as postulated earlier, restricted to gender. Age performance plays an important role in establishing independent identities in Diana Wynne Jones' *Howl's Moving Castle* and Mary Rodgers' *Freaky Friday*. Cheryl Laz makes the argument in her aptly named essay "Act Your Age" that age, like gender, is something accomplished, "not in the sense of something completed, but in the sense of something 'brought to pass' or continually carried on."[26] The common phrase she uses as the title of her essay, when uttered, is usually meant to ensure normative behaviour, but at the same time it establishes

---

[23]   Twain, Mark. *Adventures of Huckleberry Finn*. New York: Modern Library, 2001, 52. Spelling of "awkward" preserved in transcription.

[24]   Bullough, Vern L., and Bonnie Bullough, *Cross Dressing, Sex, and Gender*. Philadelphia: University of Pennsylvania Press, 1993, ix.

[25]   This prejudice is based in part on the assumption of homosexuality or an intent to be physically intimate with women as reasons for cross-dressing, as Vern L. and Bonnie Bullough explain in *Cross Dressing, Sex, and Gender* (103). However, the discussion of the relationship between cross-dressing and sexual orientation in young adult literature is outside the scope of this chapter.

[26]   Laz, Cheryl. "Act Your Age." *Sociological Forum* 13, no 1 (Mar. 1998): 100, http://www.jstor.org/stable/684926.

that age is not necessarily a fixed variable.[27] Age, like gender, is shaped by a society's expectations and the performance of a populace to achieve what can be approximated as normative behaviour. There are particular physical attributes that people use to judge someone's age, such as posture, skin texture, eye clarity, and hair colour. White, grey, or silver hair is considered a trademark of old age, even though it can occasionally occur in relatively young individuals. Certain types of clothes and accessories are often marketed to or associated with particular age groups; many department stores in the United States, for example, have a "Juniors" department for teenagers separate from the women's department. While the physical markers of age identification are intrinsically related to the ageing process, apparel and accessories are not and therefore are strongly influenced by culturally defined norms. So, too, are certain behaviours and attitudes indicative of social opinions about what is appropriate for certain chronological ages. Most of the time, we rely on myriad visual cues to inform us of a person's age; as Laz humorously points out, "we do not ask to see a birth certificate" as proof of age.[28] Because of the reliance on these visual cues and outwardly expressed behaviours, it becomes easy to mistake one's apparent age for their chronological age.

Sophie Hatter, of *Howl's Moving Castle*, is a perfect example. Despite her youth, she begins her story already acting like the old woman into which she will be turned. She insists on wearing grey shawls over grey dresses, loud noises and excitement set her ill at ease, and she spends most of her time quietly trimming hats and listening to gossip in the hat shop. She resigns herself to the fate of being the eldest of three sisters, which, in her world, is considerably unlucky: "Everyone knows you are the one who will fail first, and worst, if the three of you set out to seek your fortunes."[29] Sophie internalises this aphorism and therefore does not go out to change her situation. Her sisters, in contrast, forge their own destinies while engaging in their own bit of cross-dressing. Martha, who would rather get married and have ten children than learn magic, uses a spell to switch places with Lettie at the bakery, who wants the intellectual challenge of learning witchcraft.

To some extent, Sophie is old simply because she feels old. After the Witch of the Waste casts her spell, Sophie looks in the mirror and, upon seeing the haggard, shrivelled face of an old woman staring back at her, says, "Don't worry, old thing ... You look quite healthy. Besides, this is much more like you really are."[30] In a world where magic itself can be performative – the mushroom-pleated bonnet to which Sophie says "You have a heart of gold and someone in a high position will see it and fall in love with you"[31] is bought by Jane Farrier, who runs away with a nobleman a few weeks later – it could be that Sophie herself is at least partly responsible for her transformation. She acts according to society's expectations of

---

[27] Laz, "Act Your Age," 86.

[28] Laz, "Act Your Age," 93.

[29] Wynne Jones, Diana. *Howl's Moving Castle.* New York: Harper Trophy, 2001, 1.

[30] Jones, *Howl's Moving Castle,* 28.

[31] Jones, *Howl's Moving Castle,* 10.

an older person, and she occasionally thinks of herself as old. The Witch of the Waste merely gives her a visual manifestation of what is already present. When Howl eventually admits he knew Sophie was under a spell, he says that he "came to the conclusion that [she] liked being in disguise,"[32] indicating that she continued to perform as an old woman precisely because she wanted to, and magic helped sustain the act.

Everything changes for Sophie when she undergoes her magical metamorphosis. She awakens to the idea that her destiny is not fixed, that she can set out to make her own way, and she leaves almost immediately, cloaking herself and setting out for the hills. When Sophie comes across and helps a trapped wild dog, she remains calm, even though she had always been frightened of dogs as a girl. Upon coming across Wizard Howl's castle, she demands it to stop moving and open the door for her. To the castle inhabitants and its visitors, she behaves in an insouciant and presumptuous manner, and she acknowledges that, as a girl, she would have been embarrassed by her behaviour, but, "[a]s an old woman, she did not mind what she did or said. She found that a great relief."[33] Timidity falls away, and, as the trappings of pre-destiny had made Sophie old beyond her chronological years, her supernaturally induced senescence brings out her youthful mental and emotional vigour.

Cross-dressing as an old woman gives Sophie the chance to be involved with the world in a new way; "[b]eing the crone allows Sophie to free herself of the inhibitions of her self-conception as doomed eldest sister and make a new life for herself."[34] Instead of inheriting the hat shop, which she was never thrilled to be doing anyway, Sophie helps defeat the villains, saves Howl's life, and discovers her own magical ability to "talk life into things."[35] In the end, Sophie takes the cross-dressing for what it is: an opportunity to reinvent herself.

To Annabel Andrews in *Freaky Friday*, no one embodies the idea of the Other more than her own mother. Annabel views Mrs. Andrews' life as if it is perfect and completely unlike her own, unfairly full of freedom and the ability to "tell yourself to go out to lunch with your friends, and watch television all day long, and eat marshmallows for breakfast and go to the movies at night."[36] Common in identity reversal stories, as Caroline C. Hunt indicates, "[the hero] feels unfulfilled in some important way. In addition to not knowing *who he is*, he finds that *what he appears to be* – his existing personality – is somehow distasteful to him. Inevitably it turns out that his counterpart has exactly those qualities which he

---

[32]   Jones, *Howl's Moving Castle*, 283.

[33]   Jones, *Howl's Moving Castle*, 64.

[34]   Webb, Caroline. "'Change the Story, Change the World': Witches/Crones as Heroes in Novels by Terry Pratchett and Diana Wynne Jones.'" *Papers: Explorations into Children's Literature* 16, no 2 (2006): 156.

[35]   Jones, *Howl's Moving Castle*, 324.

[36]   Rodgers, Mary. *Freaky Friday.* New York: Harper & Row, 1972, 6.

lacks."[37] Annabel desires her mother's freedom more than anything else. When she wakes up one morning to discover she has switched bodies with her mother, she flounders with the concept of performing as an adult. Physically Annabel has an advantage because she is literally inside her mother's body, and therefore *looks* the appropriate age, but she does not act like a loving wife and mother. She punches Mr. Andrews awake, and she continues to treat her younger brother Ben as an annoying pest, not as a precious son.

Others expect Annabel to act like an adult because she appears to be one; her physical attributes are the visible markers that establish her as belonging to the adult age group. She continually surprises people by her juvenile behaviour, though not always in a negative way: the neighbour boy Boris thinks of Annabel-as-Mrs. Andrews "as a beautiful human being who still remembers how to communicate with kids. I mean, how many mothers do you know who'll sit down on the floor and play Nok Hockey with a fourteen-year-old?"[38]

Annabel's situation is a subtler example of what Laz calls an "age-click," whereby a person is suddenly and acutely aware of his or her age.[39] The source could be a number of things; it may be "from realizing that we are not acting our age or from noticing how effectively and unconsciously we have been acting our age."[40] Although Annabel's realisation is not immediate, and perhaps more relatable to a dimmer switch, her escapades as a teenager in an adult body force her to realise it was her immature, childish behaviour as a teenage-bodied teenager that was getting in the way of gaining the independence she craved. Although Annabel's performance suffers from failure after failure, the act of aged cross-dressing teaches Annabel valuable lessons that fundamentally influence her perception and construction of her identity. Instead of finding the life of the Other to be picture perfect, she realises adulthood and personal maturation require accepting difficult responsibilities along with the fun aspects of growing up.

Returning to the idea of the cross-dresser as a challenge to the status quo, the two male protagonists of *The Prince and the Pauper* do just that as a result of their class cross-dressing, ultimately bringing justice and mercy to the people of Mark Twain's England. Neither Tom Canty nor Prince Edward set out intentionally to change the very fabric of society; their cross-dressing stems from nothing more than a lark. When Tom responds positively to Edward's idea of wearing each other's clothes, Edward exclaims, "Oho, wouldst like it? Then so shall it be! Doff thy rags and don these splendors, lad! It is a brief happiness, but will be not less keen for that."[41] Yet, after the guard's mistake that lands Edward on the streets and Tom in the king's court, both boys encounter a series of events that change

[37]   Hunt, Caroline C. "Counterparts: Identity Exchange and the Young Adult Audience." *Children's Literature Association Quarterly* 11, no 3 (1986): 110. Hunt's italics.

[38]   Rodgers, *Freaky Friday*, 108.

[39]   Laz, "Act Your Age," 101.

[40]   Laz, "Act Your Age," 101.

[41]   Twain, Mark. *The Prince and the Pauper*. New York: Modern Library, 2003, 17.

the way they see the world, and what they "learn about social roles ... leads to redefined relationships to their society, and even to relatively small but nonetheless significant changes in that society itself."[42] Although Tom speaks and acts like a prince among his friends, influenced by his extensive reading and daydreaming, his manners do not quite pass muster in court. Yet nobody suspects him of not being the prince; instead, his strange behaviour and apparent memory loss are attributed to the prince having gone slightly mad. The influence of physical, visual clues of cross-dressing on perception are apparent: he looks the part, and therefore, must be the right person. However, he is cognisant enough of his performance to catch himself while blathering about his life in Offal Court and to ascribe any lapses in knowledge to his wit "clogged and dim with suffering."[43] Because the court accepts this excuse as possible, his performance is still relatively successful.

Tom's participation in cross-dressing as royalty evinces his internally developed princeliness and strengthens his identity. As John Daniel Stahl writes, "the circumstances he is thrown into ... present him with tests of character in which he must conduct himself well in order to attain a state in which his inner character is manifest and acknowledged through his social role."[44] For performing admirably in Edward's place, Tom is raised above pauperdom, given an appointment and the honourable title "King's Ward," and, fittingly, marked with a distinctive form of dress to "remind the people that he hath been royal, in his time, and none shall deny him his due of reverence."[45] Tom's uncommon way of viewing court matters, influenced by his life history and inherent sense of compassion, catalyses major social changes. His merciful decrees, such as rescinding the Duke of Norfolk's death sentence and abolishing the punishment of being boiled alive, astonish the courtiers and elicit a measure of admiration. This sets a precedence for Edward's reign, distinctively clement for its time and influenced heavily by the prince's experience as a street urchin.

In manner and attitude, Edward never varies from his princely behaviour. Yet, dressed as he is in Tom's rags, Edward is treated as the low-class waif he appears to be, shoved around and spoken to rudely. He witnesses horrifying events like a woman burning at the stake, something from which a prince would likely be sheltered. Learning the truth of how the citizenry lives and dies engenders empathy in Edward, and this enlightenment enables him to make fair-minded, compassionate judgements as king. Just as Tom has tests of character, so too does Edward: he must break from his father's harsh rule, establish one of his own making, and, in the process, affirm his selfhood.

The literary expression of class has a modern day equivalent in the social hierarchy of high school, a common theme in young adult literature. Because

---

[42]   Stahl, John Daniel. "American Myth in European Disguise: Fathers and Sons in *The Prince and the Pauper*." *American Literature* 58, no 2 (May 1986): 206.

[43]   Twain, *The Prince and the Pauper*, 85.

[44]   Stahl, "American Myth," 209.

[45]   Twain, *The Prince and the Pauper*, 207.

teenagers are dealing with the myriad changes accompanying adolescence, topics such as fitting into an established pecking order and dealing with cliques are particularly relevant. In many cases, the problems arising from this kind of setup involve an individual or group considered to be at the top of the social ladder, usually labelled as the in-crowd or the popular people, and an individual or group judged to be at the bottom or on the fringe. "Popular," in this sense, usually does not refer to someone who is well liked by his or her peers but refers almost exclusively to the "reigning" students who dominate the social scene.

Such popularity in American literature is frequently marked by expensive, trendy clothes, high-end accessories like luxury cars, and membership in highly publicised sports or clubs such as American football, cheerleading, or pep squad. When Sugar Magnolia Dempsey, the protagonist of Jennifer Ziegler's *How Not to Be Popular*, first arrives at her new school, she catalogues the groups of students she comes across, taking note of "the heads of the high school ecosystem. This category differs slightly from school to school, but usually it includes perfect poser types with an overabundance of money and power."[46] The association of wealth with popularity is reminiscent of the sumptuary laws: one must dress and accessorise accordingly to be accepted as a member of the in-crowd. By her own admission, Maggie, as the protagonist prefers to be called, usually tries to integrate with the ruling class, but she is exhausted from the effort of making friends and then losing them a few months later when she must move, due to her hippie parents' nomadic lifestyle. Setting out to be as unpopular as possible, to avoid the pain of making and breaking friendships, Maggie embraces the power of clothing as an identity marker and dresses herself in the ugliest, strangest clothes she can find because "dressing like a loser is the quickest and easiest way to make people keep their distance."[47] Her choice of clothes and accessories is not meant to distinguish herself as a member of any other particular clique but instead mark her as completely in a world of her own. She acts bizarrely when her status as "loser" is threatened: after an accidental meeting with her eventual love interest and their subsequent impromptu date, Maggie cartwheels down the aisle of the movie theatre in the attempt to drive him off.

In spite of her efforts to look and act the part of an unpopular loner, Maggie gains a modicum of popularity, in the traditional sense of the word, for what people view as her refusal to conform to conventions. Students begin replicating her unorthodox fashions and lunch box choices. She is even nominated for homecoming queen, despite not wanting the position. Although she may not recognise it, Maggie functions as the cross-dressed figure who disrupts the status quo. In time, she realises she has grown fond of the so-called freaks and geeks with whom she aligned herself and recognises in herself that she is "tired of being in the spotlight. All these years and in all those schools, I've always tried hard to be one of the superpopular people. I thought they had it so easy. But in at least one way,

---

[46]   Ziegler, Jennifer. *How Not to Be Popular*. New York: Delacorte, 2008, 14.

[47]   Ziegler, *How Not to Be Popular*, 37.

they don't. They're always being watched. And if you know you're being watched, how can you be you?"[48] By cross-dressing as someone from the lower echelons of the high school hierarchy, Maggie discovers that she is comfortable with and enjoys being outside her previous self-defined social group and acknowledges that even the in-crowd has its own issues with identity. The experience allows her to explore friendships, clubs, and activities she never would had considered in the past, giving her license to craft her own identity without conforming to standards set by high school royalty.

Kimball O'Hara, the title character of Rudyard Kipling's *Kim*, regularly reinvents himself in the veritable melting pot of ethnicities, castes, and religions of British-ruled India in the nineteenth century. As India struggles with questions of identity, so too does Kim contend with his own. His coming of age in an era of instability necessitates a hard look at himself and how he fits into the larger scheme of the world: "'This is a great world, and I am only Kim. Who is Kim?' He considered his own identity, a thing he had never done before, till his head swam. He was one insignificant person in all this roaring whirl of India, going southward to he knew not what fate."[49] Kim's chameleon-like ability to move between ethnicities facilitates the construction of his identity. He speaks multiple languages and dialects, he changes clothes and customs frequently to suit his needs, and he even changes the colour of his skin with dyes.[50] Biologically he is white, but even as the son of an Irish soldier, "his poverty weakens a racial identity implicitly based on the ideal of the Anglo-Indian gentleman."[51] He grows up mostly free from his English identity, wearing it when it is necessary for him to pass as a sahib but tending to associate himself with the people of India. When Kim agrees to go to school, he conditions his acceptance: "At the *madrissah* I will learn. In the *madrissah* I will be a Sahib. But when the *madrissah* is shut, then must I be free and go among my people. Otherwise I die!"[52] His ambivalence toward his birthright is evident from his alternating denial and acceptance of being a sahib, claiming emphatically that "I am *not* a Sahib," then not much later throwing himself "whole-heartedly upon the next turn of the wheel. He would be a Sahib again for a while."[53] Whether he is or is not, the important factor is his

---

[48] Ziegler, *How Not to Be Popular*, 326. Formatting of "superpopular" preserved in transcription.

[49] Kipling, Rudyard. *Kim*. New York: Modern Library, 2004, 119.

[50] Many examples of this behaviour can be found throughout the text, but in one instance, Kim goes to a dancing girl to ask for "a little dye-stuff and three yards of cloth to help out a jest." In leaving, he "ran down the stairs in the likeness of a low-caste Hindu boy – perfect in every detail." Kipling, *Kim*, 127–28.

[51] McBratney, John. *Imperial Subjects, Imperial Space: Rudyard Kipling's Fiction of the Native-Born* Columbus: Ohio State University Press, 2002, 106.

[52] Kipling, *Kim*, 136–37.

[53] Kipling, *Kim*, 136, 149. Kipling's italics.

conscious decision to act as he chooses: if being a sahib is beneficial to him, then he will be one. If not, then he has his own idea of how to spend his time.

Intrinsically linked to the discourse on imperialism, *Kim* and its protagonist are both necessarily influenced by the nineteenth-century colonial era. Judith A. Plotz contends that, in contrast to the idyllic, multicultural adventure Kim's journey seems to be, "the rules of the Great Game force on Kim a role that progressively impedes fully human communion between him and the Indian world."[54] To be a great spy, Kim must, by definition, remain secretive and stealthy, using his natural observation skills against the very people of whom he wanted to be a part. The success of his espionage is reliant on his convincing performance of a wide range of ethnicities and castes. As a tool of the empire, Kim fulfils his destiny by birthright, enacting the role of a loyal British subject and ostensibly embodying the sahib, and there is no doubt that Kim enjoys what he does – after all, his work engages him in ways he found pleasurable even before becoming a spy. He loved "the game for its own sake – the stealthy prowl through the dark gullies and lanes, the crawl up a water-pipe, the sights and sounds of the women's world on the flat roofs, and the headlong flight from housetop to housetop under the cover of the hot dark."[55]

Yet Kim never makes a final decision as to whom he will ultimately be; the ending "is inconclusive because Kim breaks down under a double burden of antithetical possibilities and only reconstitutes himself to uncertain purpose."[56] Within Kim is a war between taking the path assumed of him by the fact of his birth and his partiality for an Indian identity. Kim's challenge, then, is the same challenge faced by all teenagers: to discover an identity based on what the self desires, not what others dictate. Cross-dressing as a variety of ethnic personae, coupled with his multi-faceted performances of Indians and Englishmen alike, allows Kim to experience and gain awareness and understanding of the Other. Armed with the knowledge of all that is available to him, he is free to establish his own identity. At his essence, Kim is the ultimate cross-dresser. Transcending boundaries successfully and easily, he is the master of his fate, in defiance of all who may hinder him. As the lama says to Mahbub Ali regarding the options of Kim's future, "Let him be a teacher; let him be a scribe – what matter? He will have attained Freedom at the end. The rest is illusion."[57] Although the sentiment is religious in nature, the relevance to Kim's journey to selfhood is unmistakeable.

In time, all teenagers must become adults, and to some extent a balance between social harmony and independent agency must be struck in order to function in society. In this sense, a certain degree of conformity is inevitable. Commented on somewhat unfavourably by some scholars, including Garber, cross-dressing in

---

[54]   Plotz, Judith A. "The Empire of Youth: Crossing and Double-Crossing Cultural Barriers in Kipling's *Kim*." *Children's Literature* 20 (1992): 118.

[55]   Kipling, *Kim*, 5.

[56]   Plotz, "The Empire of Youth," 126.

[57]   Kipling, *Kim*, 284.

literature and film is often treated as merely a transitional state: even individuals who feel comfortable with ambiguity must eventually choose a side. Although the texts discussed here do not reveal the grown-up lives of the protagonists, and some examples do result in choosing a side, the examples of Dennis and Kim suggest crossing boundaries may yet survive into adulthood, particularly when doing so is based in part on the enjoyment of the act.

Performativity implies that repetition creates a kind of reality, and thus, the standard has the potential to change. Cross-dressing carves out places of existence in society for those who feel partly or wholly outside of it, leading to an evolving status quo. Gender in particular seems to be developing into a more fluid categorisation. The advance of women in traditionally masculine arenas over the last century implies a mercurial existence of femininity, and the recent rise of the metrosexual – heterosexual men with an interest in fashion and attention to physical appearances, which are stereotypically feminine concerns – suggest similar changes in masculinity. Other categories beyond those discussed here exist with likewise mutable facets: consider the implications of cross-species performance in the recent upsurge in Young Adult literature featuring werewolves, vampires, shapeshifters, and faeries.

Cross-dressing, in its myriad forms, is well established in Young Adult literature. The act of transgressing traditional, socially constructed, and acceptable roles allows characters to explore previously unknown territories and gain an understanding both of themselves, Others, and how they fit into place in the world. Internalising this knowledge, heroes and heroines construct a unique identity, enacting that integral process of self-creation that all teenagers, fictional and real, must undergo as they transition into adulthood.

Chapter 6
Monstrous Bodies:
Writing the Incestuously Abused Adolescent Body

Lydia Kokkola

"Why can't I see myself, *feel* where I end and begin?"[1]

The sexually abused adolescent body is quintessentially abject. Where voluntary sexual activity is often troped in literature as marking the end of childhood and entry into adulthood, the involuntary sexuality of father-daughter incest places the victim outside the semiotic order. She is no longer a child, yet she is also not an adult. More monstrous than human, the sexually abused adolescent body fills its perceiver with horror, and yet it is endlessly fascinating. This combination, I suggest, is a means by which the adolescent body can critique the aetonormative world order.[2] This chapter examines how *Push* by Sapphire represents the body of an incestuously abused adolescent. The novel depicts Precious Jones's race, body size, and pregnancy as monstrous. By probing the qualities of the horror Precious's body incites, the chapter aims to expose the power at play in such representations, and show how politically motivated writers like Sapphire may work within the tradition of adolescent fiction to challenge such views. It also exposes how potential sources of power can be evoked, and the implications of such (ab)uses of power. The discussion is set within a larger discussion of the construction of adolescence.

Writing the monstrous body: "Kids is scared of me"[3]

As this volume attests, adolescence is frequently described as a period of *sturm und drang*, thereby implying that the periods of time on either side of the teenage years are more stable and less stressful. Given how recent the notion of

---

[1]   Sapphire. *Push*. New York: Random House, 1997, 32.

[2]   Maria Nikolajeva introduces this term as an analogy to 'heteronormativity' in queer theory. For Nikolajeva, "*Aetonomativity* (Lat. *aeto-*, pertaining to age), adult normativity that governs the way children's literature has been patterned from its emergence until the present day" Nikolajeva, Maria. *Power, Voice and Subjectivity in Literature for Young Readers*. New York : Routledge, 2010, 8.

[3]   Sapphire, *Push*, 6.

adolescence is, the ubiquity of this view in Western literature is remarkable, and suggests that emphasising the turmoil of these years successfully serves larger cultural aspirations. I examine the ways a politically motivated author, Sapphire, seeks to expose the injustices she sees in the wider society by inscribing it onto the adolescent body. I argue that, in doing so, she reveals the ways different aspects of social injustice – racism, sexism and prejudices against the poor, infirm, obese and illiterate – create an interlocking system which prevents large sections of the community from thriving. By tangibly inscribing these social ills onto the body of her adolescent protagonist, Precious, Sapphire questions societal hope for change as, unlike the cases of hybrid children discussed by Beauvais above, Precious does not represent the possibility of hope in a society in conflict with itself.[4] On the contrary, the societal problems inscribed on Precious's body render her abject: she is expelled from the school, which in effect expels her from the social order and society the school represents.

I see a connection between Precious's expulsion from school and Kristeva's discussion of the expulsion of the abject. Over the course of the summer holidays, Precious's body has changed so that she is very clearly pregnant. Since she has not yet arrived at her first class, the only motivation for expelling her must be her monstrous body. She has not had a chance to behave badly. She is pushed across the boundary of the school building, rejected so that the social environment of the school is no longer affected by her presence. If social consciousness is represented in the novel by social institutions such as school and social welfare services, the unconsciousness of society – the place to which Precious is repressed – is represented in the novel through the motif of invisibility.

Precious feels that people do not *see* her, resulting in her own inability to recognise herself in her reflection. Such invisibility is a well-established theme in African American literature stemming from Ralph Ellison's *Invisible Man* and also used by writers such as Toni Morrison in *The Bluest Eye.*[5] Like the self-alienated Pecola in Morrison's novel, Precious rejects her body and fantasises about an alternative, interior, white self: "My fahver don't see me really. If he did he would know I was like a white girl, a *real* person, inside."[6] Unlike both Pecola and Ellison's invisible man, Precious appears to be very visible. She is morbidly obese and already at the age of twelve weighs more than two hundred pounds, giving her the appearance of being much older. Her obesity thus forms a physical barrier between her inner, thinking self and the outside world; a barrier that makes it literally impossible for her to be seen. In the hospital she observes

---

4   See Clémentine Beauvais, "Romance, Dystopia and the Hybrid Child," in this volume. See also Kokkola, Lydia. "Sapphire's 'Palpable Designs': Is *Push* too Pushy?" In *Literary Community-Making: The Dialogicality of English Texts from the Seventeenth Century to the Present*, edited by Roger D. Sell. Amsterdam: John Benjamin, 2012.

5   Morrison, Toni. *The Bluest Eye*. Austin: Holt, Rinehart and Winston, 1970. See for further discussion Stewart, Susan Louise. "In the Ellison Tradition: In/Visible Bodies of Adolescent and YA Fiction." *Children's Literature in Education* 40 (2009): 180–96.

6   Sapphire, *Push*, 32.

that "nobody get I'm twelve 'less I tell them,'"[7] signalling that Precious's child-self is invisible. The trope of invisibility stitches the various forms of abuse Precious faces together, and becomes (at least partially) resolved in the novel through another well-established literary motif: the struggle to become literate.

Precious's narrative starts with a series of statements which recall the opening lines of both Alice Walker's *The Color Purple*, to which *Push* makes numerous references, as well as Morrison's *The Bluest Eye*.[8] These allusions prepare the more experienced reader to expect the tropes of invisibility and literacy mentioned above.

> I was left back when I was twelve because I had a baby for my fahver. That was in 1983. I was out of school for a year. This gonna be my second baby. My daughter got Down Sider. She's retarded. I had got left back in the second grade too, when I was seven, 'cause I couldn't read (and I still peed on myself). I should be in the eleventh grade ... But I'm not. I'm in the ninfe grade. I got suspended from school 'cause I'm pregnant which I don't think is fair.[9]

Like both Walker and Morrison, whose novels were published in 1983 when Precious gave birth to her first child, Sapphire starts her narrative *in medias res* with a character describing a very young African American girl who is pregnant by her father. Precious's idiolect keeps her ethnicity in the forefront, whilst the text exposes other sources of injustice: her father's sexual abuse, her daughter's infirmity, the poor quality of her education. A few pages later, we learn that she is morbidly obese, and before the end of the first chapter Precious reveals that her mother also physically, mentally, and sexually abuses her.

As these opening lines also reveal, the numerous social ills *Push* addresses are intimately interwoven, and some of their connections are obvious. One cannot consider her sexual abuse without also taking her femininity into account. The resulting pregnancies have affected the size of her body. The poor quality of the education she receives is largely due to the poverty in which she and her family live. But there are also slightly less obvious connections between these various problems woven into the narrative. For instance, the various descriptions of meals Precious prepares reveal a diet made from inexpensive ingredients which are high in fat and starch but low in fibre and vitamins, which denotes the family's poverty, whereas Precious's excessively large portion sizes are part of her mother's abuse. In this way, Sapphire forces her readers to consider Precious intersectionally: she does not allow the various 'strikes' against Precious to be arranged hierarchically but, rather, forces us to bear witness to how these various sources of injustice fuse with one another as they are written onto Precious's body.

---

[7]   Sapphire, *Push*, 11.

[8]   Walker, Alice. *The Color Purple*. London: The Women's Press, 1983. Morrison, *The Bluest Eye*.

[9]   Sapphire, *Push*, 3.

Although the various strands of abuse are tightly interwoven, I shall tease them apart in order to shed more light on how sexual, physical, and mental abuse, pregnancy, lack of education, and race render Precious's teenage body abject. In doing so, I leave her femininity, her poverty, her HIV infection, and her obesity in the shadows, not due to irrelevance or self-evidence, but simply because these are issues which have been discussed more fully elsewhere.[10] I conclude by discussing Precious's partial return to the social order through her struggles to become literate and questioning how much we can generalise from Sapphire's representation of this monstrous, young body to wider debates on the nature of adolescence.

Losing sight of the body: "Why can't I see myself?"[11]

The abject is a primal fear that cannot be expressed through language (the semiotic order, which is associated with the adult world), and so it is expelled or repressed within the subconscious (within the symbolic order, which is associated with the pre-verbal child). As Barbara Creed explains "The place of the abject is where meaning collapses, the place where I am not."[12] Typically, this associated with collective fears (such as the fear of death) and responses to trauma. As a result of her multiple experiences of abuse, Precious's sense of self has been totally destroyed; she asks "Why can't I see myself, *feel* where I end and begin?"[13] But as Kristeva also points out, the abject cannot be fully repressed, the abuse that has been wrought on Precious's body becomes manifest through disturbances in her language. Silent and illiterate at the start of the novel, Precious's self-healing is expressed in the text through her increased ability to express herself both orally and in writing. The novel does not, however, suggest that the healing process is completed or that Precious achieves full autonomy. Absence and language disturbance pervade the entire novel. The mind-body split, however, is most powerfully introduced into the narrative in conjunction with specific acts of sexual abuse.

Recalling nights when Carl would alternate between having sex with Precious and with her mother, Precious connects these acts of violence with her body-self split.

---

[10]   See Kokkola, "Sapphire's 'Palpable Designs'"; Thompson, Mary. "Third Wave Feminism and the Politics of Motherhood." *Genders OnLine Journal* (2006), 43; Highberg, Nels P. "The (Missing) Faces of African American Girls with AIDS." *Feminist Formations* 22, no 1 (2010): 1–20.

[11]   Sapphire, *Push*, 32.

[12]   Creed, Barbara. "Lesbian Bodies: Tribades, Tomboys and Tarts." In *Sexy Bodies: The Strange Carnalities of Feminism*, edited by Elisabeth Grosz and Elspeth Probyn, 86–103. London: Routledge 1996.

[13]   Sapphire, *Push*, 32.

Carl come over fuck us'es. Go from room to room, slap me on my ass when he through, holler WHEEE WHEEE! Call me name Butter Ball Big Mama Two Ton of Fun. I hate hear him talk more than I hate fuck. Sometimes fuck feel good. That confuse me, everything get swimming for me, floating like for days sometimes. I just sit in back classroom, somebody say something I shout on 'em, hit 'em; rest of the time I mind my bizness. I was on my way to graduate from I.S. 146'n the fuckface Miz Lichenstein mess shit up. I ... , in my inside world, I am so pretty, like a advertisement girl on commercial.[14]

As the borders of Precious's body are physically violated, her mind collapses. Note that she finds Carl's sex talk worse than his bodily violations. Usually, she is invisible to him and usually Precious is distressed when rendered invisible. Carl's name-calling, however, distresses her because she *cannot* remain absent. His words define her as a woman who enjoys the sexual attention she is receiving. Precious longs to reject this definition, but knows from experience that resistance (physical or verbal) will result in a beating. Carl interprets Precious's silence as agreement. Her body seems to collude with him as she involuntarily orgasms; a response which leaves her "swimming" in a state of confusion. These involuntary orgasms disgust Precious: "I HATE myself when I feel good."[15] She responds by smearing her face with her own faeces, and engaging in other self-harming acts such as mutilating herself with a razor.[16] Her goal s not to kill herself, simply to expel her body which has let her down.[17] But, since her body cannot be expelled, she suffers a mind-body split: "My body not mine, I hate it coming."[18] This leads her to feel confused, as though she is "floating"; she does not recognise herself. When she is held back in school, thereby losing the opportunity to become a writing subject, she becomes absent in her own text. Representing herself by absence – the three dots signalling an omission ("I ... ,") – the text recalls Kristeva's comments on the abjection of a corpse: "It is no longer I who expel. 'I' is expelled."[19] Precious cannot expel her knowledge of her father's abuse or of her physical response to that abuse, and so she expels her self. Her use of a symbol, "... ," that represents an omission to refer to herself signals the return of the abject as it reasserts itself through a disturbance in language.

Precious's healing begins only once she has reimposed her own language onto her body by labelling Carl's actions as rape, which she connects to race: "I think I was rape. I think what my fahver do is what Farrakhan said the white man did

---

[14]   Sapphire, *Push*, 35; punctuation as in original.

[15]   Sapphire, *Push*, 58.

[16]   Sapphire, *Push*, 111–12.

[17]   Creed, Barbara. "Horror and the Monstrous Feminine: An Imaginary Abjection." In *Feminist Film Theory: A Reader*, edited by Sue Thornham, 252–53. New York: New York University Press, 1999.

[18]   Sapphire, *Push*, 111.

[19]   Kristeva, Julia. *The Powers of Horror: An Essay on Abjection*. New York: Columbia University Press, 1982, 4.

to the black woman ... Farrakhan say during slavery times the white man just walk out to the slavery Harlem part where the niggers live ... and he take any black woman he want.[20] Precious relates Carl's behaviour back to the racialised history of sexual abuse in much the same way that Morrison motivates Cholly's rape of Pecola in *The Bluest Eye* through the sexual abuse he experienced at the hands of the white men. Unlike Morrison, however, Sapphire does not excuse Carl's abusive behaviour as a result of living in a racist society. Precious notes that racism may have contributed to her father's violent behaviour, but she still holds him personally responsible. Similarly, Mama's crimes are not reduced. On the contrary, the more readers come to know about Mary's complicity in Carl's abuse, as well as the abuse she, too, has inflicted upon her daughter, the more monstrous Mary becomes. She breaches the incest taboo, our ideas about motherhood and the same-sex taboo. Combined, Precious's initial homophobia – a topic to which I shall return – is very credible.

In *The Poetics of Childhood*, Roni Natov notes how the metaphors of the mother's body as a place of safety are woven into many works of children's literature, especially those intended for very young readers.[21] Typically, the child character (or anthropomorphic animal character) expresses the desire to return to the safe haven of the mother's body. But for Precious, the mother's body was never a place of safety. Her forced return to the maternal body is presented amidst images of death. Precious describes her mother's fingers as a "creepy spider, up my legs, in my pussy";[22] an image that recalls the widow spider discussed by Grosz in terms of the *vagina dentata*.[23] Mary is depicted as a predatory beast whose sexuality threatens Precious's very existence. Like her responses to her father's sexual abuse, Precious's reactions to her mother's body are decidedly visceral. The mother's body is abjected not, as in Kristeva's discussion, in order for Precious to become an autonomous subject, but as a survival strategy. Precious recalls being forced to perform oral sex on her mother as though it were happening to someone else. She cannot expel the mother's body, but rather the "'I' is expelled." The result is another mind-body split:[24]

> That night I dream *I am not in me* but am awake listening to myself choking, going a huh a huh A HUH A HUH A Huh. I am walking around trying to find where I am, where the sound is coming from. I know I will choke to death I don't find myself. I walk to my muver's room but it look different, she look different. I look like a baby almost. She is talkin' sweet to me like Daddy talks. I am choking between her legs A HUH A HUH. She is smelling big woman smell. She say suck it, lick me Precious. Her hand is like a mountain pushing my

[20]   Sapphire, *Push*, 68.

[21]   Natov, Roni. *The Poetics of Childhood*. New York: Routledge, 2003, 63–90.

[22]   Sapphire, *Push*, 21.

[23]   Grosz, Elizabeth. "Animal Sex: Libido as Desire and Death." In *Sexy Bodies*, ed. Grosz and Probyn, 278–99.

[24]   Kristeva, *The Powers of Horror*, 4.

head down. I squeeze my eyes shut but choking don't stop, it get worse. Then I open my eyes and look. I look at little Precious and I feel hit feeling, feeling like killing Mama. But I don't, instead I call little Precious and say, Come to Mama but I means me. Come to *me* little Precious. Little Precious look at me, smile, and start to sing: ABCDEFG[25]

Elizabeth Grosz has examined the embodied nature of responses of the subject to the abject: "it is usually expressed in retching, vomiting, spasms, choking – in brief, in disgust."[26] Precious attempts to expel the abject; in this instance, her mother's clitoris. She chokes, but cannot expel her mother's body because Mary is clamping her head in place. This results in another kind of splitting of the self as Precious separates what is left of her self as she attempts to mother her child self. The child-Precious provides the key to reconnecting the fragmented parts of Precious's selfhood: literacy. By becoming a speaking, writing subject, Precious will return her experiences to the symbolic order, become an autonomous adult and regain the sense of self that we see erased in both this scene and when she is raped by her father.

Although the works Beauvais discusses above take place within fantasy worlds and *Push* is set within a grittily stark rendition of Harlem of the 1980s, the sexual brutality and resulting pregnancies evident in all the novels suggest that these fictional teenagers address larger social issues. Beauvais observes that the single sexual encounter resulting in conception in both *Breaking Dawn* and *Noughts and Crosses* "enacts, at the level of adolescent libido, the social struggles of the adult-orchestrated world."[27] Precious's frequent sex with her father can also be read in a similar light. Carl's repetitive abuse reflects a society which bludgeons certain sectors of the community into submission, where the solitary sexual encounters of Sephy and Bella prior to the conceptions of their respective daughters preserves the notion of the innocent child even after *de facto* virginity has been lost. Moreover, the sexual encounters of all three adolescent girls are decidedly ambivalent in terms of sexual desire. Sephy and Bella both select their sexual partners themselves, but their first sexual experiences are tinged with violence. Precious's situation reverses the emphasis – her father's sexual violence is tinged with sexual pleasure – but the parallels between these events and their depictions in three very different novels produced within the same decade suggests to me that the pregnant teenage body is itself abject: it signals the return of a widespread fear that Western society has attempted to suppress. It seems to me not coincidental that all three novels foreground issues of race (or "species" in Meyer's *Twilight* series). But where the hybrid off-spring Beauvais discusses present ambivalent attitudes towards increasing racial mobility, *Push* addresses the racist sexual stereotype

---

[25]   Sapphire, *Push*, 58–59; first italics mine.

[26]   Grosz, Elizabeth. "The Body of Signification." In *Abjection, Melancholia and Love: The Work of Julia Kristeva*, edited by John Fletcher and Andrew Benjamin, 89. London: Routledge, 1990.

[27]   Beauvais, in this volume.

of the promiscuous African American woman. These connections between race, pregnancy, and the abject are symptomatic of a decidedly ambivalent view of society.

The sexual, pregnant adolescent body: "Did you ever get to be a chile?"[28]

The first obvious act of discrimination against Precious that readers witness – her expulsion from school – arises as a direct result of her pregnancy. What is not obvious is why she needs to be expelled. She is capable of attending school, and indeed the success of her placement at the alternative school reveals that there is nothing about being pregnant that presents an obstacle to Precious's ability to learn. Thus her expulsion can be assumed to take place solely because the presence of a pregnant adolescent in the school is considered something which disturbs the "civilised" world of the school. Beauvais argues that, in the novels she discusses, the adult world is *"waiting"* for the children to disturb it.[29] If the same were true for *Push*, it would explain the necessity of maintaining the notion that adolescence is a period of *sturm und drang*. By creating a definable, limited period during which society can be questioned, adolescence becomes a carnival period that offers the potential for renewal and reform. That this potential for change is made manifest through the birth of a child is not surprising in itself, but the connections between pregnancy and abjection offer further insight into the nature of the fears these texts address.

In *The Powers of Horror*, Kristeva argues that the female body is abject because it is not fixed: it swells during pregnancy and contracts after birth, it bleeds, lactates, and is open to penetration.[30] This permeable, unfixed body, Kristeva argues after Bakhtin, is grotesque: it destabilizes the boundaries between the civilised and the uncivilised, between animal and human. With the onset of puberty, the adolescent body also becomes abject as it destabilises the boundary between the child and the adult and draws attention to the adolescent's sexuality.[31] The pregnant adolescent is thus doubly marginalised, and when, as is the case of Precious, the pregnancy results from incest the result is quintessentially abject.

The abject, as Kristeva has explained, cannot remain suppressed into the symbolic order; it re-emerges as disturbances in language. Ms Lichtenstein expels Precious's abject body from the social (civilised) world of the school. She refuses to label what she sees, but instead uses a euphemism: "I see we're expecting a little visitor."[32] The particular 'disturbance in language' Ms Lichtenstein uses, "a little visitor," implies that Precious's child will not be staying for long. Indeed,

---

[28]   Sapphire, *Push*, 13.

[29]   Beauvais, in this volume.

[30]   Kristeva, *The Powers of Horror*, 102. See also Creed, "Lesbian Bodies," 87.

[31]   Grosz, Elizabeth. *Volatile Bodies: Toward a Corporeal Feminism.* Bloomington: Indiana University Press, 1994, 75.

[32]   Sapphire, *Push*, 6.

all the figures of authority that we see in the novel – teachers, social workers, and nurses – all confirm that they expect Precious to give her son up for adoption. Both Precious's pregnant body and the idea of her as a mother disturb the adults around her, and it is the precise nature of that disturbance that I wish to probe. Why does the pregnant teenage body incite such fear and fascination? How does it challenge the aetonormative world order?

The abject signals a breakdown of some boundary we revere: the physical boundaries of the body are a case in point. Teenage sex does not only signal the breaching of bodily borders; it also breaches the border between adulthood and childhood. For although "rigid oppositions between childhood innocence and adult passion, particularly sexual passion, are difficult to maintain," sexuality has retained its significance in adult-adolescent power relations.[33] Even though adolescence is a recent concept in Western history, it has already become a powerful conceptual tool that pervades areas as seemingly diverse as the legal system, medical science, and the fashion and banking industries, to name just a few examples. The result is a disjuncture that Higonnet questions: "Absolute distinctions between child and adult leave [teenagers] stranded on a very uncomfortable boundary. How can children possibly become adults from one instant to the next? The English and American cultures which above all others have glorified the ideal of childhood innocence deal badly with adolescence."[34] This inability to "deal" with adolescence is painfully evident in *Push*, where Precious's body is stranded between the worlds of adulthood and childhood. Rejected from both worlds, Precious is *unheimlich*, a disturbing presence whose pregnant body questions the credibility of the adult-adolescent border.

In *Push*, this rejection of Precious-as-child appears overtly in a nurse's comment made shortly after Precious has given birth to her first child, Little Mongo (so called because she is 'mongoloid,' i.e., she has Down's Syndrome). Upon realising that the baby was conceived incestuously, the nurse, 'Nurse Butter,' asks "'Was you ever, I mean did you ever get to be a chile?' Thas a stupid question, did I ever get to be a chile? I *am* a chile."[35] Nurse Butter's well intentioned remark reveals that she recognises Precious has not engaged in consensual sex. Nevertheless, she expresses her pity in a form that reveals that, as a result of her abuse, Precious is no longer a child. Even though Precious's sexual experiences take place involuntarily within abusive, incestuous relationships, the knowledge gained from these experiences pushes her outside the boundaries of childhood. She is not a child, but neither is she an adult. She is expelled from both categories.

In *Disturbing the Universe*, Trites argues that "Sexual potency is a common metaphor for empowerment in adolescent literature, so ... for many characters in YA novels, experiencing sexuality marks a rite of passage that helps them define

---

[33] Higonnet, Anne. *Pictures of Innocence: The History and Crisis of Ideal Childhood*. London: Thames & Hudson. 1998, 10.

[34] Higonnet, *Pictures of Innocence*, 194.

[35] Sapphire, *Push*, 13.

themselves as having left childhood behind."[36] Trites's argument is built on a discussion of works depicting voluntary sexual activity. Precious's experiences of sex have not been voluntary, and her behaviour cannot as such be characterized as "active"; yet, she is a "knowing" child and is perceived as such. Ms Lichtenstein and those nurses who do not know that Precious has been raped read her pregnant body in terms of the power play Trites outlines. They assume that she has deliberately encroached upon adult claims to power and is thus defiant and uncooperative.

The reader, however, witnesses how these readings of Precious's body continue the cycle of abuse. For instance, when Precious returns to the hospital in search of help after being attacked by her mother, she has to wait for Nurse Butter to become available. Whilst waiting, another nurse speaks to her. "She say she sorry to see me back here, had hoped I be done learned from my mistakes. What kinda shit is that! I didn't make no mistake unless it being born."[37] As Highberg observes, "The truth becomes secondary to [the nurse's] personal assumptions, which push her to dismiss Precious as unworthy of any further attention, deeper thought or basic help."[38] The assumption of superiority implicit in the nurse's comment is evidence of how aetonormative hegemony disempowers adolescents who attempt to use their sexuality to negotiate the adult-adolescent boundary. However, Precious is not deliberately posing a threat to the adult world, she is simply "trying to survive" the abuse she suffers.[39] Since her father's abuse results in further societal rejection, as evidenced in the nurse's reaction, Precious is further separated from the limited sources of help and empowerment she might access. As far as the nurses, who represent the society, are concerned, Precious is simply "a problem got to be out they face," something which must be expelled from the civilised world of the hospital.[40]

The incestuously abused, pregnant, teenage body breaches our most revered boundaries: not only those concerned with bodily integrity and adult-adolescent boundaries, but also those that govern familial relationships. Thus the abject challenges our fundamental understanding of how the world is structured. We long to reject the idea of children becoming parents and, as a result, cope badly when they do. Precious, like teenage mothers in the real world, is expelled: she is no longer a child, but since she cannot be considered an adult, she is simply monstrous. However, as a young mother, Precious also sheds light on the power of maternal privilege.

---

[36] Trites, Roberta Seelinger. *Disturbing the Universe: Power and Repression in Adolescent Literature*. Iowa City: University of Iowa Press, 2000, 84.

[37] Sapphire, *Push*, 75.

[38] Highberg, "The (Missing) Faces," 12.

[39] Sapphire, *Push*, 124.

[40] Sapphire, *Push*, 77.

Evoking maternal privilege: "Take Abdul I don't have nothing"[41]

Motherhood and reproductive rights and, to a lesser extent, privileges have always been heatedly debated topics within feminism. In recent years, much of this discussion has revolved around the concept "new Momism": a concept which shows how motherhood has been intertwined with and partly legitimised by consumer spending. In her comparison of *Push* with a collection of autobiographical stories written by mothers – *Breeder*, edited by Gore and Lavender – Thompson shows how the legitimisation of these 'new Moms' "is based upon an invisible, cultural de-legitimization of other 'breeders.'"[42] The term "breeder," which Gore and Lavender co-opt for political purposes, is a racist label which originally denoted slave women who "bred" children for their owners and which later came to be applied to black mothers who were deemed to be leeching money from the welfare system through careless reproduction. In their collection of autobiographical narratives, Gore and Lavender "affirm alternative family structures and question the assumed normalcy of the hetero-normative, two parent family."[43] However, as Thompson goes on to demonstrate, this questioning only applies to rigidly delineated aspects of motherhood. The "new Mom" in Gore and Lavender's collection is a superwoman who strives "'to have it all,' a problematic message because it cannot be achieved by all women ("having it all," in a feminist sense would presumably include equal pay, freedom from sexual violence, and reproductive rights – to name a few unmet desires)."[44] Precious is something of a superwoman in the way she raises herself up and improves her situation. Through her committed endeavours to become literate and care for her son, she achieves a far better living situation at the end of the novel than she was at the beginning – even though she is still "½way between the life [she] had and the life [she] want[s] to have."[45] Nevertheless, Precious's struggles do not result in a decent wage, she has only just begun to process her history of sexual violence, and, unlike the film adaptation, she will never regain custody of her daughter. "[E]qual pay, freedom from sexual violence, and reproductive rights" are indeed "unmet desires" for Precious.[46]

Thompson discusses "new Momism" in terms of *maternal privilege*; a privilege which initially seems empowering and benign. Sephy and Bella also evoke maternal privilege, and their determination to prioritise their accidentally conceived children over the survival of either the child's father (in *Noughts and Crosses*) or mother (in *Breaking Dawn*) is celebrated in the novels Beauvais

---

[41] Sapphire, *Push*, 70.
[42] Thompson, "Third Wave Feminism and the Politics of Motherhood," paragraph 2.
[43] Thompson, "Third Wave Feminism," paragraph 7.
[44] Thompson, "Third Wave Feminism," paragraph 18.
[45] Sapphire, *Push*, 84.
[46] Thompson, "Third Wave Feminism," paragraph 18.

discusses.[47] However, as Thompson shows, the celebration of motherhood, as opposed to parenthood, downplays the role of fathers: in Blackman's saga, Callum dies so that Callie can live, and in *Push*, Carl dies of AIDS, leaving Precious with one less problem to face. Thompson also questions the societal legitimisation of self-sacrifice and the abandonment of the mother's sense of autonomy, a theme which is particularly evident in Meyer's saga.[48] Finally, her discussion of how reproduction and consumerism have become entwined "tacitly affirm[s] reproductive choice as the privilege of the educated, predominantly white, middleclass."[49] Precious's reception as a mother affirms Thompson's arguments. After the birth of Abdul, Precious is forced to use her nascent literacy skills to defend her right to motherhood.[50] It is her determination to care for Abdul that forces her out of her mother's home, and which renders her eligible for the kind of care she needs from the social welfare system. Her resolve to raise Abdul and ensure he becomes literate helps her maintain momentum as she strives for a better life for them both. So, despite the opinions of those around her, Precious draws strength from her position as mother. This evocation of maternal privilege as a source of power, Duncan has found, has real-world significance where becoming a mother provides underprivileged youngsters with a means of improving their social outcomes.[51]

Despite other people's opinions, Precious is proud of herself for becoming a mother, even though both children are the result of rape. Indeed, it is her pride in being a mother that pushes Precious to continue to strive towards literacy, caring for her child "*while*, not *instead of*, following [her] dreams" of becoming literate and gaining autonomy.[52] When Precious arrives at Each One Teach One, she takes (and presumably fails) a preliminary literacy test, but she refuses to be put down: "I look bitch teacher woman in face, trying to see do she see *me* or the tess. But I don't care what anybody see. I see something, somebody. I got baby. So what. I feel proud 'cept it's baby by my fahver and that make me not in picture again."[53] Motherhood is one of Precious's few sources of strength in a world that renders her invisible; having a baby makes her feel "proud." Before returning to the trope of invisibility, I would like to briefly consider Precious's other form of privilege: her heterosexuality.

---

[47]   Beauvais, in this volume.

[48]   Hendershot Parkin, Rachel. "Breaking Faith: Disrupted Expectations and Ownership in Stephenie Meyer's Twilight Saga." *Jeunesse: Young People, Texts, Cultures* 2, no 2 (2010): 61–85.

[49]   Thompson, "Third Wave Feminism," paragraph 24

[50]   See Kokkola, "Sapphire's Palpable Designs," for a fuller discussion of Precious's nascent literacy skills and her use of these in defending her right to be a mother.

[51]   Duncan, Simon. "What's the Problem with Teenage Parents? And What's the Problem with Policy?" *Critical Social Policy* 27 (2007): 307–334.

[52]   Gore, Ariel, and Bee Lavender. *Breeder: Real-Life Stories from the New Generation of Mothers*. Seattle, Wash.: Seal Press, 2001, xiii.

[53]   Sapphire, *Push*, 33.

Evoking heterosexual privilege: "I cannot see how I am the same as a white faggit."[54]

Sapphire allows space for readers to reflect on the ways Precious exploits the very few privileges she has. As I have acknowledged from the outset, Precious is trapped in a complex web of social injustices, and there is no doubt that she is a figure who is intended to inspire pathos. However, it is also worth noting how Precious herself is willing to exploit the other point of access to power she has besides that of maternity: heterosexual privilege. Precious may be disgusted by her bodily responses to her father when she orgasms, but her responses confirm her sexual orientation as heterosexual, especially as she has had experience of same-sex sex with her mother. Like her hard won maternal privilege, Precious is willing to use her heterosexuality to her advantage. However, the way in which she does so differs markedly from her use of maternal privilege. Working within the Foucauldian tradition, Marilyn French discusses how "power *to*" differs markedly from "power *over*."[55] Her arguments aptly distinguish between the ways Precious negotiates her maternal and heterosexual privileges. Whereas her role as a mother provides the impetus and power for Precious *to* leave her abusive home and continue on her path to literacy, she constantly evokes power *over* homosexuals in her homophobic dismissal of "faggits" and "butches."

Given that Sapphire is a politically active lesbian writer, one can assume that she does not want readers to emulate Precious's homophobia. She uses Precious's evocation of heterosexual privilege as a means of challenging such views. Precious's class at Each One Teach One is all female. One of her classmates, Jermaine, and her teacher, Ms Rain, are lesbians. Whilst Precious is initially dismissive of Jermaine, she changes her attitudes. This is partly a result of her discovery that her much loved teacher is also a lesbian, and partly because she hears about the abuse Jermaine has suffered as a result of her sexual orientation. She mellows to the point at which she realises that "I never be butch like Celie but it don't make me happy – make me sad. Maybe I never find no love, nobody."[56] This change of heart does not extend to gay men, however. When she discovers she has HIV, her friend Rita tries to explain that "All people with HIV or AIDS is innocent victims" but Precious "cannot see how I am the same as a white faggit or crack addict."[57] Sapphire does not resolve this problem, but leaves the question hanging in the air for the reader to answer, thereby forcing them to consider the privileges afforded by heterosexuality.

Precious's access to maternal and heterosexual privilege do not, however, compensate for her sufferings. As I have shown, each act of oppression is written

---

[54]   Sapphire, *Push*, 108.

[55]   French, Marilyn. *Beyond Power: On Women, Men, and Morals*. New York: Summit, 1985, 504–512.

[56]   Sapphire, *Push*, 95.

[57]   Sapphire, *Push*, 108.

onto her body, creating a monstrous figure. Precious describes the experience of being "more than dumb, we invisible" in terms of vampirism.[58] Vampires "eats, drinks, wear clothes, talks, fucks, and stuff but when you git right down to it they don't exist. I big, I talk, I eats, I cooks, I laugh, watch TV, do what my muver say. But I can see when the picture come back I don't exist. Don't nobody want me. Don't nobody need me. I know who I am. I know who they say I am – vampire sucking the system's blood."[59] As Stewart observes, "Precious is not a ghost ... but the characterization of herself as a vampire signals that same eerie, frightening response. Her cultural and historical heritage – a product of a violent history – contributes to her dislocation and displacement."[60] By situating *Push* in a wider discussion of African American literature, Stewart observes how the seemingly very visible, fat, Black body Precious inhabits is rendered invisible.[61]

Reclaiming the body through language: "What it take for my muver to see me?"

As I noted at the beginning of this chapter, the trope of invisibility is used throughout *Push* to express society's failure to respond to Precious's needs and to express her self-alienation. Susan Stewart explains, "Precious ... becomes invisible because those who hold the power of the gaze, most of whom are white, refuse to see her. This diminishes agency and transforms what would be the subject (or object) of the gaze into nonexistence."[62] Stewart's brief overview of the trope of invisibility in Young Adult fiction traces connections back to Ellison's *Invisible Man*, to show how the metaphor has become "an intertextual shortcut" for loss of subjectivity.[63] Her review foregrounds race and sexual abuse and, although she does not comment on it, this has the unfortunate consequence of conflating them. Highberg takes up this common conflation of "down-low" sexuality and race in his discussion of the invisibility of African American girls with HIV. He observes that "The long history of American racism has created a situation where any serious discussion of how race intersects with any social ills usually reverts to the most dominant and destructive of master narratives."[64] From the point of view of my discussion here, the important point Highberg makes is that the trope of invisibility connects each of the forms of discrimination and social ills Precious faces, but foregrounds racism.

---

[58]   Sapphire, *Push*, 30.

[59]   Sapphire, *Push*, 31.

[60]   Stewart, "In the Ellison Tradition," 185.

[61]   Lieber, T.M. "Ralph Ellison and the Metaphor of Invisibility in the Black Literary Tradition." *American Quarterly* 24 no, 1 (1972): 86–100.

[62]   Stewart, "In the Ellison Tradition," 186.

[63]   Stewart, "In the Ellison Tradition," 180.

[64]   Highberg, "The (Missing) Faces," 4–5.

Readers first become aware of Precious's invisibility in the school context. Piecing her story together, we learn that by the second grade she has already been force fed by her mother and repeatedly raped by her father. The abuse literally renders her immobile: she sits silent at her desk for the whole day. Invisibility initially seems to be a voluntary survival strategy. At first she is taunted by her classmates. Unpleasant as these taunts are, they reveal that Precious's obese body was visible. By refusing to respond, she becomes so invisible "Kids is scared of me."[65] She becomes so dependent on her self-imposed invisibility that she does not dare to move, and so wets herself on a daily basis. The school's response is simply to make her repeat the year. They do not seek the source of the problem. She becomes so invisible that she is allowed to pass through the system, even though, at the age of sixteen, despite regular attendance, "page 122 look like page 152, 22, 3, 6, 5 – all the pages look alike to me."[66] As Stewart observes:

> On one level, it is not difficult to understand why Precious feels as though she is invisible, for what she experiences reflects a type of wholesale socio-economic and cultural blindness wherein "turning a blind eye" takes on a literal meaning for Precious's circumstances. No one wants to see her.[67]

Although the school contributes to Precious's invisibility, it also provides the key to her ability to regain her visibility when she starts specialist literacy classes. The literacy classes enable her to reclaim her body through language; the abjected body enters the symbolic order as Precious finds ways to express what has happened to her first in writing and then in speech.

As a result of her struggles to become literate, Precious finds ways to first speak and then write her incestuously abused body into existence. However, the return to visibility is not unmitigatedly pleasant. For the first time in her life, Precious starts to feel lonely. Up until now, she explains, the constant sexual, physical and mental abuse from both her parents and the constant humiliations at school and on the street have left no room such a "small thing" as loneliness.[68] Finding her voice through her literacy classes brings Precious to a new view of herself; she carries her pregnancy visibly and shows bodily pride. She feels seen by her classmates: "At least when I look at the girls [in her class] I see *them* and when they look they see *ME,* not what I looks like."[69] This leads her to reconnect the parts of herself which, were described as having split during her abuse:

> I always thought I was someone different on the inside. That I was just fat and black and ugly to people on the OUT-SIDE. If they could see the *inside* me they would see something lovely and not keep laughing at me, throwing spitballs ...

---

[65] Sapphire, *Push*, 6.

[66] Sapphire, *Push*, 5.

[67] Stewart, "In the Ellison Tradition," 185.

[68] Sapphire, *Push*, 62.

[69] Sapphire, *Push*, 95.

and polly seed shells at me, that Mama and Daddy would recognize me as ... as, I don't know, Precious! But I am not different on the inside.[70]

Splitting and invisibility have both been survival strategies Precious has needed to survive her abuse. In the healing process, she must unlearn these strategies and so reclaim her abjected body.

Encountering the monstrous adolescent body: "Forgit the WHY ME shit and git on to what's next"[71]

In conclusion, I wish to consider the wider implications of Sapphire's monstrous creation. Precious is not merely an individual, she represents a view of the world. What does the novel say about the state of adolescence? In *Radical Children's Literature*, Kimberley Reynolds astutely observes:

> The wounded child may symbolise a damaged self, but it may equally stand for a damaged culture; this means that if the image of the self as a child can be kept intact and unviolated, the myth of innocent childhood that Rose maintains is central to the well-being of adults and the work of children's literature remains in place individually and socially.[72]

The glimpses we have of Precious's life as a child do not reveal a romanticised, innocent child. Towards the end of the novel we learn that that Carl began sexually abusing her when she was still in nappies. Precious has never known a time when she was "intact and unviolated," and if she represents a culture, then it is a culture that has suffered constant abuse. Ingrained sexisim, racism, negative attitudes towards the obese and poorly educated, and the long-term impact of grinding poverty prevent Precious from flourishing as an individual, but they also prevent the society in which she lives from flourishing.

However, the Precious who serves as narrator is *not* a child, but an adolescent. She represents a society on the brink of collapse. Caught at the last possible moment when change is possible, she challenges the adult world to see her and alter their views. We witness Precious abandon her homophobic views, thereby modelling the changes in attitude the novel promotes. Most importantly, she challenges negative stereotypes surrounding teenage motherhood. Her ability to mother her son, Abdul, is vastly superior to the way her mother and grandmother have raised their children. Sapphire draws on stereotypical notions about the child as the hope for the future, but also uses the idea of adolescent *sturm und drang* as challenging the status quo and opening up the possibility of change. The adults,

---

[70]   Sapphire, *Push*, 125.

[71]   Sapphire, *Push*, 139.

[72]   Reynolds, Kimberly. *Radical Children's Literature: Future Visions and Aesthetic Transformations in Juvenile Fiction*. Basingstoke: Palgrave Macmillan, 2007, 90.

especially Carl and Mary, present equally stereotypical views of adulthood as a time of stasis and stagnation, and offer no hope of redemption. Even the more positive adult figures, including Ms Rain, show no signs of changing as a result of their encounters with Precious.

But Precious cannot overcome her history: her HIV infection symbolises the lasting damage done to her youthful body. She will never be able to escape the forces she faces, and as a representation of the society in which she lives, Precious comes to stand for all that is wrong with that world, all that we would like to abject. Yet, despite the fears she embodies, Precious's capacity to improve her situation fascinates readers and challenges them to consider an alternative world where such monsters could be tamed. Previous is a 'heavy' character not only in terms of her body size: she signifies a weight of cultural messages about the forces that prevent individuals and communities from thriving. These are not topics many of us choose to engage with of our own volition. By evoking the abject, Sapphire has created a character who fascinates whilst she educates.

Chapter 7
"The Beat of your Heart":
Music in Young Adult
Literature and Culture

Karen Coats

Teenagers use music, perhaps more than any other language or cognition-related activity, to regulate and alter their moods, establish and consolidate both core and tribal identities, celebrate the joys of embodiment, sublimate aggressive sexual or violent feelings, mourn relational losses, generate courage for new endeavours, affirm their values and beliefs, and worship their gods. They are voracious consumers of music; indeed, research shows that, in general, people are more likely to be avid music listeners between the ages of fourteen and twenty than they are at any other time in their lives, with consumption of music doubling between the tween and teen years.[1] In our lifetimes, we have seen a rapid evolution of personal music technology that has facilitated the private consumption of music. At home, clunky personal turntables turned bedrooms into places for teenage girls in particular to dance and dream,[2] while living-room HiFis with enormous speakers and complex toggle switches to engineer the sound allowed families to share their tastes with one another, willingly or not. On the road, car stereos not only picked up music radio, but could be upgraded with 8-track tape players, cassettes in the 1970s and 1980s, and now CD players, satellite radio, and MP3 devices. Outside the car, teens in the second half of the twentieth century used transistor radios and other portable music devices, and gathered around boomboxes on basketball courts, parking lots, and beaches, developing a public culture of music and dance that sometimes turned into a competitive substitute for gang violence as crews showed their superiority and turf ownership through break dancing rather than breaking heads. Today, it is rare indeed to see a teenager who isn't occasionally, if not often, plugged into an iPod.

Considering the ubiquity of portable music in teenage culture, it is odd that authors of Young Adult literature often overlook the importance of music in their

---

[1]   Roberts, Donald F., and Ulla G. Foehr. *Kids and Media in America*. Cambridge: Cambridge University Press, 2004, 86.

[2]   See McRobbie, Angela, and Jenny Garber. "Girls and Subcultures: An Exploration." In *Resistance Through Rituals: Youth Culture in Postwar Britain*, edited by Stuart Hall and Tony Jefferson, 220. New York: Routledge, 2003; Frith, Simon. *The Sociology of Rock*. London: Constable, 1978, 66.

writing, or even sometimes get it wrong in terms of technology or currency (in fact, this is one of the things that marks a book as consistent in its time period). Unless the book is specifically about a teenager's relationship to music, many authors either omit any mention of it, or else they use it as a more or less atmospheric marker of setting, unimportant to character development.[3] For authors sensitive to the full materiality of the teenager's world, however, music becomes an important code for social and individual identity formation, much like it functions in actual teenager culture. The sociological literature features rich and varied accounts of the role of music in youth culture, mostly focusing on the ways in which music functions to manage affect and enable self-fashioning at an individual level, and how it establishes and maintains group boundaries at the level of social identity; emerging research in cognitive neuroscience nuances our understanding of those processes by considering how the brain processes music and what implications that might have in our understanding of adolescent development. In what follows I will attempt to map some of the insights found through these studies onto the way music functions in contemporary adolescent literature, and how this coordinated approach can enrich our understandings of identity formation, which is arguably the key project of adolescence. My textual examples are by no means meant to be exhaustive, but rather point to some ways in which the uses of music in texts can be understood and interpreted.

Gender and ideology in music

In a 1992 article, Perry Nodelman notes a trend in Young Adult literature where male protagonists use music to foil an oppressive patriarchal order that insists on a form of masculinity that truncates the full expression of selfhood. Music in the novels he examines flourishes only in a feminine space, and the boys enter into that space as "an act of defiance against his father's conventional male values,"[4] discover their ability to express their "true" selves through music, and emerge as males more acceptable, according to Nodelman, to an ideology that values the softer side of masculinity: "A female music represents the essence of their presumably male selfhood."[5] In other words, music in these novels, all written in the late 1970s to late 1980s, enables boys to negotiate their Oedipus complex with a decidedly second-wave feminist twist in the outcome.

Certainly, many contemporary novels fall into a similar pattern, but as teenagers fashion their identities in a post-Oedipal economy, gender becomes more of a

---

[3]   Interestingly, tween survival literature (such as George's *My Side of the Mountain*, Farmer's *A Girl Named Disaster*, Hesse's *The Music of Dolphins*, etc.) includes, as part of the protagonist's path to self-sufficiency, the need and ability to produce music of some sort.

[4]   Nodelman, Perry. "Males Performing in Female Space: Music and Gender in Young Adult Novels." *The Lion & the Unicorn* 16, no 2 (1992): 224.

[5]   Nodelman, "Males Performing in Female Space," 224.

fuzzy set, and the semiotics of music in teenager texts responds. Some expressions remain starkly traditional; for instance, in John Green and David Levithan's *Will Grayson, Will Grayson*,[6] the gay main character is obsessed with directing a campy high school musical extravaganza, musical theatre having become associated in the public imagination with gay men. But in other books, music is specifically cited that challenges tidy associations between character type and music genre. Moe, for instance, in Frank Portman's *King Dork*,[7] is a wannabe rock guitarist who dresses in his father's old army coat and pretends to be edgy and unstable, and yet he describes his fondness for Bubblegum music, acknowledging that, although it was written for younger kids, it is "brilliant by accident" and "the best rock and roll music there ever was."[8] His love of this particular kind of music adds a layer to the central theme of the book, namely, Moe's relationship to childhood itself. He positions himself as the anti-Holden Caulfield, rejecting Holden's romanticized view that growing up means leaving something beautiful and worth cherishing behind, and yet his love of teenybopper music and his ironic nickname, Chi-Moe, short for child molester after a career survey indicated that he might make a good priest, belies the straightforwardness of his disdain for all things child. But it also positions him as someone who crosses gender lines in terms of musical taste. Angela McRobbie and Jenny Garber, as well as Simon Frith, clearly position Bubblegum as the kind of music specifically embraced by teenyboppers, that is, prepubescent girls,[9] and Moe's embrace of it is at first reactionary. He says, "maybe I got into it at first because it was so clearly the opposite of what everyone else liked,"[10] but he goes on to claim his rediscovery of the genre as form of superiority in both taste and knowledge, a position that reinforces his defensive self-positioning as not like what he calls "the normal people," people who fall into traditional gender and clique categories.

A more extensive and subtle example of gender blurring through musical taste appears in Steven Chbosky's *The Perks of Being a Wallflower*.[11] A playlist drawn from that novel positions Charlie, the protagonist, in an ambiguous gendered space in terms of his musical taste, as he listens to music that is traditionally coded masculine (Pink Floyd, Nirvana), and feminine (Simon and Garfunkel, Suzanne Vega), as well as music that blurs those categories (The Smiths, Genesis, Procol Harum, The Moody Blues). Much of the music Charlie listens to falls under the label of "emo," a musical aesthetic that is illustrative of the blurring of gender boundaries in that it encourages both boys and girls to explore the range of emotions that have traditionally fallen into rigid gender binary associations. Emo as a label

---

[6]   Green, John, and David Levithan. *Will Grayson, Will Grayson*. New York: Dutton Juvenile, 2010.

[7]   Portman, Frank. *King Dork*. New York: Delacorte, 2006.

[8]   Portman, *King Dork*, 84.

[9]   McRobbie and Garber, "Girls and Subcultures"; Frith, *The Sociology of Rock*.

[10]   Portman, *King Dork*, 84.

[11]   Chbosky, Steven. *The Perks of Being a Wallflower*. New York: MTV Books, 1999.

engenders strong responses among young people who either identify or actively dis-identify with the tag, but as a musical style, it emerged out of hardcore punk in the 1980s as a reaction to the violence inherit in the staccato rhythms, harsh dissonance, and intentionally shocking lyrics of that genre. Bands began to adopt a more distinctive melodic line and varied rhythms, and wrote lyrics that were deeply nostalgic and personal and elicited strong emotional responses, including cathartic tears, from their audiences. As Philip Tagg's research shows, listeners tend to create verbal and visual images that are strongly tied to conservatively understood gendered representations while listening to music; hardcore punk's commitment to fast, staccato rhythms, consistently loud volume, and rhythmic syncopations code it as male, while emo's central characteristics of slower tempos, smooth legato rhythms, varying volumes, and descending melodic lines registers the music itself as feminine in most people's estimations.[12] Charlie's introspective narration utilizes a traditionally feminine genre – the epistolary novel form – and yet it is his taste in music that truly ambiguates his gender presentation.

Janet K. Halfyard relates Tagg's findings to the opening theme songs of the TV series *Buffy the Vampire Slayer* and its companion series *Angel* to demonstrate how the characters in those series play with gender boundaries, not to blur them, she concludes, but to display and then intentionally cross them in order to emphasize the moral, emotional, and material complexity of the world the two series create.[13] Throughout the *Buffy* series, music plays an intentionally narrational role explored in detail by Amanda Howell.[14] In her essay, Howell also considers the music in terms of the way it plays with traditional conventions of gender. Since the 1950s, rock music has established particular roles for males and females, roles that of course have shifted somewhat over time but still largely reinforce the image of the male rebel, restless for independence and sexual conquest, and his female object, a support who nevertheless holds him down with her demands for romantic love. According to Howell, *Buffy* complicates these images on multiple fronts, from its ironic play with 1950s and 1970s images of rock-and-roll rebel bad boys in the characters of Angel and Spike, to its literalisation of the musical metaphors

---

[12]   Tagg, Philip. "An Anthropology of Stereotypes in TV Music?" *Swedish Musicological Journal* (1989): 19–42. http://www.tagg.org/articles/xpdfs/tvanthro.pdf. Retrieved February 20, 2011.

[13]   Halfyard, Janet K. "Love, Death, Curses and Reverses (in F minor): Music, Gender, and Identity in *Buffy the Vampire Slayer* and *Angel*." *Slayage: The Online Journal of Buffy Studies*. http://slayageonline.com/PDF/halfyard.pdf. Retrieved 20 February 2011. It can also be argued, using Tagg's findings, that the title music for *Girlfight* provides a more straightforward expression of Diana's "feminine masculinity." The staccato beat basically is the melodic line, coding the music as distinctly masculine, and yet its sound is that of a thin percussion instrument reminiscent of hand claps or a double-dutch jump rope, a traditionally female pastime.

[14]   Howell, Amanda. "'If we hear any inspirational power chords ...': Rock Music, Rock Culture on *Buffy the Vampire Slayer*." *Continuum: Journal of Media & Cultural Studies* 18, no 3 (2004): 406–22.

of pain and death in the field of romance, to its expansion of ubiquitous rock romantic lyrics to include broader senses of loss than the break-up of a couple. At the centre of these explorations is Buffy herself, whose coming-of-age narrative is intensified by her development into a mature warrior, and whose moments of transition and loss are almost always accompanied by haunting soundtracks with female vocalists that explore the line between the traditional pangs of romance and more profound expressions of subjective loss and destitution, scores that Howell sees as "more of an expansion of – rather than a departure from – the space conventionally delineated for female artists, listeners, and audiences by rock music and its commercial culture."[15] Howell concludes by agreeing with and expanding upon Halfyard's reading of the series theme song, emphasizing how the power guitar, which has become a hallmark signifier of masculine heroism in the field of rock and beyond, is ironically associated with Buffy's emergence and limitations as a female warrior who is also a commercial product.

In the recent Young Adult film *Fish Tank*, the music presents challenges to gender in a different way.[16] Mia, the protagonist, retreats into the private sanctuary of an empty apartment to dance, dreaming about the possibility of dancing professionally. This might appear to be a traditionally feminine activity, but her music and dance style of choice is hip hop, a form whose lyrics are usually angry and often misogynistic, and she dances in a hoodie and baggy sweats, clothes designed to hide her body rather than put it on display. When she does manage to get an audition to dance professionally, it is clear to everyone except Mia, at first, that the kind of dancing she does is not the kind the promoters are after, and when she realizes that they want her to dance in a seductively feminine way, she runs out. Music is a complex signifier in this film; it augments Mia's character development as an angry, defiant young woman, which in and of itself challenges the more traditional teen trope of the angry young man. However, her anger as represented by hip hop is clearly a survival mechanism; when she lets her guard down and attempts to adopt a more traditionally feminine, dependent role in response to her mother's new boyfriend by choosing his favourite song (Bobby Womack's cover of "California Dreamin") to dance to, she ends up exploited and hurt. She and her mother finally bond while dancing to Nas's "Life's a Bitch," a hip hop song that speaks to both of them of the gritty realities of their limited choices as poor, single women for whom anger is a hedge against despair.

The powerful associative qualities of gender in music consumption thus allow writers to use it as a signifier of character development in various ways to reinforce, challenge, or even blur gender norms and category distinctions.

---

[15]   Howell, "If we hear any inspirational power chords ...", 414.

[16]   *Fish Tank*. Dir. Andrea Arnold. 2009. IFC Films 2011. DVD.

Beyond gender: Music and identity

While gender stereotypes do not seem to have become less rigid in a post-Oedipal economy, the performance of gender among teenagers, as the above examples illustrate, is being called into question, and seems to allow for more transgression and finer gradations within other identity-marking discourses. Niche identities are more common and more pronounced, as young people struggle to assert themselves as individuals in a culture where the self has been characterized as both "empty"[17] and "saturated."[18] What Cushman means by characterizing the self as empty is that we have abandoned the position that the self has some sort of pre-existent core of originality and authenticity that seeks expression; thus the project of 1960s teenagers to "find themselves" was always already doomed to fail because there never was a self to find, only one to fashion through the adoption of beliefs, values, material artifacts, and narratives made available through culture. This notion of an empty self was cynically perpetuated, according to Cushman, by both the advertising and the therapeutic industries of post-WWII America so that they could induce an identity crisis and offer ready-made, consumer-based solutions. Gergen then follows up by examining the effect of advertising and media image on young people; with so many voices coming at them from so many sources, teenagers are saturated with proliferating, competing messages on who to be and how to live, and no compelling narrative emerges to take precedence and sort out the relative importance of the conflicting voices. Teenagers have adapted by becoming experimental with their identities, trying on various roles and subject-positions. Young Adult literature of the twenty-first century reflects this new form of self-fashioning in various ways, but positioning music as the centre of the project of a character's identity formation occurs less often in the literature than in real life. Indeed, Nicholas Cook goes so far as to say, "In today's world, deciding what music to listen to is a significant part of deciding and announcing to people not just who you 'want to be' ... but who you *are*. 'Music' is a very small word to encompass something that takes as many forms as there are cultural or sub-cultural identities."[19]

Studies of teenagers and their music abound, usually focusing on the subcultures that grow up around specific types of music, such as rap, hip-hop, rock, etc. Many studies focus on what Simon Frith termed "bedroom culture," examining the use of music in private spaces, since, according to educational psychologist Reed

---

[17] Cushman, Philip. *Constructing the Self, Constructing America: A Cultural History of Psychotherapy.* Reading, Mass.: Addison-Wesley, 1995.

[18] Gergen, Kenneth. *The Saturated Self: Dilemmas of Identity in Contemporary Life.* New York: Basic Books, 2000.

[19] Cook, Nicholas. *Music: A Very Short Introduction.* Oxford: Oxford University Press, 2000, 5.

Larson,[20] adolescents are more likely to explore multiple possibilities for identity construction and negotiate stress and negative emotion while engaged in solitary media use. But Frith challenges the idea of music as expressive of some sort of core identity:

> The question we should be asking is not what does popular music *reveal* about "the people" but how does it *construct* them ... popular music is popular not because it reflects something, or authentically articulates some sort of popular taste or experience, but because it creates our understanding of what popularity is.[21]

Frith goes on to argue that popular music serves three functions: 1) to create, in a very direct way, "a particular sort of self-definition"[22] that establishes both identity and non-identity, 2) to provide language for feelings that might otherwise be unavailable to us, or else depressingly banal, and 3) to situate and organize our experiences of the past and the present.[23] These functions of music all mediate the space between the public and the private, and hence prove crucial in the project of identity formation, because the most important outcome of identity experimentation is whether and by whom the identity is recognized and valued; identities are always crafted in and through a process of social mirroring and feedback. These functions play out in interesting ways in literature that pays attention to the role of music in teenagers' lives.

King Dork's Moe demonstrates the way in which music can negotiate a public persona and enable connections between people, as well as with the past and future. As he struggles to craft a reasonable sense of who he is, he is hampered by the loss of his father, who died when he was young. He tries to connect with the memory of his dad by reading his books and listening to music his dad would have listened to as a teenager, and then he uses his knowledge of retro music to try to connect with his well-meaning stepfather, Little Big Tom. LBT, an aging hippie, clearly wants to have a meaningful relationship with Moe, and music helps them to share a language. Meanwhile, Moe and his best friend Sam have an ongoing shared fantasy of becoming a famous band. They treat their ambition with a large measure of irony, however, by continually changing the name of the band, the role of the players (although Moe is almost always on guitar, Sam's contribution varies to include things like "bass and calisthenics,"[24] or "bass and

---

20   Larson, Reed. "Secrets in the Bedroom: Adolescents' Private Use of Media." *Journal of Youth and Adolescence* 24, no 5 (October 1995): 535–50.

21   Frith, Simon. "Toward an Aesthetic of Popular Music." *Music and Society: The Politics of Composition, Performance, and Reception*, edited by Richard Leppert and Susan McClary, 137. Cambridge: Cambridge University Press, 1987.

22   Frith, "Toward and Aesthetic of Popular Music," 140

23   Frith, "Toward and Aesthetic of Popular Music," 140–42.

24   Portman, *King Dork*, 91.

gynecology"[25]), and inventing first album titles, all aimed at poking some measure of fun at conventional rock band names. He also ridicules classmates whose self-identity is tied too closely to the fashion of rock:

> I don't dress up like anything. True, I did let my hair grow a little longer and started to wear flared jeans over the summer when I got more into seventies bands and stuff, as a sort of tribute to their fine work; and I've got the army coats, though that's more of a practical tool than a fashion statement. But I don't "dress punk," or mod or metal or goth or garage or rockabilly or anything. I don't wake up every morning and put on a music-genre-oriented-youth-culture Halloween costume – that's what I'm saying.[26]

And yet Moe takes music very seriously as an integral marker of both who he wants to be and who he is. He cherishes the common boy fantasy that being in a band will impress a girl he's just met, and, as noted above, he champions lesser-known genres as a way to distinguish himself as superior to his peers. "I'm quite confident," he says, "that when we're all dead, history will clearly conclude that my retro rock revival was years ahead of everyone else's retro rock revival."[27] In these ways, he demonstrates the limitations Frith notes about the role of music in constructing rather than expressing the self: Moe uses music to insist on his separation from others by deploying the kinds of collective fantasy clichés that culture makes available – that rock stars get girls, and that history vindicates the outsider.

The title character of Robin Benway's *Audrey, Wait*[28] also demonstrates Frith's social functions of music, but in a less jaded way. Audrey becomes wildly famous when her boyfriend writes a song about their break-up. The break-up itself was full of the usual phrases and awkward silences, but the song has an infectious beat that transcends age boundaries and makes Audrey a household name not just among indie music fans, but among most households. Frith points out that the most intense experiences of our lives tend to be accompanied by the most ordinary and uninspired language; it is pop music that makes our feelings seem grander and less clichéd than they are.[29] This is clearly what happens with Audrey's song; it strikes a chord with audiences that gives it global appeal. The book focuses on the problematics of a private life gone suddenly public; Audrey is in many ways betrayed by the force that inspires her. She defines herself by her relation to indie music, so the popularisation of the song threatens to redefine her without her permission. Her best friend, Victoria, however, understands better than Audrey the ephemeral nature of what she's experiencing; she is willing to admit and embrace that part of the enjoyment of the music is immersion in the chaotic scene it creates, while Audrey herself wants to continue to insist on some sort of purity in her

---

[25]   Portman, *King Dork*, 97

[26]   Portman, *King Dork*, 83.

[27]   Portman, *King Dork*, 84.

[28]   Benway, Robin. *Audrey, Wait*. New York: Razorbill, 2008.

[29]   Frith, "Toward and Aesthetic of Popular Music," 141.

interaction with the music itself. Further, she experiences herself as somehow separate from the hype that surrounds the kind of music she likes: As an indie music fan, she inhabits a niche identity that establishes her sense of style, her pastimes, even her ways of speaking as independent, that is, not mainstream; she and Victoria get it, and the rest of the world doesn't. But when her life becomes fodder for paparazzi and internet lore, her style is blown out everywhere, and pop culture becomes a much too public mirror. The situation thus mounts a critique of the way a private life can become a commodity through song, while acknowledging that this process has become a necessary feature of individual access to the emotions made available through pop music in contemporary culture.

An unusual casting of identity construction through music is found in Antony John's *Five Flavors of Dumb*.[30] Main character Piper is intensely irritated with the way things are going at school and at home. A local high school rock band, Dumb, has won a competition, and their front man, whom Piper can't stand, is acting like a conceited jerk. She challenges the band's arrogance, reminding them that despite the win, they have no paying gigs coming up, and they take her up on their challenge by making her their manager for a month. Piper has no idea whether the band has any talent, because she herself is deaf, but she can tell by the way they interact that they are not working as a team onstage or off. This lack of synchronicity, which is available to Piper despite her inability to hear their music, threatens their future, but also acts as a metaphor for both Piper's inner turmoil and her anger toward her parents, who have drained her college savings for a cochlear implant for her baby sister, which she takes as a rejection of her as a person on multiple fronts. Piper's involvement in the band requires that she enlist the help of both a close friend and her brother to take care of the musical quality side of things, while she manages the personal relationships that are required to enable a group of teenagers to make music together. As she works with the band and overcomes multiple challenges to their success, including most of all their individual narcissisms, she develops a stronger sense of self that allows her to confront her parents regarding how she feels about her sister's implant and their attitude toward her own deafness. The spirit of coordination that she seeks becomes a thing that she enables, thus crafting a sense of herself in community to replace the sense of herself as alone and undervalued.

In each of these texts, music has a clear role to play in creating and sustaining an identity that has value both to the individual and to the social groups that they care about. While Moe uses music affiliations to exalt his fragile sense of self and craft an oppositional identity to the cultural mainstream, Piper uses music as a bridge to create communities between herself and her family, as well as among the members of the band she's trying to manage. Audrey's sense of herself as a fan is challenged when she becomes part of the music she idolizes, but when she can cut through the clutter and sordidness of the music business, she can still find the exhilarating emotional release of losing herself in a good song.

---

[30]   John, Antony. *Five Flavors of Dumb*. New York: Dial, 2010.

Music, emotion, and the adolescent brain

The emphasis on identity construction is perhaps enough of a reason to focus on the place of music in Young Adult literature, but recent research into cognitive neuroscience and the specific area of adolescent brain development renders the topic even more salient for scholars of youth literature. According to David Levitin,[31] an intensified interest in music comes online for children around the age of ten or eleven, and continues through their teenage lives, so that, for most adults, the music that we hold in highest sentimental regard is the music of our adolescence. He cites cases of Alzheimer's patients suffering from severe memory loss yet still able to recall the songs they knew when they were fourteen. Adolescence is a time of fundamental changes in brain structure: the prefrontal cortex, which is the known as the CEO of the brain, responsible for planning, assessing risk, impulse control, and reasoning, goes through a growth spurt just prior to puberty, followed by a period of pruning and organizing of the neural pathways, strengthening those pathways that are in use, and pruning away or dead-ending those pathways that are not reinforced through activity and experience. Meanwhile, imaging shows that the teenage brain is more dependent on the limbic system and the amygdala, the emotional centre of brain activity, for its responses to stimuli. Scientists speculate that, along with a surge in hormonal activity, this is why teenagers have a harder time regulating their emotional responses than most adults – an underdeveloped prefrontal cortex coupled with a perfectly responsive limbic system means that teenagers tend to lead with their emotions rather than their reasoning faculties.

In terms of responding to music, the limbic system is in charge of emotional responses, while the cerebellum, which is also undergoing a period of dynamic growth during adolescence, coordinates movement responses to music, such as foot tapping, dancing, or playing an instrument. So it would seem to follow that adolescents are more attuned to music than they are to argument when it comes to organizing their social lives, regulating their responses, and constructing their identities. In the process of neural maturation, connections between the prefrontal cortex and the amygdala are strengthened, and the cerebellum, which coordinates thinking processes as well as motor processes, becomes more adept at doing its job. Music may intervene in these processes by helping to order the connections; that is, music has immediate emotional accessibility through systems that are already highly developed, but it is also an art form that is regulated through rhythm, structure, and anticipation. Therefore, it makes sense to think that young people may use music to forge and strengthen connections between the limbic system and the prefrontal cortex. The result of those connections, for most people, is that emotional responses get tempered by what we have learned of consequences, as well as what we can imagine through reasoned creativity. But our adult reasoning skills are still informed by the emotional education we

---

[31]   Levitin, David J. *This is Your Brain on Music: The Science of a Human Obsession.* New York: Dutton, 2006.

received throughout our adolescence, because our strongest memories always have an emotional component, and because the neural pruning we undergo is structured by experience, particularly repetitive experiences such as listening to the same songs or types of music.

I have argued elsewhere that what we have learned about the adolescent brain and its reliance on emotional response should make a difference in the way we approach and critique literature written for this age group.[32] Literature that we might consider melodramatic and insubstantial is in fact developmentally appropriate and important if we consider a more robust theory of identity than we have traditionally espoused as education practitioners and/or literary theorists. In general, our approach to criticism of Young Adult literature has tended to focus on a cognitive/linguistic model, surfacing conflict and growth in terms of finding one's voice and negotiating an ethical response to power and otherness, with our understanding of ethics leaning toward Kantian abstractions. But as psychoanalytic thinker Mark Bracher points out, this is an anemic approach to understanding the complexity of identity.[33]

Bracher argues that our most persistent desire is for a coherent identity that has meaning in the world. He proposes a theory of identity that aligns with the Lacanian registers of the Real, the Imaginary, and the Symbolic. In the register that imperfectly reflects the Lacanian conception of the Real, we experience our bodies at the level of emotion and feeling; the differentiation imposed by image and language is overwhelmed by oceanic feelings of relative connectedness, well-being, or dis-ease. This emotional register leads us to seek both the mirroring and the amplification of our emotions through others in order to validate and affirm those emotions. Songs that lead to social bonding, as well as religious songs that affirm the presence of the divine, especially when those songs are sung or experienced in the company of others, enable that sort of validation. The Imaginary register is the register of perception and images, particularly body image, where we seek to affirm our sense of self through our competencies at the level of the body. Whereas in literary criticism it is a commonplace to associate agency nearly exclusively with voice as linguistic competence, Bracher situates agency at the level of embodiment: we each have things that we do well, that make us feel good about ourselves, and hence when we feel uneasy or at odds in our emotional register, we can use our bodies to change our feelings, either by making ourselves look good, or by doing something, like jogging, woodworking, performing music, dancing, or knitting, that makes us feel more aligned with our ideal image of ourselves. Finally, there is the cognitive/linguistic component of

---

[32] Coats, Karen. "Young Adult Literature: Growing Up, In Theory." In *The Handbook of Research on Children's and Young Adult Literature*, edited by Shelby A. Wolf, Karen Coats, Patricia Enciso, and Christine Jenkins, 315–29. New York: Routledge, 2011.

[33] Bracher, Mark. *Radical Pedagogy: Identity, Generativity, and Social Transformation*. New York: Palgrave Macmillan, 2006.

our identity, where we attempt to situate our perceptions and emotions within specific signifiers that have value in the larger culture.

At any given moment, we experience challenges to one of the components of our identity, and we turn to the other components to compensate for perceived inadequacies. For instance, suppose, for purposes of an academic audience, we get an article rejected, or a bad teaching evaluation. This constitutes an assault on our linguistic/cognitive sense of self insofar as we desire to be perceived as intelligent scholars with publishable ideas, or dynamic teachers who desire appreciation from our students. We might respond by doing something nonscholarly that bolsters our perceptual/imagistic identity, or we might get drunk, which temporarily alters our emotional state. Eventually, though, since most of us are overly invested in our linguistic/cognitive identity component, we go back to our cognitive activities and work even harder to earn the signifiers that we have come to value.

Consider, however, that most teenagers, because of their brain structure, are more invested in the emotional and perceptual aspects of their identity. They, like adults, are actively seeking communal affirmation for their self-presentation, but they are more likely to seek that affirmation at the level of emotional mirroring, which is readily accessed through music. Benway's Audrey, for instance, doesn't just listen to music, she goes to concerts and positions herself near the speakers so that there is nothing but the sound of the music, the feel of the rhythm, and the press of bodies all around her. This practice effects a complex silencing technique that teens everywhere replicate by listening to their music *loud*, sometimes loud enough so that even the words cease to have their traditional semantic dimension, and become overwritten by their sound. Consider the following passage from Brenna Yovanoff's *The Replacements*:

> It wasn't like the other songs. There was no story, no conversation. This was just the feeling, without words or pictures, and it had nothing to do with Luther or his clean, singing guitar.
>
> It was the sound of being outside, of being alien. It was the pulse that ran under everything and never let you forget that you were strange, that the world hurt just to touch. Feelings too complicated to ever say in words, but they spilled out of the amplifiers, seeping into the air and filling up the room.
>
> Out in the crowd, everyone had stopped moving. They stood in the pit, staring up at me, and when I stopped playing, they started to clap.[34]

Yovanoff captures the experience of emotional mirroring and amplification that happens in a musical transaction. Operating outside of representation through image or language, the music in this passage "spills" and "seeps" directly from the consciousness of the artist to the consciousness of his listeners, relaying

---

[34]   Yovanoff, Brenna. *The Replacements*. New York: Razorbill, 2010, 141–42.

rather than actually articulating an experience of loss that resonates thematically throughout the book.

In much fantasy literature, music acts as an irresistible emotional lure, beckoning humans to join a world where reason is abandoned and hedonistic pleasures triumph. Obviously, this usually results in capture or death for the human so seduced, exemplifying our cognitive bias. But in realistic fiction, music, even the kind that beckons a character beyond reason, can function in a healing context. Such is the case in Jennifer Donnelly's *Revolution*.[35] Oddly, the jacket text mentions nothing about the importance of music, which is central to the book. The first words of the book, "Those that can, do. Those that can't, deejay,"[36] immediately establish a musical hierarchy of insiders and outsiders. Within the first few sentences, phrases like beat-match, trip-hop, and Memphis mod, and name drops like John Lee Hooker and Beale Street similarly position readers and characters – you're cool if you know what these things mean, and uncool if you don't. Andi Alpers, the main character, clearly is an insider, particularly to the emotions of the blues. She is grieving the accidental death of her little brother, a death for which she feels wholly responsible. Meanwhile, she's surrounded by a gaggle of superficial, rich poseurs who don't know a thing about real sadness and who are in love with their own pretentiousness:

> "But, really, you can't even *approach* Flock of Seagulls without getting caught up in the metafictive paradigm," somebody says.

> And "Plastic Bertrand can, I think, best be understood as a postironic nihilist referentialist."

> And, "But, like, New Wave derived its meaning from its own meaninglessness. Dude, the tautology was *so* intended."[37]

The use of music to establish the boundaries of her social group foreshadows the central role it will play in establishing Andi's character; the implicit sneer with which she reports their conversation emphasizes the distance she feels from those around her, even though they are all part of the same social and economic set: "No Billboard Hot 100 fare for us. We're better than that,"[38] she snarks, relegating pedestrian pop music to those who attend public school, not the elite of Brooklyn with their posh private school credentials. These snippets of reported speech and her commentary are immediately followed by someone complimenting her on her guitar playing; she, unlike her fellows, has real talent, but right now it's in the service of her guilt, as she deliberately plays until her fingers rip and bleed.

---

[35]   Donnelly, Jennifer. *Revolution*. New York: Delacorte, 2010.

[36]   Donnelly, *Revolution*, 3.

[37]   Donnelly, *Revolution*, 5.

[38]   Donnelly, *Revolution*, 5.

While her headmistress chides her for using her music as an outlet for her pain, Andi focuses on the work she does with her guitar teacher, Nathan, a 75-year-old Holocaust survivor who does not try to talk her out of her grief. Instead, he supports her need to keep her wound open, offering her the authority of those whom she respects: "This word closure ... it is a stupid word, *ja*? Bach did not believe in closure. Handel did not. Beethoven did not. Only Americans believe in closure because Americans are like little children – easily swindled. Bach believed in making music, *ja*?"[39] However, Andi's circumstances will not allow her to focus all of her attention on her grief and guilt as she wishes; she must complete a senior thesis or she won't graduate. She has chosen a (fictional) eighteenth-century French composer named Amadé Malherbeau, who wrote mainly for the six-string guitar and, for the purposes of the story, was known for experimenting with minor keys, refusing traditional harmonies, and integrating the augmented fourth, also known as the Diabolus in Music, into his compositions. At first she refuses to write her thesis, but then her estranged, Nobel-prize-winning father gets involved, and she is forced to accompany him to Paris for winter break to work on her thesis while he works on a genetic mystery – the determination of whether a heart that has been recovered really belongs to the young Dauphin slowly tortured to death in the years following the French Revolution.

As the story progresses, so does the metaphor of the Diabolus in Music. The augmented fourth is a tritone – a musical interval that stretches across three tones – used to create an unresolved dissonance in the music.[40] As Andi tells her father, it's "kind of like asking a question that can't be answered."[41] He doesn't understand why that's devilish, and he wouldn't, because he is a scientist and a rationalist, and to his way of thinking, all questions eventually have an answer, even if that answer can't be found with current technologies or ways of thinking. But Andi is attuned to her emotions, and she, like Nathan, knows that there are some questions that not only can't be answered, but shouldn't be, such as why little brothers can be swept up into someone else's madness and killed as a result. Eventually, Andi meets a fellow musician in Paris on whom she develops a crush, and they connect through their music, playing their favourite songs for each other, sparking a small seed of hope in Andi's bleak landscape. But it is not until she travels back in time (either a result of too many anti-depressants combined with wine and a blow to the head, or the introduction of magic realism into the text – either possibility is cleverly left open to interpretation) that she is finally able to work through the complex nexus of guilt and grief that has threatened to take her life. While in eighteenth-century Paris, she is indeed able to effect closure through finishing the

---

[39]   Donnelly, *Revolution*, 20.

[40]   Interestingly, the vampire Spike uses tritones when he sings in "Once More with Feeling," the musical episode of *Buffy the Vampire Slayer* in Season 6. His predicament, of being hopelessly love with Buffy, is echoed in his solo, which is sung in a minor key with lingering tritones; he is, literally, the devil in music.

[41]   Donnelly, *Revolution*, 84.

work of Alexandrine, a girl who has been the Dauphin's companion and is trying to keep his spirits up through the use of fireworks as he is being held and tortured in a tower. While there, she also discovers the true identity of Mahlerbeau and helps him through his composer's block by exposing him to Radiohead and Led Zeppelin on her iPod.

Andi's journey through grief to healing could not have been effected without her involvement in music on multiple levels. The "devil in music" is effective not simply on the metaphorical, semantic level, as an unanswered question, but as a material signifier – the sound of a tritone actually makes one feel off balance, as if one is, like Andi, in the midst of something unresolved. Like Charlie's in *Perks*, and Audrey's in *Audrey, Wait*, Andi's music is real, and is a reflection of her emotional state, and readers who are familiar with the songs cited will have one more level of engagement with the characters as they participate in the silent reading of their stories. More importantly, however, they will know that these characters and authors actually understand the importance of music to the development of a meaningful sense of identity. Because music, says Andi, "It gets inside of you, ... and changes the beat of your heart."[42]

---

[42] Donnelly, *Revolution*, 436.

Chapter 8
Emotional Connection: Representation of Emotions in Young Adult Literature

Bettina Kümmerling-Meibauer

The newly arisen interest in the representation of emotions in literature, fine arts, media, and other cultural artefacts has caused an "emotional turn" in cultural studies since the beginning of the twenty-first century. Several disciplines are involved in this process: cognitive psychology, philosophy, pedagogy, linguistics, neuroscience, and literary studies, among others. This enumeration clearly demonstrates that a complex phenomenon such as the development and impact of emotions can only adequately analysed by a juxtaposition of different academic perspectives, thus eliciting an interdisciplinary perspective. One important aspect of the study of emotions is the phenomenon of empathy, a term coined by the American psychologist Edward Bradford Titchener in 1909. This term, which has etymological roots in Antique Greek and might be literally translated as "compassion," was Titchener's translation of the German notion "Einfühlung" (i.e., the German translation of the Antique Greek term), which was a seminal concept in German aesthetics and philosophy at the turn of the century. Nonetheless, this concept was strictly refused by philosophers and psychologists inspired by new realism in the 1920s, because they claim that this idea is based on a non-analytical access.

To begin with, the notion of "empathy," as it is defined in modern psychology and sociology, should be determined. The American scholars Hastings, Zahn-Waxler and McShane classify this term as "the ability to understand another's perspective and to have a visceral or emotional reaction."[1] This definition clearly shows that empathy is both understanding of other people's points of view and recognition of one's own intuitive and emotional reaction. The above-mentioned scholars additionally emphasize that empathy combines affective, cognitive and physiological processes. The affective process is determined by emotional sympathy, the cognitive process refers to the possibility to perform a change

---

[1] Hastings, Paul D., Carolyn Zahn-Waxler, and Keely McShane. "We Are, by Nature, Moral Creatures: Biological Bases of Concern for Others." In *Handbook of Moral Development*, edited by Lin Melanie Killen and Judith G. Smetana, 484. Mahwah/London: Erlbaum, 2006.

of perspective and to put oneself in the position of another person, and the physiological process concerns autonomous activities of the nervous system, for example to empathize with another's joy, anxiety, or pain.[2]

In this regard empathy is often confused with sympathy. However, the difference between both emotional conditions should be highlighted, because empathy does not infer that the person with whom one empathizes with should automatically be classified as sympathetic. On the contrary, the interesting point is the observation that one usually is even able to empathize with other people's emotional conditions, even if these respective people are regarded as unfriendly or unappealing. In order to demonstrate this close relationship, this chapter focuses on recent research in cognitive psychology and neurobiology stressing adolescents' psychological and emotional development, especially the impact of the discovery of mirror neurons, and the findings by cognitive psychologists about the multi-levelled acquisition of emotional competence that influences the complex concept of empathy.

On the basis of these theoretical issues I will discuss how emotions are presented in three adolescent novels: *Ich ganz cool* (I very cool, 1992) by Kirsten Boie, *The Curious Incident of the Dog in the Night-Time* (2003) by Mark Haddon, and *Tenderness* (1998) by Robert Cormier.[3] *Ich ganz cool* was nominated for the German children's literature award in 1993 and received wide acclaim in Germany. Haddon's novel received the Whitbread Award and is often mentioned as a prototypical crossover novel, read by young people and adults alike, while Cormier's Young Adult novel provoked intense discussions, especially in the U.S. In the following analysis, I want to show that Boie, Cormier, and Haddon created demanding novels that challenge the reader to reflect upon the relative quality of emotions and their impact on the developing sense of empathy for mentally and emotionally handicapped figures.

The protagonist Steffen in Boie's novel is a thirteen-year-old boy, half-heartedly attending secondary modern school, living with his single mother and two half-siblings in a precarious household, always longing to get in contact with his father and to find a "real friend" among his peers. His everyday life is determined by quarrels, silly games such as "courage jogging" (i.e., rapidly crossing a road when a car is approaching) or "surfing with a sub-urban train" (i.e., travelling on a sub-urban train's roof), watching TV, or playing brutal video games. Because of his social and familiar background and the obvious negligence by his mother, who is more concerned about her new boyfriend, Steffen seems to be a loser who has not much in common with all those smart kids that mainly appear in novels for young adults.

---

[2]   Cosmides, Leda, and John Tooby. "Evolutionary Psychology and the Emotions." In *Handbook of Emotions*, edited by Michael Lewis and Jeannette Haviland Jones, 91–115. London: Sage, 2001.

[3]   Boie, Kirsten. *Ich ganz cool*. Hamburg: Oetinger, 1992; Haddon, Mark. *The Curious Incident of the Dog in the Night-Time*. London: Jonathan Cape, 2003; Cormier, Robert. *Tenderness*. New York: Delacorte, 1998.

Another case of an apparent "loser" is Christopher Boone, the protagonist in Haddon's novel, who lives alone with his father in a small town. His mother left the family some times ago, since she could not stand the extraordinary challenges that are caused by Christopher's psychological disposition. Christopher is handicapped by Asperger syndrome, but the notion "autism" or "Asperger" is only mentioned in the blurbs, not in the text. For this reason his social relationships are restricted to just some people who are accustomed to his sometimes weird behaviour and demands, i.e., he dislikes to be touched by other people, but he also dislikes specific colours, numbers, signs, and meals. He is additionally dependent on a strict time schedule in order to avoid chaotic circumstances that might disturb his everyday life. Moreover, Christopher has problems understanding other people's jokes, ironic remarks, and facial expressions, since – due to his disability – he did not acquire the ability to reflect upon other people's feelings and beliefs.

The protagonist in Cormier's novel, Eric Poole, however, is far from simply an unusual loser. He is a psychopath and serial killer who is only sexually exhilarated by young slender girls with long dark hair whom he strangles during sexual intercourse. Since he has to wait some years before he can get a driving license, he concocts a hideous plan in order to prevent the police detecting his criminal disposition. He then murders his mother and stepfather, feigning that they have maltreated him severely, and is then sentenced to spend three years in a youth prison until he attains full age. Although the chief inspector mistrusts Eric and sets a snare using a decoy after his release from prison, Eric is far too clever to be taken in by this trick, stays on the lookout for new prey and is additionally supported by a young girl who falls in love with Eric and warns him about the chief inspector's pitfall.

The protagonists of these three novels have one important feature in common: they are not (or at least in a restricted sense) able to have empathy for other people, so that they give rise to ambivalent, even negative, feelings in the beginning. However, a thorough analysis of the authors' narrative strategies emphasizes that in the course of the respective narratives, the reader might develop a sense of empathy – not sympathy – for the main figures, although they represent a social outsider and loser (Boie), a psychotic killer (Cormier), and a boy with Asperger syndrome (Haddon).

The new interest into the phenomenon of empathy was caused by recent findings of neurobiological science, particularly the discovery of mirror neurons by the Italian neuroscientists Giacomo Rizzolatti and Leonardo Fogassi in 2003. Their research is regarded as a milestone in the investigation of human emotions. Accidentally, Fogassi discovered in an experiment with apes that their brains are structured by neuronal nets that help them to imitate or mirror other animal's or human people's activities in their own brain. In a next step, Fogassi found out that these neurons are situated in the lower pre-motor cortex. Since these neurons stimulate the imitation of other people's behaviour and activities, he described them as mirror neurons. With the help of further experiments he demonstrated that these mirror neurons also exist in the human brain. Therefore, intuitive understanding and empathy could be traced back to a neurological basis.

However, these abilities are not innate, but must be acquired in a complex process. Cognitive psychologists distinguish at least four seminal stages in this acquisition process. The first stage is coined as tendency of imitation that already functions with infants and toddlers who attempt to imitate other people's facial expressions. This first stage, called "global empathy," presents the pre-condition for the acquisition of identity and is responsible for the construction of synapses in the infant brain that lead to the development of mirror neurons. While the tendency of imitation is acquired before the first birthday, the second stage, called "egocentric empathy," will be acquired seemingly later, at age two. Pre-conditions for the acquisition of egocentric empathy are the experience of object permanency and the distinction between one's own identity ("I," "Me") and other people's identity ("You," "He/She," "They").

When they are approximately four years old, children usually develop "empathy for another's feelings."[4] In order to reach this third stage, children must learn to empathize with other people's feelings, beliefs, and ideas. This ability is known as "Theory of Mind," abbreviated as TOM. This concept demands the ability to understand other people's feelings and thoughts, but also the ability to purposefully map activities. As Lagattuta and Wellman have shown, "empathy for another's feelings" is acquired at age four in a basic sense. When children grow older, at approximately age seven to eight, they are able to understand that persons might, say, be bad-tempered in a positive and stimulating surrounding, because these emotional shifts are caused, for instance, by unpleasant memories or a more general state of unease. At this age children start to make comments about other people's mental and psychic state of mind. Therefore, they are also able to anticipate other people's emotional condition.[5] The fourth and last stage, "empathy for another's life condition," will be achieved at age ten to eleven.[6] This phase of empathy is far more complex and abstract, since it demands discernment of not only individuals' feelings, but also those of groups, such as the peer group, a sports team, or an ethnic, social, or religious group. It is typical for this stage of life that children are then enabled to hide their own feelings and thoughts by feigning different attitudes or feelings.

The acquisition of these four stages of empathy belongs to the realm of emotional competence, a major concept that embraces all phenomena dealing with

---

[4]   Hastings, et al. "We Are, by Nature, Moral Creatures," 487.

[5]   Deham, Susanne, Marie von Salisch, Tjerrt Olthof, Anita Kochanoff, and Sarah Caverly. "Emotional and Social Development in Childhood." In *Blackwell Handbook of Childhood Social Development*, edited by Peter K. Smith and Craig H. Hart, 307–328. Oxford: Blackwell, 2002; Eisenberg, Nancy, Tracy L. Spinrad, and Adrienne Sadovsky. "Empathy-Related Responding in Children." In *Handbook of Moral Development*, edited by Killen and Smetana, 517–49.

[6]   Hastings et al, "We Are, by Nature, Moral Creatures," 487.

emotions.[7] Emotional competence is comprised of five essential features: firstly, the knowledge that emotions can be experienced and expressed, secondly, the ability to have empathy, which is strongly tied to Theory of Mind; thirdly, the acquisition of emotional scripts, i.e., encoded emotions; fourthly, the knowledge that multiple emotions can occur at the same time or displace another in a emotional chain; and finally, the acknowledgment that a feeling causes different emotional reactions. It is not quite clear in this context how literary texts or pictures actually challenge emotions. Although literary works clearly do evoke emotions, one has to consider that the reader is only *indirectly* confronted with these emotions and feelings. When intensively reading a novel, poem, or drama, the written text nevertheless might cause emotions, such as empathy, joy, fear, and sadness. In this regard a transfer process is more or less successfully negotiated that relies on the reader's ability to activate his or her knowledge of emotions. Although readers usually are aware of the characters' fictional status, they are nevertheless able to feel charity, animosity, affection, or empathy towards them. Therefore, the investigation of the representation of emotions in literary works demands the analysis of multiple aspects, for instance the author's intention, the reception by the reader guided by his or her perceptions and assumptions, and the literary work's emotional structure – i.e., signals and markers that refer to emotional conditions and govern the reader's attitude towards the text.

Nevertheless, although it is an unsolved question how emotions are expressed in literary works, concentrating on the literary techniques that represent emotional conditions might provide the best approach. Here two aspects are relevant: foregrounding and enhancement of awareness. Both features exert a powerful influence on the reader's reception. Foregrounding refers to those literary passages and elements that are clearly marked by the author (for example: code switching, unusual lexicon, neologisms, irony, different points of view, change of typography, contradictory assertions) in order to emphasize certain emotional conditions, while enhancement of awareness applies to literary strategies, such as overstatement, enrichment, and repetition, which draw the reader's attention to the text's seminal passages and assertions.

Here authors deliberately deploy these cognitive strategies to present specific emotions. In order for these to be effective, writers assume that the majority of their readers have common knowledge about the characteristics of emotions, in which situations they usually occur, and how they should be linguistically and bodily conveyed. Most often some sentences and/or expressions are sufficient in order to evoke a mental representation of a specific emotion. In cognitive psychology, this strategy is characterised by "emotional settings" or "emotional scripts" that rely on certain encoded emotions; i.e., a common knowledge exists about the representation of emotions such as anger, jealousy, joy, or sadness in

---

[7]   Rosenblum, Gianine, and Michael Lewis. "Emotional Development in Adolescence." In *Blackwell Handbook of Adolescence*, edited by Gerald R. Adams and Michael D. Berzonsky, 273. London: Blackwell, 2003.

facial expression, gesture, posture, and language.[8] For this reason authors certainly make efforts to present key emotional scenarios so that the reader will recognize the specific emotional situation on the one hand, and to stimulate certain emotional reactions on behalf of the reader on the other hand. These literarily imagined emotions are created to activate stimuli that should elicit the reader's notional empathy with the figures presented in the text.

In this regard, the following distinctions are discernible: a) the reader permanently sympathizes with a literary figure; b) the reader has a consistent animosity towards a literary figure; c) the reader develops a changing attitude towards a figure which is characterized by a partial solicitousness or rejection respectively. While many children's books, especially for younger children, contain somewhat two-dimensional characters that are defined by belonging to morally and socially adjusted criteria which enable the readership to easily attribute a character as either "bad" or "good," more complex children's books, and particularly works targeted at older children and young adults, refrain from this strict assignment, thus challenging the reader to comprehend a character's process of development. This process might evoke a changing attitude towards characters insofar they are not easily characterized as definitely "bad" or "good" anymore, therefore putting the figures' moral appraisal and social estimation into perspective. In this regard, emotions play a significant role, because characters are classified by means of their emotional state of mind – this characterization is supplemented by their outlook, social status, intellectual ability, and imaginative power as well. Although empathy is tightly connected with moral evaluation, both aspects might evoke different reactions. On the one hand, a person or character might be morally condemned because of her behaviour and beliefs; on the other hand, one is nevertheless able to comprehend the same person's or character's feelings and thoughts.

This distinction is even more challenging when individuals are either confronted with characters that have not developed the ability to have compassion with other people or with characters that provoke antipathy. The protagonists in the three novels by Boie, Cormier, and Haddon belong to at least one of these categories. Nevertheless, it is my contention that the reader develops a sense of empathy towards the main characters during the reading process. In the subsequent passages I will show which narrative strategies are used by the authors in order to achieve this changing attitude and what cognitive abilities are required on behalf of the reader.

Kirsten Boie's *Ich ganz cool* confronts the reader with an unusual situation. Steffen's everyday life and imagination is dominated by different media, such as

---

[8]   Barkow, Jerome, Leda Cosmides, and John Tooby, eds. *The Adapted Mind. Evolutionary Psychology and the Generation of Culture*. Oxford: Oxford University Press, 1992; Hoffman, M.L. "Empathy, its Development and Prosocial-implications." In *Nebraska Symposium on Motivation Social Cognitive Development*, edited by H.E. Howe and C.B. Keasy, 169–217. Lincoln: University of Nebraska Press, 1977.

television, computer games, and cassettes. Living with his single mother and two half-siblings, he is longing to meet his father, whom he does not know personally. After an arranged meeting with his gentrified father that does not satisfy Steffen's expectations, Steffen changes the subject of his daydreams. Instead of a father who is stylised as a super hero and all-round-man, Steffen starts to imagine a mate of the same age. His daydreams are obviously inspired by video films and advertising spots, especially by a video clip stressing the intimate and rough friendship among motorcyclists roaming around in their Harley-Davidsons and enjoying wild life in the uncivilized country. This novel demands a high reading competence because of its seemingly fragmentary structure and the overarching use of youth slang that is characterised by neologisms, onomatopoetic expressions influenced from comics, and an elliptic sentence structure dominated by repetitions and hiatus.

> So, courage jogging, ey, you are just allowed to run when the car is fully on the cross-roads; the cooler must be behind the shop window of Edeka, otherwise it is not correct. There is no exception, Recep says, a fat lot I care, whether one is smaller or has shorter legs, never mind. Whoever wants to join in, equal rules of play. The trick is you have to run exactly at that place, where the building lot is, the cars cannot draw aside. They cannot even brake, we have checked that. You are either quick enough, or bommmppp!, game over. Everything is sludge then, bad luck. (My translation)

In an interview, the author claimed that she attempts to present an almost authentic youth language that is largely influenced by oral speech. Her knowledge of youth slang is mainly based on her experience with young people whom she observed and listened to in suburban trains. Nevertheless, her novel is not a linguistic report of youth slang used at the beginning of the 1990s in Germany, since Boie successfully intertwines different speech levels and linguistic codes into her work. Moreover, the protagonist's process of development is not linearly presented, since the text mainly consists of interchanging passages that either describe Steffen's daydreams or his everyday life. This aesthetically demanding novel requests a high level of concentration and attention from the reader. Although Steffen always tries to be "cool" (as indicated by the book title), he is obviously hiding his feelings. He is longing for acceptance and love which he does not find in his own family: his mother is an alcoholic with changing boyfriends, his little sister – his mother's favourite – is mentally retarded, and his older brother is just interested in brutal computer games and his peer group. The familiar situation is characterized by indifference, negligence, aversion, and missing communication. The family members usually do not talk to each other; by contrast, they exchange four-letter-words, curse or yell at each other. In this situation Steffen is longing for his unknown father, with whom he would like to get in contact. In his daydreams he anticipates that he and his father would be close friends, riding on their motorcycles, making trips through the desert, going fishing, and sitting together at a campfire while smoking cigarettes, a daydream that is obviously influenced by TV-spots for the cigarette brand "Marlboro." Steffen additionally daydreams that his father is a ninja warrior whose identity must be kept secret.

These mental images highly contrast with his real father's behaviour and outlook. When Steffen finally meets him in a coffee shop, he is disappointed, because his father is a narrow minded and bossy supermarket manager who does not show any interest in Steffen's personality. After this meeting Steffen retreats into his shell, not acknowledging that his classmate Schnulli (= little pacifier) is deeply interested in becoming close friends with him. The turning point happens when Steffen is confronted with his brother's grief about his best friend who was killed during a trial of courage, i.e., suburban train surfing. In this situation, because of his anxiety, Steffen turns towards his classmate at whom he formerly sneered. He finally accepts Schnulli's proposal to go fishing. The novel finishes with Steffen's last daydream that is characterised by peacefulness and joy, thus emphasizing the beginning friendship between Steffen und Schnulli.

The interplay between the steady everyday life that evokes the impression of stagnation, and the allusions to Steffen's changing state of mind, explained by means of his daydreams, largely contributes to the novel's ambiguity. This ambiguous attitude influences the reader's attitude towards the protagonist. In the beginning Steffen seems to be more or less disagreeable: he is quarrelling with his family, watching horror videos, idling away the days, not interested in school, education, and learning. However, when intensively reading the first chapters, it becomes obvious that Steffen's life and feelings are from the start dominated by his desire to find real friendship and love. A close reading of the text reveals that despite his familiar background, Steffen is sensitive and clever. In the course of the novel, the reader is able to empathize with the protagonist, since she witnesses Steffen's experiences and acknowledges that the open ending indicates a spark of hope. Although Steffen's social background will not change in the end, the reader is invited to develop an attitude towards the protagonist that is mostly characterised by empathy, maybe even sympathy.

The author accomplishes this changing attitude by two main narrative strategies: Boie introduces Steffen as a first-person narrator who tells his own story without interfering comments that should qualify Steffen's descriptions and powerful daydreams. Moreover, she imparts to him an authentic aura insofar as the text is dominated by impudent youth slang. These strategies challenge the reader to engage with Steffen's world view free of any moral judgement by an omniscient narrator. This novel requests a reader who is poised for an attentive reading, always looking for clues that suggest different interpretations of Steffen's experiences and daydreams. In addition, in order to develop empathy for a character who is not well educated and appealing, readers must have acquired stage 3 and stage 4 of emotional competence; i.e., "empathy for another's feelings" and "empathy for another's life conditions." In case they have just acquired the third stage of emotional competence, they might not be able to understand the impact of Steffen's difficult life condition on his restricted articulateness, sometimes aggressive conduct, and odd behaviour, which on closer consideration reveals a deep vulnerability, high sensibility, and an overarching longing for friendship and acceptance.

In Mark Haddon's novel, *The Curious Incident of the Dog in the Night-Time*, the protagonist Christopher suffers from Asperger syndrome. Therefore, he has difficulty understanding jokes and metaphors and, more importantly, he is unable to tell lies: "I do not tell lies. Mother used to say that this was because I was a good person. But it is not because I am a good person. It is because I can't tell lies."[9] People suffering from Asperger syndrome have a couple of mental disabilities that mostly concern their social and emotional relationships. While Christopher Boone is highly skilled in maths and possesses a so-called photographic memory, he has severe problems comprehending other people's emotional and mental state of mind; in other words, he has not developed a Theory of Mind.[10] Therefore, he is not able to predict other people's behaviour or to empathize with others. Besides his parents, teachers, and neighbours, he regards all other people as strangers and therefore as possible danger, because he doesn't know anything about them. He dislikes "small talk" (as talking without words and sense), specific colours and meals, and he gets angry when touched by strangers, even by his parents:

> Father was standing in the corridor. He held up his right hand and spread his fingers out in a fan. I held up my left hand und spread my fingers out in a fan and we made our fingers and thumbs touch each other. We do this because sometimes Father wants to give me a hug, but I do not like hugging people, so we do this instead, and it means that he loves me.[11]

He usually avoids looking into other people's faces, because he is distressed by their facial expression which he cannot decipher. Moreover, he is unable to create mental images or new ideas. He only memorizes those events and things which he has seen in reality, therefore he feels threatened by unknown people and situations. Although Christopher has difficulty understanding other people's feelings and thoughts and imagining a story, he successfully attempts to write a murder mystery novel about the neighbour's dog that has been killed. Since he refers to events that he experienced himself and chooses Arthur Conan Doyle's detective stories about Sherlock Holmes as model, he has a prototypical pattern that supports his literary efforts.

How can a reader empathize with a character who doesn't show empathy with other people? Mark Haddon attempts to accomplish this effect by two narrative strategies. The novel is a first-person narrative written from Christopher's perspective, and Christopher never speaks about his own feelings and emotions. Thus, the reader's perception is indissolubly connected to Christopher's restricted point of view. Like Christopher, the reader has to check the information given in the text in order to create an overall picture of the events and situations. Since the first person narrator only conveys fragments, leaving many gaps, the reader

---

[9]   Haddon, *The Curious Incident,* 24.

[10]   Bruning, N., Kerstin Konrad, and Beate Hepertz-Dahlmann. "Bedeutung und Ergebnisse der Theory of Mind-Forschung für den Autismus und andere psychiatrische Erkrankungen." *Zeitschrift für Kinder- und Jugendpsychiatrie und Psychotherapie* 33, no 2 (2005): 77–88; Happé, F.G.E. "The Role of Age and Verbal Ability in the Theory of Mind Task Performance of Subjects with Autism." *Child Development* 66 (1995): 843–55.

[11]   Haddon, *The Curious Incident,* 21.

is put into the position of having to decipher the meaning of the fragmentary text as if composing jigsaw pieces. This narrative strategy conveys an uncertainty whether Christopher's descriptions are reliable due to his restricted world view. By an in-depth reading process the reader might be able to get an impression of the chronological order of the story and of the characters' feelings and intentions. Hence, because Christopher hasn't developed the ability to analyse his parents' aims the reader has the task of decoding these aims in order to comprehend the parents' and teachers' reactions towards Christopher. The task to make the events' coherence accessible is left to the reader, while the first-person narrator fails to understand the full meaning of the events he represents in his narrative.

Another narrative strategy, namely multiperspectivity, is used in Robert Cormier's *Tenderness*. Multiperspectivity as a change of perspectives demands the ability to understand other people's points of view, because the presentation of situations or events from different angles is indispensable for the comprehension of a narrative structured by multiple perspectives. The appeal of this narrative strategy consists in the acknowledgement of different points of view, thus stimulating the reader to reflect upon the relationship between different narrators telling the same story from their respective perspectives, but also upon the reliability of their comments and assertions.

The story in *Tenderness* is told, alternately, by two narrators. While the passages dealing with the girl Lori are written as first-person narrative, presenting the events from Lori's point of view, the parts focusing on fifteen-year-old Eric Poole are constructed as third-person narrative. Both Lori and Eric have psychic problems: Lori always falls in love with young men whom she watches on TV, becoming fixated on the idea to meet and kiss them. When she is able to accomplish this endeavour, she is cured from this specific anchorage; however, she then turns toward a new one. Eric Poole, by contrast, is a psychopath and murderer, who kills three young innocent girls while caressing and cuddling them. He also murdered his parents, feigning that they sadistically mistreated him. Sentenced for homicide in self-defence, he spent a couple of years in prison. Although the police inspector, Lieutenant Procter, suspects him of murder, he doesn't have proofs for this assumption. By accident, Lori watches Eric on TV. She is fascinated by his facial expression and moves heaven and earth in order to meet him. Eric is irritated by Lori's affection, unable to kill her. Both gradually develop a strange relationship, characterised by mutual dependency and growing uncertainty about their own feelings.

During the interrogations at the police station and in jail, Procter characterises Eric as a "monster." This characterisation perfectly matches with Eric's behaviour in the beginning. He doesn't show any emotions, he just satisfies his sexual drives when killing young girls. Therefore, the reader certainly reacts with irritation when confronted with the description of Eric's murderous and brutal activities, recognising that Eric is highly skilled and determined on the one hand, but that he is driven by sexually abnormal behaviour on the other hand. After the initial encounter with Lori, Eric discovers that he develops a sort of affection towards the girl. He feels compassion for her after she told him about her desperate childhood, and he is even able to be grateful: saying "thank you" for the first time in his whole life, after Lori warned him that the young girl with the black hair is a decoy sent by Procter. Unfortunately, Lori drowns during a boat trip with Eric. Eric is arrested for murder, although it was an accident. By night Eric is tormented by nightmares, which mainly consist of his memories about the girls' murder and his mother's death. Eric tries in vain to banish these memories, since the former feelings of tenderness and sexual desire give way to anxiety and malaise. Eric's wish to forget Lori's face and her appeal to love her is not fulfilled. By contrary, overwhelmed by guilt and fear, Eric begins to cry. The novel finishes with these descriptions, giving the work a quite disturbing and perplexing ending.

Actually the reader should be relieved about this final turn; nevertheless, a close reading of the last chapter reveals that Eric has been changed during the course of the novel. The relationship with Lori exerts a great influence on Eric; insofar he gradually admits his feelings towards her. The reader also acknowledges that Eric was sexually abused during his childhood so that he was forced to hide his real feelings behind a mask. Characterised by callousness from the beginning, Eric has a breakdown in jail when he is tormented by his awful memories. The final decision of whether this happen because of guilt, horror, or remorse is left to the reader. In this masterpiece, Cormier succeeds in arousing the reader's empathy – not sympathy – with Eric. The reader is tempted to adopt Eric's point of view, thus comprehending the causes for his psychopathic behaviour. Although Eric's actions will be despised for moral reasons, the reader might nevertheless be able to understand Eric's disposition. In the end, the reader probably might even sense compassion for him, acknowledging Eric's loneliness and grief.

This novel especially challenges the reader's cognitive abilities through being confronted with different perspectives: Lori's homodiegetic point of view, Procter's factual observations, and the heterodiegetic narrative about Eric's background. While the reader easily empathizes with Lori, the third-person narratives about Eric and Procter create a certain distance towards these respective characters. By means of retrospect that informs about the protagonists' pasts, and by internal monologues that provide insight into the characters' inner feelings and beliefs, the reader is caught in a net of contrary emotions, desires, and anxieties. Thereby, the reader loses a superior position, entrapped by the events' maelstrom. Cormier ingeniously succeeds in procuring a complex pattern of emotions that rely on mental schemata but exhibit innovative aspects. This process is mainly achieved by the insertion of internal monologues and memories that reveal the characters' emotional states of mind. However, Cormier enriches the readers' "encoded" knowledge about emotions by confronting them with new experiences and nuances.

To sum up, it is my contention that the three novels by Boie, Haddon, and Cormier are benchmarks in the history of Young Adult fiction insofar the three authors present characters that are unappealing, weird, and, in Cormier's novel, even disgusting, yet they each successfully manage to arouse empathy with their protagonists. The authors reach this goal by complex narrative strategies that express emotions and provoke changes in the reader's attitude towards the protagonists. One important narrative strategy is the selection of a first-person narrator who tells the respective story from a restricted point of view. This strategy is then complemented by other narrative devices: youth slang in order to evoke the impression of an authentic report (Boie), focus on the perspective of a character who suffers from Asperger syndrome and therefore is not able to have empathy with other people (Haddon), and multiperspectivity (Cormier).

Last but not least, I would like to consider what young adults should learn about empathy when reading these three novels, which are targeted at an audience older than thirteen years of age. At this age level, the four stages of empathy have been usually acquired allowing a new, complex emotional competence. The authors demonstrate the wide range and variety of emotions by referring to "encoded" knowledge about emotions on the one hand, and by requesting readers to supplement and scrutinize their former knowledge. In this regard, they are challenged on both the emotional/affective and on the cognitive level. This process proceeds in three to four steps. Firstly, readers have to recognize the presented emotions in order to assign them to "emotional scripts." If they will not or just rudimentarily succeed with this transfer process, they are secondly prompted to classify the "new" emotions according to their knowledge. Thirdly, this experience causes a learning process that leads to the enlargement and differentiation of emotional competence.[12] The result of this learning process consists in a mental representation of the respective emotional situation in memory. Fourthly, readers are determined to reflect upon their level of knowledge before and after the reading of the respective novel. Thus, the readers are prompted to be conscious that they acquire new knowledge about emotions and empathy. Moreover, they acknowledge that it is possible to acquire this knowledge by means of literature, in this case novels written for young adults. This phenomenon, which should be classified as "meta-cognitive" orientation, accounts for the ability to reflect upon the emergence and change of knowledge in general.[13] Finally, the reader is challenged morally to judge the respective characters and their behaviour; however, the multiple points of view and the variety of emotions presented in the texts demand a re-evaluation of moral norms. In sum then, Boie's, Cormier's, and Haddon's literary achievements should be highly praised, since they succeed in artistically creating an emotional network that stimulate readers to reflect upon the protagonists' emotional development and to transfer this learning process to their everyday life experiences. When reading these novels, readers will be confronted with the cognitive challenge not only to have "empathy for another's feelings," but also to develop "empathy for another's life conditions."[14]

---

[12] Tooby, John, and Leda Cosmides. "Does Beauty Build Adapted Minds? Towards an Evolutionary Theory of Aesthetics, Fiction, and the Art." *SubStance. A Review of Theory and Literary Criticism* 30, nos 1 & 2 (2001): 6–27.

[13] Byrne, James P. "Cognitive Development During Adolescence." In *Blackwell Handbook of Adolescence*, edited by Adams and Berzonsky, 227–46.

[14] Voss, Christiane. *Narrative Emotionen. Eine Untersuchung über Möglichkeiten und Grenzen philosophischer Emotionstheorien.* Berlin: de Gruyter, 2003.

Chapter 9

Brain and Behaviour:
The Coherence of Teenage Responses to
Young Adult Literature

Shirley Brice Heath and Jennifer Lynn Wolf

"The teenage brain" has been a favourite topic of popular writers since the turn of the twenty-first century.[1] Television programs, news features, and radio talk shows have joined ranks with popular science magazines to tell the public about the adolescent brain. These stories suggest that hormonal explosion, sleep deprivation, neuron-pruning, and multiple developmental demands on the teenage system combine to mean that adults must somehow find a way to take charge of what is going on inside the teenage brain. Such news blasts invariably focus on what teenagers do not do, no longer do, cannot do, and what they therefore must have by way of both stimulation and restraint from parents and educators. Centred somewhere in these blasts comes a reminder of the long and consistent history of worrying about how, when, and what young people read or why they do not read or how when they do read they do so in ways that make adults cringe. These defamations of teens have come along with an increasing number of studies that point to the competition for time and resources that electronic media offer adolescents who might otherwise commit to reading. Research reports on the effects of multi-tasking make it clear that reading and writing extended texts, such as those of Young Adult literature, will forever be incompatible with multi-tasking.[2]

This chapter clarifies some popular-press claims about the "teenage brain" and points to the difficult nature of research on the human brain when subjects are engaged in complex cognitive tasks such as reading. The gist of our argument echoes that of many scholars in the neurosciences: no brain study, especially when reported in the popular press, should be simplified and transformed into implications for practice in other fields.[3] The first section of this chapter provides an

---

[1]   See, for example, Feinstein, S.G. *Secrets of the Teenage Brain*. Thousand Oaks, Calif.: Corwin. 2009.

[2]   A useful summary is provided by Wallis, Claudia. *The Impacts of Media Multitasking on Children's Learning and Development: Report from a Research Seminar*. New York: The Joan Ganz Cooney Center at Sesame Workshop, 2010.

[3]   For a summation of where neuroscience and reading research stand in relation to one another, see Hruby, George. C., and Usha Goswami. "Neuroscience and Reading: A Review for Reading Education Researchers." *Reading Research Quarterly* 46, no 2.4 (2011): 156–72.

overview of findings regarding brain maturation and cognitive development during adolescence. The second section reviews behavioural evidence on adolescents as they read and reflect on "their" literature – the world of Young Adult fiction. Here we examine anthropological studies of how young adult readers behave in their reading. What do they do with the book in their hand and their eyes on the page? How do they view the book, their reading, and ways of making meaning?

For more than a decade, Heath and Wolf have studied how young people who work in collaboration with adults in theatre, literary reading and writing, and community development projects perceive and shape their own pathways of learning. We have worked with a team of young ethnographers who spend long periods of time hanging out with adolescents while they are engaged in activities outside their hours in school or with their families. We have learned much about what young people do, how they view their own competencies, what they believe they need and want from adults, and how they use language.[4] The findings we report here relate primarily to what and how adolescents read the literature written for and by teenagers. The chapter needs a brief word about what may seem the odd combination of findings from the brain sciences with research studies done by anthropologists. Heath first became interested in cognitive neuroscience nearly a decade ago when she wanted to push beyond the behaviours of young people recorded through longitudinal observation and participation and interviews to understand more fully what happens as young people learn during those times when they themselves voluntarily undertake cognitively demanding tasks such as reading Young Adult literature. The desire to push beyond observable behaviour to brain behaviour led to the need to stay abreast of findings from the neurosciences.

Wolf's interests in young people and the arts immersed her in youth theatre, visual arts, and the lives of adolescent readers of Young Adult fiction. She undertook a longitudinal study of young readers in a public library located in an urban centre in northern California. The specific site of her ethnographic research was a section in the library dedicated to Young Adult literature. Here young people were welcome at all times and were expected to review, help select, and take some operational responsibilities for this part of the library. The population of young people who frequented this library on a regular basis included homeless youth, dropouts, irregular school attendees, star academic performers, and students who saw school as part of their lives, to be sure, but not as the most important thing in their lives.

---

[4]   A perspective on how older children and teenagers in working-class families changed their views on these matters between 1981 and 2011 is given in Heath, Shirley Brice. *Words at Work and Play: Three Decades in Family and Community Life.* Cambridge: Cambridge University Press, 2011.

Mapping brain maturation

Commonly claimed in the popular media in the first decade of the twenty-first century was the "synaptic pruning" said to happen during adolescence. However, no simple picture emerges from fMRI studies that show that the volume of cortical grey matter and cortical thickness decreases while white matter increases, bringing greater intra-cortical connectivity. Specifically, fibres that connect Broca's region with Wernicke's speech region increase. Though more studies remain to be done on the behavioural implications of this increase in connectivity, we can observe that adolescence is a time of increased potential for linguistic fluency and range of genres. Following functionally from the gains in white matter may well be the increased ability of older children and adolescents to share information more rapidly and efficiently between the fronto-cortical circuits and the frontal cortex and other cortical and subcortical regions. In comparison with younger children, adolescents can handle more difficult semantic structures for meaning-making, a skill especially critical in reading, a cognitive process that in contrast with listening requires activation across a greater number of cortical areas.[5]

Methodological challenges confront neuroscientists seeking to improve their understanding of how structural and functional maturation of neural pathways work together for highly complex tasks such as reading. A critical question is whether repeated use of a given structure in the brain leads to morphological change. This question in turn relates to sociocultural factors (e.g., familial and peer-related) that influence frequency, types, and models of reading and readers as well as contextual supports for oral language development in genre variation, metaphor usage, and shifts in key (e.g., irony, parody).[6]

Structural changes such as those examining both the relationship between growth in white matter and grey matter and increases in myelination of cortico-hippocampal relay pathways may be relevant for functional processes that underlie social cognition. For adolescents, these centre in "executive" functions that relate to working memory and response inhibition – both of which are repeatedly and richly illustrated within Young Adult literature, as are emotion-related processes.

---

[5]   Broca's area is usually associated with language output or the production of language, while Wernicke's area is associated with the processing of language input. For many years, scientists thought of these two areas as distinct regions. However, research in recent years has shown the extent of their interconnectivity through bundles of nerve fibres that increase with maturation. Paus, T. "Mapping Brain Maturation and Cognitive Development During Adolescence." *Trends in Cognitive Sciences* 9, no 2 (2005): 60–68; Berl, M.M., E.S. Duke, J. Mayo, L.R. Rosenberger, E.N. Moore, J. VanMeter et al. "Functional Anatomy of Listening and Reading Comprehension During Development." *Brain and Language* 114, no 2 (2010):115–25.

[6]   For a useful summary on reading and oral discourse or extended text, see Perfetti, C.A., and G.A. Frishkoff. "The Several Bases of Text and Discourse Processing." In *Handbook of the Neuroscience of Language*, edited by B. Stemmer and H.A. Whitaker, 165–74. Burlington, MA: Academic Press, 2008.

Both structural and functional maturation have strong implications for peer-peer interactions and influences as well as for the processing of verbal and non-verbal cues that are highly critical in the social life of adolescents who constantly need to "read" signals of anger and acceptance and to make judgements about the consequences of actions.

Cognitive and social neuroscience research

Cognitive neuroscientists have led the way in trying to understand executive functions. Their studies relate to key areas of concern about both psychiatric disorders (such as depression, substance abuse, and anxiety disorders) as well as risk-avoidance and integrative understanding of action and consequence.[7] Their findings support the following general points:

A) Young people who engage with electronic media's micro-moments more than two hours each day are less likely to sustain visual and attentive focus than those who spend more time in direct personal interactions.

B) Multi-tasking has a negative effect on concentration, attentiveness, and memory.

C) Downtime for processing new experiences in learning aids retention of information and depth of skill understanding.

D) Mobile software developers have successfully turned the entertainment world available in hand-held devices into cognitive retraining for increasingly brief intervals of focused attention. Their games encourage micro-moments of attention, rapid shifts in visual and memory focus, and reduced exposure to extended verbal texts.

The influence of social interactions behind these findings on cognitive functioning has led neuroscientists to propose a new field termed "social neuroscience."[8] Highly interdisciplinary, this field challenges social scientists to bring their sustained and systematic observations of oral and written language behaviours to bear in the learning sciences. Their need is especially critical with relation to visual focus, envisionment, embodiment, and emotive engagement. The following discussion suggests areas in which social and cognitive may come together as researchers seek to improve our understanding of adolescent brain development and their reading behaviours. Young Adult fiction offers a body of texts rich in potential for examining some initial linkages.

Most of us know how a young adult reader, immersed in the newest volume of a favourite series, behaves when caught in the obsessive urge to just keep reading

---

[7]   Paus. T., M. Keshavan, and J.N. Giedd. "Why Do So Many Psychiatric Disorders Emerge During Adolescence?" *Nature Reviews*, (2008): 947–57.

[8]   Meltzoff, A., P.K. Kuhl, J. Movellan, and T.J. Sejnowski. "Foundations for a New Science of Learning." *Science* 325 (2009): 284–89.

– through calls to dinner, friends' phone calls, and homework demands. What we cannot see is the cognitive training of neural structures in the brain that take place as the reader practices the complex interdependent and cross-modal tasks involved in young adult reading. Avid Young Adult literature readers easily log the magical 10,000 hours that make them expert – a popular conclusion essayist Malcolm Gladwell gleaned from his studies of research on what it takes to make an expert. These fiction readers are simultaneously engaged in the tasks of processing extended text, sustaining visual attention, decoding and encoding "rare vocabulary" and complex dialogue, and putting together current actions with a foreshadowing of future events and consequences to come (e.g., "envisioning"). Beyond these tasks, how do adolescents, whose parents and teachers often see them as unable to follow the simplest instructions, voluntarily practice repeatedly the imaginative constructions and deciphering of maps, codes, mathematical riddles, foreign languages, and scientific information that Young Adult novels offer? Answers lie in the relationships and sense of ownership and inclusive role that these texts – whether printed-word, mixture of print and graphic illustration, or graphic novel – give readers.

Teenagers build relationships through the demands from Young Adult literature that readers foresee scenarios from given circumstances, understand character development, and invent and co-create narrative worlds that replicate the actual physical world of teenage readers. Maps, signs, emails, mixed media, multiple messages on the same point, and simultaneous (and often conflicting) narratives come at adolescents incessantly in the information age. However, ways of taking in information from multiple structured symbol systems (alphabetic, numerical, cartographic) must be learned. The interdependence of the brain's modal systems (for vision, language, motor control, balance, etc.) ensures that these ways of taking encompass image and verbal retention in long-term memory, analogical reasoning, reinstigation of skills learned in other settings, and narrative retellings of experiences. Grounded cognition is a field that takes advantage of cognitive models as well as research made possible by fMRI and related technologies that allow neuroscientists to see the neural work of different sections of the brain working in synchrony with one another. This interdependence enables humans to take advantage of specific contextual experiences (such as close involvement with another human being within guided participation) that influence attentiveness, visual focus, eye-hand coordination, and a sense of self within a variety of roles.[9]

Vision is our most efficient sense. The term "envisionment" encompasses both our ability to look and see and our capacity to perceive cognitively and to predict or envision – see in our heads – what can happen. New technologies in the neurosciences allow scientists to see that when we create images in our mind or *visualize scenes, characters*, or *actions*, memory, language fluency, and mental

---

[9] Barsalou, L.W. "Grounded Cognition." *Annual Review Psychology* 59 (2008): 617–45.

images benefit.[10] Visual thinking, mental modelling, and envisionment of act and consequence in future scenarios take place in parts of the brain that work in coordination with language centres.[11]

Taking in words means simultaneously building visual images in the head that often go well beyond what can be expressed verbally. For example, brain research shows the high overlap in neural networks between visual perception of details and mental imagery. Visualizing is essential to verbal processing. Grounded cognition enables us to move back and forth between mental images and verbal recall. In other words, "see it as you read it" is not so simple an instruction as we may think. The more frequently individual readers have either seen or done actions they read about, the more complex the mental images they build as they process words, and the more likely they are to handle analogical reasoning. It may seem curious, but young readers who are likely to say "I don't know this word" or "what's that word?" are those who have higher visual acuity and brain activity in the vision centres of the brain than do those who do not admit that they don't know the meaning of a word. It seems that visually acute readers accept that they have to "look around" to figure out what they don't know; in other words, the mental picture they create from the words they know point them to the meaning of words they do not know.[12] We see this same phenomenon working in sequence when learners say: "I can see what I want to say, but I can't put it into words yet."

For older readers, such as those of Young Adult literature, visual images, whether from the actual world experienced or created as mental images from words on the page, aid both memory and amplification as well as extension of verbal information. Perhaps most important, envisionment through mental images facilitates the use of mental models in problem-solving and reasoning through abstract ideas.[13] In comparative experiments, imagery appears repeatedly to take precedence over language in developmental learning with regard to both maturational age and levels of conceptual difficulty. A picture that we form in

---

[10]   Ramadas, J. "Visual and Spatial Modes in Science Learning." *International Journal of Science Education* 31.3 (2009): 301–318.

[11]   Suwa, M., and B. Tversky. "What Architects and Students Perceive in their Sketches: A Protocol Analysis." *Design Studies* 18 (1997): 385–403; *The Handbook of Communication Science*, edited by C. Berger, M. Roloff, and D. Roskos-Ewoldsen. 2nd ed. Thousand Oaks, Calif.: Sage, 2009.

[12]   Merriman, W.E., and J.M. Marazita. "Young Children's Awareness of their own Lexical Ignorance: Relations to Word Mapping, Memory Processes, and Beliefs about Change." In *Thinking and Seeing: Visual Metacognition in Adults and Children*, edited by D.T. Levin, 57–74. Cambridge, Mass.: MIT Press, 2004.

[13]   Kosslyn, S.M., W.L. Thompson, and G. Ganis. *The Case for Mental Imagery*. Oxford: Oxford University Press, 2006; Latour, B. "Visualization and Cognition: Thinking with Eyes and Hands." *Knowledge and Society* 6 (1986): 1–40; Uttal, D.H., and K. O'Doherty, "Comprehending and Learning from 'Visualization': A Developmental Perspective." In *Visualization: Theory and Practice in Science Education*, edited by J.K. Gilbert, M. Reiner, and M. Nakhleh, 53–72. London: Springer, 2008.

our minds of a concept, scene, or sequence of actions hangs in memory more efficiently than do words of text. In other words, a picture is worth a thousand words, and a picture is all the better when it is a picture created in the reader's mind from words as well as experiences recalled.

Once visually perceived, details tend to transform as depictive and abstracted in both working and long-term memory. This means that making images in the mind (or through active drawing or using other means of visually rendering or representing these images – doodling, sketching, building models, for example) as one reads words on the page helps readers remember and later verbalize what they have read. This boost in memory power works for both depictive material and abstract ideas.[14] Young Adult books increasingly take advantage of this aspect of cognitive learning by using maps, graphic design, and codes that make clear authors' expectations that young readers will carry these visual images in their heads as they read the verbal text.

Authors also expect readers to grasp actions conveyed through words on the page by seeing ahead of the actions described in words on the page. Readers must "see" current actions in order to look ahead to create future scenarios and to visualize possible narrative trajectories. Modal overlapping in the brain enables readers to develop pictures in their heads of what they have not seen. These often become quite fixed – so much so that when Young Adult books become movies, young readers object strenuously to filmmakers' visual images. For readers, the images they create in their own heads as they read can become what cognitive scientists sometimes term "future memories." These enable readers to see ahead in order to foretell and forecast events and consequences that may follow actions currently underway in the text. Cognitive neuroscience makes clear how important this "looking ahead" is for memory and for internal plan-making and mental monitoring.[15]

Simulation complements the envisioning that readers do along the way. When successful readers see text that describes an action, they embody the action, simulating associated movements deep within the neural structures of the brain. Humans (along with other higher order primates) have mirror neurons that enable motor neurons to register or simulate an action either physically seen or mentally envisioned while reading about or hearing descriptions of actions. Motor neurons mirror actions we observe attentively. When outside observers watch readers engaged with written texts, it is not possible to see any evidence of actual movement of body parts in the silent still reader. Yet fMRI technology tells us that motor neurons are activated when readers take in information that conveys motor

---

[14] Intons-Peterson, M.J. "Imaginal Priming." *Journal of Experimental Psychology: Learning, Memory and Cognition* 19, vol 1 (1993): 223–35; Ramachandran, V.S., and E.M. Hubbard, "Synaesthesia: A Window into Perception, Thought and Language." *Journal of Consciousness Studies* 12 (2001): 3–24.

[15] Ingvar, D. "Memory of the Future: An Essay on the Temporal Organization of Conscious Awareness." *Human Neurology* 4/3 (1998): 127–36.

actions. For example, mental rotation of visual objects is accompanied by motor simulations in the brain in making these objects turn. Linkage between visual imagery and the motor system supports theories of language comprehension (a view increasingly evidenced in the work of reading researchers).[16] The modal structuring of the brain enables simultaneous neural work of simulation, situated action, and bodily states. The cognitive work of understanding, "seeing," or "perceiving" the verbal text does not get accomplished without grounding in simulation, the situating of actions in line with foreshadowing and contextualising, and the sensing of the bodily states of characters behind and within actions.

Though theatre companies that work with young people in the writing and enacting of their own stories may seem to have more claim on embodiment than does Young Adult literature, it is critical when we think of young adult readers to note that their verbal renderings of what they have read, as well as their translation into comics, maps, and visual illustration of any kind, demonstrate the extent to which spatial arrangements and movements through space figure in their memories of these works. Young Adult literature relies on words showing the movements of bodies – on the ground, through the air, and even within the dream images of characters.

Young readers also identify emotionally with characters, creating a sense of the "joint attention" of reader and character on the same situation. Thus as adolescents read, they benefit from the "double exposure" of reading about what someone else does, thinks, or feels and seeing this as being "the same as me." This doubling is important for Young Adult literature readers, because behaviours in the textual world that they perceive as "like me" serve as proxy for their own behaviours without the inefficiency and dangers involved in their actually taking the risks that literary characters may pursue.

Neuroscientist Anthony Damasio first alerted the field of cognitive neuroscience to the heft that emotional engagement gives to memory, adaptation of what is seen and heard, and facility in developing future scenarios for action of the self.[17] As adolescents recruit what they see, experience, and sense as they read, they bring to bear the worlds of acting, thinking, and feeling with which they identify. Thus they make use of human resources for both reasoning and feeling their way through new tasks and new settings. Young Adult literature, as much or more than most resources upon which adolescents call in their leisure time, facilitates much-needed practice in fundamental cognitive behaviours: envisioning and embodying for positive emotional fuelling. Neuroscientists stress the power of the social nature of environment on cognitive responsiveness. Information is less stored

---

[16] Speer, N.K., J.R. Reynolds, K.M. Swallow, and J.M. Zacks. "Reading Stories Activates Neural Representations of Visual and Motor Experiences." *Psychological Sciences* 20.8 (2009): 989–99.

[17] Damasio, Anthony. *Descartes' Error: Emotion, Reason, and the Human Brain.* New York: Avon, 1998; Damasio, Anthony. *Looking for Spinoza: Sorrow, and the Feeling Brain.* Orlando, Fla.: Harcourt, 2003.

than situated in bodily patterns and senses remembered and projected. "Future memories" enable readers to envision, embody, and reason about future actions by remembering affordances that environments or situations have given them or could provide. The modalities of the brain work as dynamic systems.

As adolescents read, they collect envisionment, embodiment, and emotive engagement toward goals self-derived and adopted. Adolescents make clear in their reports of processes of which they are aware during their reading that they bring their intuitive ideas to bear. These ideas work as productive resources from which more systematic and integrated knowledge come as they reorganize existing pieces of knowledge in line with additional information that is "like me."[18] The large, complex mental structures that coordinate activation of specific knowledge according to context are termed "coordination classes." Conceptual understanding, looked at through this theory, amounts to knowing how to see concepts in action in order to learn how to look at the right things and to make correct inferences. As young adults learn to do this, they need representations of actions and consequences that "stand still" (as written texts do) so that they can return to these scenes again and again or through reading books in a series. They need to see and see again specific aspects of a phenomenon or concept, and each time they return to a literary text, they see something different and thereby increase their integration of knowledge.[19] "Conceptual ecology" – the ability to make ideas portable by making them visible for testing against intuitive ideas and grounded action – is what cognitive science terms "a good idea." This back-and-forth between what characters in Young Adult literature have experienced, want to experience, or could experience (and feel) supports adolescents in developing and testing their own intuitions and considering their own actions. Young Adult fiction readers do this best by relating (that is, developing a relationship with) and re-lating (internally comparing as well as talking with other young adult readers). Relating means participating.

No one knows this better than Young Adult literature readers.

Young Adult literature readers in action

In this second portion of this chapter, we show how adolescents in their behavioural interactions with Young Adult literature put their neuronal capacity for envisionment and embodiment into play. The changing conventions of Young

---

[18] DiSessa, A. "Meta-representation: Native Competence and Targets for Instruction." *Cognition and Instruction* 22.3 (2004): 293–331; DiSessa, A., and B. Sherin. "What Changes in Conceptual Change?" *International Journal of Science Education* 20, no 10 (1998): 1155–91; Parnafes, O. "Self-generated Representations for Promoting Conceptual Understanding." *Proceedings of the Chais Conference on Instructional Technologies Research 2009*. Raanana: The Open University of Israel, 2009.

[19] Scherz, R., and S. Oren. "How to Change Students' Images of Science and Technology." *Science Education* 90 (2008): 965–85.

Adult texts draw readers in, and the publishing industry responds to how, when, and what their readers want. Of primary importance to Young Adult fiction readers is the ability to form social relationships through participating with the characters, plot, and strategies of texts. In what follows, we lay out the features of Young Adult literature that make possible the relationship-building that forms the foundation of readers' participation with the texts they read and write.[20]

The most obvious feature relished and required by teenage readers is the reordering potential of Young Adult literature. Adolescents take charge of the order in which they will read their books. They want their books to be written so that they may replace the traditional story order of beginning, middle, and end with any one of several means of reordering how events turn out. In Young Adult literature reordering, young readers take control of aspects of both the sequencing and the scope of emergence – their own and those of the characters and actions in the books they read. For example, they do so when they read the endings of books first. Adult readers often see the get-the-ending-first as a form of cheating or evidence of refusal to delay gratification. Teenage readers see this reordering as a way to sharpen their critical perspective on the book. Holding the end in mind, they read and assess "lead-up" elements, asking "Does this fit together?" Such critical reading leads these readers (in general) to assess the first book in almost every series as the best. One young reader had this assessment of the second book in the series in which *The Hunger Games* was the first volume: "In *The Hunger Games*, she [the author Suzanne Collins] tied it all together, but in the second, she was too rushed. It was confusing, and in some parts I didn't get it."[21] This young reader hastened to express confidence that the author would get "things straight" by the third book.

Authors of Young Adult literature take note of the fact that the reordering potential must be in place and is likely to be invoked by an end-first approach. In John Green's endnote to *An Abundance of Katherines*, he writes: "The footnotes of the novel you just read (unless you haven't finished reading it and are skipping ahead, in which case you should go back and read everything in order and not

---

[20]   Young Adult works cited in this section: Collins, Suzanne. *Hunger Games*. New York: Scholastic, 2008. Rowling, J.K. *Harry Potter and the Chamber of Secrets*. New York: Scholastic, 2000. Green, John. *An Abundance of Katherines*. New York: Dutton, 2006. Taylor, Lani. *Lips Touch, Three Times*. New York: Scholastic, 2009. Rosoff, Meg. *How I Live Now*. New York: Random House, 2006. Chambers, Aidan. *Postcards from No Man's Land*. New York: Random House, 1999. Johnson, Angela. *The First Part Last*. New York: Simon & Schuster, 2003. Tolkien, J.R.R. *The Hobbit (1937)*, New York: Houghton Mifflin, 2007. Larsen, Rief. *The Selected Works of T.S. Spivet: A Novel*. New York: Penguin Books, 2009. Anderson, M.T. *The Astonishing Life of Octavian Nothing, Traitor to the Nation, Volume I: The Pox Party*. Cambridge, Mass.: Candlewick Press, 2006. Meyer, Stephenie. *Twilight*. New York: Little, Brown, 2005. The Harvard Lampoon. *Nightlight, A Parody*. New York: Random House, 2009. Dokey, Cameron. *Beauty Sleep*. New York: Simon & Schuster, 2002. Campbell, Patty. "The Sand in the Oyster." *The Hornbook* 69, no 6 (1993).

[21]   Collins, *The Hunger Games*.

try to find out what happens, you sneaky little sneakster) promise a math-laden appendix. And so here it is." An additional example comes in the volume *Lips Touch Three Times* by Laini Taylor. This book, mixing text and graphic illustration in three sequenced clumps, tells the story first in graphic form, thereby revealing ending before beginning – of the written text version, that is. The volume also takes advantage of the reality that when we read stories several times over different periods of time (and in different modes), we perceive how the "real" story or plotline or moral can be read differently each time. Thus the graphic "fronted ending" of *Lips Touch Three Times* does *not* truly capture any finality about what the textual version may reveal. The reverse is also true.

Meg Rosoff, author of *How I Live Now*, captures the end at the beginning, while also noting through reminders of "supposedly," "mostly," and "can't remember much" that we never "actually" relive or accurately remember what happened before, even if we "know" the ending. She writes in the opening pages: "But the summer I went to England to stay with my cousins everything changed. Part of that was because of the war, which supposedly changed lots of things, but I can't remember much about life before the war anyway so it doesn't count in my book, which this is. Mostly everything changed because of Edmond. And so here's what happened."

Young Adult literature honours the reordering penchant of its adolescent readers through the frequent use of flashbacks (e.g., *Catcher in the Rye* and *The Outsiders*). This device enables authors to foretell as well as to foreground. Patty Campbell, a Young Adult fiction librarian and columnist for The Horn Book Magazine, suggests that the generic happy ending of children's literature grows up and becomes more complicated in Young Adult literature. She tells us that this literature offers "endings that read as beginnings." Campbell further argues that while clear-cut "happy" resolutions are no longer guaranteed (and indeed may be frowned upon) by Young Adult literature readers, they want to look forward and see development. But we would also add that they acknowledge as well the fact that chance plays a big part in dislodging paths of development for many teenagers. Thus acceptance and adaptation, as well as invention of creative solutions (often through magic realism, science fiction, fantasy, or dreams), come about for young adult characters.

A second means by which these adolescent readers manage their reordering is by putting into place their own navigational routings through Young Adult novels. The case of Cathy, a sixteen-year-old secondary school student illustrates this point. On the day the book group met to critique Aidan Chamber's novel *Post Cards from No Man's Land*, Cathy stood out as casting the most enthusiastic vote for the title (which went on to win both the Printz and Carnegie awards). While her peers found the book "wordy" and "confusing in the way its chapters bounced back and forth between historical eras and characters," Cathy prized the book for its dual narration. She explained: "At first, the flashback chapters threw me. So then I decided to just read the teenager's chapters, the chapters that the modern teenager tells ... Then I went back and read the chapters from the elderly lady ...

At first I thought I would forget stuff, but this way it really stuck in my mind. It let me see how both the characters were really questioning themselves about life."

Aidan Chambers alternates between a contemporary teenager's point of view as he travels through Europe and an elderly woman's point of view as she flashes back to memories of when she was young during the war. When this order doesn't work for Cathy, she reorders the narrative to her liking. While Chambers' choice to alternate between these two characters gives a particular structure to his novel, it also allows, even makes it easier, for readers to enter into and travel through the narration on their terms. A further example comes in the volume *The First Part Last*, by Angela Johnson. Seemingly titled to entice alternative-direction Young Adult literature readers, the novel explores a character often ignored in Young Adult literature and beyond – the teenage father. The slim novel begins with a two-page passage labelled "Now," followed by another two-page passage labelled "Then." Passages switch between the *now* after the birth of Bobby's daughter and the *then* passages before the birth.

A third means by which these readers manage their reordering within their readings comes through the, often unchallenged, dominance and authority teenagers claim over language, mathematical tricks, and the science in science fiction. Young Adult books often seem to adults to have too much fantasy, too many complex science fictive worlds, and an excess of secret codes, formulae, maps, and languages. But we might consider the alternative view that Young Adult fiction readers enjoy donning the mantle of authority for fictive worlds in which they can draw on mathematical, geographic, and scientific reasoning.

Consider the case of Ryan, an eighteen-year-old who dropped out of his urban high school at the age of sixteen and elected to take courses at a local community college in topics and subjects that interested him. He was an avid fantasy reader, who saw Tolkien's works of the *The Hobbit* and *Lord of the Rings* trilogy as the gravitational centre and standard-bearer for all fantasy. Ryan took every opportunity to draw *The Hobbit* into his conversations, wanting to let others know that he spent significant amounts of time learning the fictional language of Elfin that Tolkien created for his characters. In interviews with anthropologist Wolf, Ryan directed her attention to one of the first pages of *The Hobbit*, where Tolkien writes what reads like a historio-linguistic description of the made-up language, complete with an invented "transcript" of a salvaged portion of its alphabet. Tolkien issues his readers the challenge of cracking the code of Elfin and becoming fluent in this fictional language, a challenge Ryan was proud to have met. It is a written rather than a spoken language, and Ryan showed Wolf the loose-leaf notebook he filled with his Elfin writings, which he explained as illustrating his progress from novice to expert. For the Tolkien books, Ryan could easily turn to text portions in Elfin and translate these into English.

The draw of co-texts is not lost on publishers. *The Selected Works of T. S. Spivet* by Reif Larsen, a volume published to much acclaim in England, Germany, and the United States in 2010, uses maps created by a young boy. It is not possible to read the printed words without also reading deeply into the maps, for without these, no meaning can be gleaned from the written text. The popularity of this book, marketed entirely for the adult market, may well have come from readers who recall mapping the worlds of Tolkein as teenage readers. All such maps, partial as they are, subscribe to Herman Melville's dictum from *Moby Dick:* "It is not down in any map; true places never are." Maps offer their own narratives, just as do the many other genres collaged into Young Adult novels: emails, letters, diary entries, newspaper articles, receipts. In recent years, the two volumes of M.T. Anderson's *Octavian Nothing* have engaged some Young Adult fiction readers who report that they enjoy the challenge of interpreting multiple modes along with conflicting narratives in order to create their own sense of outcome or ending.

A fourth means by which Young Adult literature readers manage their own reordering comes through the repeat reading habits of adolescents. They read the same types of books repeatedly, and they also read the same individual books again and again. When Wolf asked a teenage reader who seemed to be complaining about "It's just the same genre over again," why he read the same kind repeatedly if he did not like knowing how it would all turn out, he replied vehemently: "But that's not it. You don't know. The books go at it the same, but I like to make them all different in my mind by mixing up what happens in the ones I've read lots." He knew why he liked what seemed to others a punishing redundancy over which he could assume complete control for creating newness.[22]

When adults see their adolescent children reading the same books again and again, they often question such repeat reading just as they do reading the endings first. Are teenage readers stuck in certain genres, unwilling to challenge themselves with new reading experiences? Could they be simply doing what comes easily now that they have done the same thing over and over? Adolescent readers see repeat reading differently. They see it as a means of creating close-up and personal relationships. They see their repeat readings as comforting, building their expertise as readers digging deeply into meanings, memorizing certain passages, knowing character traits and idiosyncrasies. With this expertise, they negotiate their roles and status within specific reading communities where this kind of knowledge is prized.

The Harry Potter series allowed, even encouraged, repeat readers. If the first wave of the Harry Potter effect brought young readers (children with the first volumes, teenagers with the later volumes, as Harry himself becomes a teenager) out into the open, proud to carry around long books in public, then the second wave of the Harry Potter effect spotlighted young readers proud to have read the books more than once. Why now? Teenage readers say they take up these books a second time or more for several reasons: to prepare for movie viewing or reading

---

[22] Similar points about repeat and genre reading are considered in John G. Cawelti's *The Six Gun Mystique*. Bowling Green, Ky.: Bowling Green Press, 1975; David Hajdu's *The Ten-¢ent Plague: The Great Comic Book Scare and How it Changed America.* New York: Farrar, Straus and Giroux, 2008; and Janice Radway's *Reading the Romance: Women, Patriarchy & Popular Literature.* Durham: University of North Carolina Press, 1984.

of a next instalment in the series, to spot re-read to be ready for interactions with other Harry Potter readers, to play Harry Potter trivia with friends and parents, to communicate in Harry Potter chat rooms and on Harry Potter internet social sites, and to secure bragging rights by knowing the most esoteric fine-grained detail about a particular character or event.

Two further notes on the behaviours of teenagers as they read are especially relevant as technologies and multiple media seem to be taking over the world of the book. Apple created in 2011 a virtual bookstore that provided not only text, but also pictures that unfolded, characters that talked, words that could pronounce themselves, and music. Many wonder if this kind of digital interactivity will engender mental passivity and further the inclination of the young to want to be entertained passively rather than to undertake the kind of active engagement with young adult reading we have laid out here. Foretelling this future is best done by looking not only at surveys of the reading habits and preferences of the young, but also by studying closely what they do with reading.[23]

How Young Adult literature readers relate to single titles and to rewrites/ reworkings of classics may give some indication of what they will do as options for representing stories increase. Single titles have capitalized on the popularity of rereading within the adolescent realm. Traditional or nostalgic readers may assume that having read one version or form of a story, a reader may not feel the need to read any other. These literature readers would not agree, since they see that different versions of the same text offer ample rereading and relationship-building opportunities. The mega-best seller *Twilight* by Stephenie Meyer comes in multi-modal ways: Young Adult fiction readers can read the original novel (544 pages of text), listen to the audio reading of the novel (at 12 hours and 52 minutes), read the graphic novel (224 pages of pictures and text), watch the movie (121 minutes), and read the satire novel, *Nightlight* (160 pages).

These readers view fairy tales, as well as the best-known works of writers such as Jane Austen or Charlotte Bronte, in the same way as allowing different channels for rereading – even in parodic forms. Consider the case of Willow, a thirteen-year-old Young Adult fiction reader who frequents her urban library and dresses in ruffled skirts, lacy scarves, and strings of pearls along with her combat boots, shaved hair and safety pin earrings. As her fashion style might suggest, Willow is a reader of fractured fairy tales. Willow reports having read "all the fairy tales" as a child, and she now enjoys reliving her own childhood memories in rewoven Young Adult novels. Beyond triggering nostalgia, Willow enjoys encountering the new: new motivations, new personality components, new kinds of magic, new tests and trials.

Willow engages with reconstructed fairy tales in a particular way. She reads forward into the novel looking for the places where the new story "surprises" her. When it does, that's a good thing; Willow sees herself as someone who knows

---

[23]   See, for example, Gutnick, A.L., M. Robb, L. Takenchi, and J. Kotler. *Always Connected: The New Media Habits of Young Children*. New York: Joan Ganz Cooney Center and Sesame Street, 2010.

fairy tales "inside out, in (her) sleep," as a reader who has "pretty much seen it all in fairy tales," and so is a reader who is especially challenging to surprise. Once surprised, she reads backwards, collecting literary verification that the new information actually "fits" into the framework of the original tale. Willow explained what she meant by "fit": "The author can't just stick something in there, just to be crazy. It has to, you know, *fit*. It has to, you know, keep with the things that *have* to happen in that fairy tale."

To critique whether a Young Adult author has been successful in both fracturing and reconstructing a favourite fairy tale, Willow re-reads the re-told tale, and also reads back into the original tales – in her own extensive collection, and into library versions of "originals," such as Andrew Lang's colour-coded fairy volumes, Hans Christian Andersen's text, and tales of the Brothers Grimm. She scours the original tales, both text and graphics, for any small hints that might suggest the turn the contemporary Young Adult writer has taken. If she can find such a clue, a symbol, piece of foreshadowing, or subtle motif, that too is a good thing. It tells Willow that the author of the fractured tale read the original "so, so up close" that she saw something that even Willow did not see.

Willow favours the fractured fairy *Beauty Sleep* by Cameron Dokey, and she explains the many things she likes about this adjusted version. She likes that it offers a "finally" plausible explanation of why Aurora pricks her finger on her sixteenth birthday. Many traditional tellings have the King and Queen leave the castle and their daughter unsupervised for that day – a device that always bothered Willow. Why would her parents forget that it was her sixteenth birthday? Willow likes that she can see through the first person narration of Dokey's novel into what the Princess is thinking, and that she can see the seeds of independent, defiant thinking. In this retold tale, Aurora will ultimately choose to prick her own finger to manipulate the spell against her father's wishes in order to save the kingdom. And her plan will succeed. Willow likes most of all that this new revelation about the story "fits" into the confines of the original tale about a royal baby born to a fated spell. Willow takes new meaning from her favourite childhood fairy tale: it is possible to transform fate into agency; adolescence has a dark and powerful relationship with magic; and, finally and perhaps best of all – good things can happen when teenagers rebel against their parents.

When Young Adult literature readers take up a series or "follow" (as Willow does) certain aspects of this literature, many do so through loyalty to a particular sub-genre (such as fairy tales), but more often to specific characters (rebelling teens) and, in some cases, to particular authors. In their descriptions of the characters they follow and sometimes seem to adopt from their readings, teens often speak as though through the mind of these characters. They speak with empathy or a sense of the ethical choices that teens face in handling relations with adults (especially parents who abandon, mistreat, or ridicule their children). In their Young Adult literature reading, teenagers "rehearse" the talk of hard choices, deliberated decisions, and rough challenges in forming and sustaining the most common relationship – that between parent and child – assumed to be the norm in modern nations.

Conclusion

To pull together what we have said about brain development during adolescence and habits of reading that teenagers follow, we conclude with the views of author Ursula Le Guin. She expresses a point of view that offers a guiding principle for scholars and educators to consider as they follow the on-going research of neuroscientists and social scientists.

> I believe that all the best faculties of a mature human being exist in the child and that if these faculties are encouraged in youth they will act well and wisely in the adult, but that if they are repressed and denied in the child they will stunt and cripple the adult personality. And finally, I believe that one of the most deeply human, and humane, of these faculties is the power of imagination.[24]

Brain maturation makes the envisionment, embodiment, and empathy that readers of Young Adult literature bring to bear in their reading possible. Together, these give the cognitive insights and social foundations critical to adolescents' development of judgement and foresight. These in turn benefit from the rehearsals and mental practice that result from the "power of imagination" that Young Adult reading expects.

---

[24] Le Guin, Ursula. *Essays on Fantasy and Science Fiction.* New York: Putnam, 1979, 44.

Selected Bibliography

Primary sources

Alvarez, Julia. *Before We Were Free*. New York: Random House, 2002.
Alvarez, Julia. *How the Garcia Girls Lost Their Accents*. New York: Penguin, 1991.
Alvarez, Julia. *Something to Declare*. Chapel Hill: Algonquin Books, 1998
Anderson, M.T. *The Astonishing Life of Octavian Nothing, Traitor to the Nation*. Cambridge, Mass.: Candlewick Press, 2006.
Benway, Robin. *Audrey, Wait*. New York: Razorbill, 2008.
Blackman, Malorie. *Noughts and Crosses*. London: Random House, 2001.
Blackman, Malorie. *Knife Edge*. London: Random House, 2004.
Blackman, Malorie. *Checkmate*. London: Random House, 2005.
Boie, Kirsten. *Ich ganz cool*. Hamburg: Oetinger, 1992.
Burgess, Melvyn. *Lady: My Life as a Bitch*. Harmondsworth: Penguin, 2003.
Chambers, Aidan. *Postcards from No Man's Land*. New York: Random House, 1999.
Chbosky, Steven. *The Perks of Being a Wallflower*. New York: MTV Books, 1999.
Collins, Suzanne. *Hunger Games*. New York: Scholastic, 2008.
Cormier, Robert. *Tenderness*. New York: Delacorte, 1998.
Danticat, Edwidge. *Breath, Eyes, Memory*. New York: Soho Press, 1994.
Danticat, Edwidge. *Behind the Mountains*. New York: Orchard Books, 2002.
Dokey, Cameron. *Beauty Sleep*. New York: Simon & Schuster, 2002.
Donnelly, Jennifer. *Revolution*. New York: Delacorte, 2010.
Glass, Linzi. *Ruby Red*. London: Macmillan, 2007.
Glass, Linzi. *The Year the Gypsies Came*. London: H. Holt, 2006.
Green, John. *An Abundance of Katherines*. New York: Dutton, 2006.
Green, John, and David Levithan. *Will Grayson, Will Grayson*. New York: Dutton, 2010.
Haddon, Mark. *The Curious Incident of the Dog in the Night-Time*. London: Jonathan Cape, 2003.
Halberslam, Gaby. *Blue Sky Freedom*. London: Penguin, 2008.
The Harvard Lampoon. *Nightlight, A Parody*. New York: Random House, 2009.
John, Antony. *Five Flavors of Dumb*. New York: Dial, 2010.
Johnson, Angela. *The First Part Last*. New York: Simon & Schuster, 2003.
Jones, Diana Wynne. *Howl's Moving Castle* (1986). New York: Harper, 2001.
Kipling, Rudyard. *Kim* (1901). New York: Modern Library, 2004.
Larsen, Rief. *The Selected Works of T.S. Spivet: A Novel*. New York: Penguin, 2009.

McCaughrean, Geraldine. *Not the End of the World*. Oxford: Oxford University Press, 2004.

Meyer, Stephenie. *Twilight*. London: Atom, 2005.

Meyer, Stephenie. *Breaking Dawn*. London: Atom, 2008.

Morrison, Toni. *The Bluest Eye*. Austin: Holt, Rinehart and Winston, 1970.

Paver, Michelle. *Chronicles of Ancient Darkness*. London: Orion, 2004.

Perrault, Charles. "Donkeyskin," In *The Classic Fairytales*, edited and translated by Maria Tatar. New York: Norton, 1999.

Pierce, Tamora. *Alanna: The First Adventure*. New York: Atheneum, 1983.

Portman, Frank. *King Dork*. New York: Delacorte, 2006.

Riordan, Rick. *Percy Jackson & The Olympians*. New York: Hyperion, 2005.

Rodgers, Mary. *Freaky Friday*. New York: Harper & Row, 1972.

Rosoff, Meg. *How I Live Now*. Harmondsworth: Penguin, 2004.

Rowling, J.K. *Harry Potter and the Chamber of Secrets*. New York: Scholastic, 2000.

Sapphire. *Push*. New York: Random House, 1997.

Shan, Darren. *The Saga of Darren Shan*. London: HarperCollins, 2006.

Slovo, Gillian. *Every Secret Thing: My Family, My Country*. London: Abacus, 1998.

Stockett, Kathryn. *The Help*. New York: Penguin, 2010.

Taylor, Lani. *Lips Touch, Three Times*. New York: Scholastic, 2009.

Tolkien, J.R.R. *The Hobbit (1937)*, New York: Houghton Mifflin, 2007.

Twain, Mark. *The Adventures of Huckleberry Finn* (1884). New York: Modern Library, 2001

Twain, Mark. *The Prince and the Pauper* (1881). New York: Modern Library, 2003.

Twain, Mark. *The Adventures of Tom Sawyer* (1876). Harmondsworth: Penguin, 1985.

Veciana-Suarez, Ana. *Flight to Freedom*. New York: Orchard Books, 2002.

Walker, Alice. *The Color Purple*. London: Women's Press, 1983.

David Walliams, *The Boy in the Dress*. New York: Razorbill, 2009.

Weatherly, L.A. *Angel*. London: Usborne, 2010.

Yovanoff, Brenna. *The Replacements*. New York: Razorbill, 2010.

Ziegler, Jennifer. *How Not to Be Popular*. New York: Delacorte, 2008.

Secondary sources

Anderson, Susan. "The Child in the World: Challenges to Traditional Literary Landscapes in the Young Adult Fiction of Meg Rosoff." In *Deep Into Nature: Ecology, Environment and Children's Literature*, edited by Jennifer Harding, Elizabeth Thiel, and Alison Waller. Lichfield: Pied Piper, 2009.

Ashliman, D.L. *A Guide to Folktales in the English Language: Based on the Aarne-Thompson Classification System*. New York: Greenwood Press, 1987.

Auerbach, Nina. *Communities of Women: An Idea in Fiction*. Cambridge, Mass.: Harvard University Press, 1978.

Barkow, Jerome, Leda Cosmides, and John Tooby. Eds. *The Adapted Mind. Evolutionary Psychology and the Generation of Culture*. Oxford: Oxford University Press, 1992.

Barsalou, L.W. "Grounded Cognition." *Annual Review Psychology* 59 (2008): 617–45.

Bennett, Michael. "Jeremiad, Elegy and the Yaak: Rick Bass and the Aesthetics of Anger and Grief." In *The Literary Art and Activism of Rick Bass*, edited by O.A. Weltzein. Salt Lake City: University of Utah Press, 2001.

Baxter, Kent, *The Modern Age: Turn-of-the-century American Culture and the Invention of Adolescence*. Tuscaloosa: The University of Alabama Press, 2008.

Berger, C., M. Roloff, and D. Roskos-Ewoldsen, eds. *The Handbook of Communication Science*. 2nd ed. Thousand Oaks, Calif.: Sage, 2009.

Berl, M.M., E.S. Duke, J. Mayo, L.R. Rosenberger, E.N. Moore, J. VanMeter et al. "Functional Anatomy of Listening and Reading Comprehension During Development." *Brain and Language* 114, no 2 (2010): 115–25.

Bhabha, Homi. *The Location of Culture*. New York: Routledge, 2005.

Bracher, Mark. *Radical Pedagogy: Identity, Generativity, and Social Transformation*. New York: Palgrave Macmillan, 2006.

Bradford, Clare. *Unsettling Narratives: Postcolonial Readings of Children's Literature*. Waterloo: Wilfred Laurier University Press, 2007.

Brocklebank, Lisa. "Rebellious Voices: The Unofficial Discourse of Cross-Dressing in d'Aulnoy, de Murat, and Perrault," *Children's Literature Association Quarterly* 25, no. 3 (2000).

Bruning, N., Kerstin Konrad, and Beate Hepertz-Dahlmann. "Bedeutung und Ergebnisse der Theory of Mind-Forschung für den Autismus und andere psychiatrische Erkrankungen." *Zeitschrift für Kinder- und Jugendpsychiatrie und Psychotherapie* 33, no 2 (2005): 77–88.

Buell, Laurence. *The Future of Environmental Criticism: Environmental Crisis and Literary Imagination*. Oxford: Blackwell, 1995.

Bullough, Vern L., and Bonnie Bullough. *Cross Dressing, Sex, and Gender*. Philadelphia: University of Pennsylvania Press, 1993.

Butler, Judith. *Gender Trouble: Feminism and the Subversion of Identity*. 2nd ed. New York: Routledge, 1990.

Byrne, James P. "Cognitive Development During Adolescence." In *Blackwell Handbook of Adolescence*, edited by Gerald R. Adams and Michael D. Berzonsky, 227–46. London: Blackwell, 2003.

Campbell, Patty. "The Sand in the Oyster." *The Hornbook*. 69, no 6 (1993).

Cart, Michael. *From Romance to Realism. 50 Years of Growth and Change in Young Adult Literature*. New York: HarperCollins, 1996.

Cawelti, John G. *The Six Gun Mystique*. Bowling Green, Ky.: Bowling Green Press, 1975.

Chodorow, Nancy. *The Reproduction of Mothering. Psychoanalysis and the Sociology of Gender*. Berkeley: University of California Press, 1978.

Coats, Karen. *Looking Glasses and Neverlands. Lacan, Desire, and Subjectivity in Children's Literature*. Iowa City: Iowa University Press, 2004.

Coats, Karen. "Young Adult Literature: Growing Up, In Theory." In *The Handbook of Research on Children's and Young Adult Literature*, edited by Shelby A. Wolf, Karen Coats, Patricia Enciso, and Christine Jenkins, 315–29. New York: Routledge, 2011.

Cock, Jacklyn. *Maids and Madams: A Study in the Politics of Exploitation.* Johannesburg: Raven Press, 1980.

Cook, Nicholas. *Music: A Very Short Introduction.* Oxford: Oxford University Press, 2000.

Cosmides, Leda, and John Tooby. "Evolutionary Psychology and the Emotions." In *Handbook of Emotions*, edited by Michael Lewis and Jeannette Haviland Jones, 91–115. London: Sage, 2001.

Creed, Barbara. "Lesbian Bodies: Tribades, Tomboys and Tarts." In *Sexy Bodies: The Strange Carnalities of Feminism*, edited by Elizabeth Grosz and Elspeth Probyn, 86–103. London: Routledge, 1996.

Creed, Barbara. "Horror and the Monstrous Feminine: An Imaginary Abjection." In *Feminist Film Theory: A Reader*, edited by Sue Thornham, 252–53. New York: New York University Press, 1999.

Crew, Hilary S. *Is it Really "Mommie Dearest"? Daughter-Mother Narratives in Young Adult Fiction.* Lanham, Md.: Scarecrow, 2000.

Cushman, Philip. *Constructing the Self, Constructing America: A Cultural History of Psychotherapy.* Reading, Mass.: Addison-Wesley, 1995.

Damasio, Anthony. *Descartes' Error: Emotion, Reason, and the Human Brain.* New York: Avon, 1998.

Damasio, Anthony. *Looking for Spinoza: Sorrow, and the Feeling Brain.* Orlando, Fla.: Harcourt, 2003.

Davis, Rocío G. "Children on the Edge: Leaving Home in Sandra Cisneros's *The House on Mango Street* and Lois-Ann Yamanaka's *Blu's Hanging.*" In *Literature on the Move: Comparing Diasporic Ethnicities in Europe and the Americas*, edited by Dominique Marçais et al. Heidelberg: Universitätsverlag Winter, 2002.

Deham, Susanne, Marie von Salisch, Tjerrt Olthof, Anita Kochanoff, and Sarah Caverly. "Emotional and Social Development in Childhood." In *Blackwell Handbook of Childhood Social Development*, edited by Peter K. Smith and Craig H. Hart, 307–328. Oxford: Blackwell, 2002.

Dillabough, Jo-Ann, and Jacqueline Kennelly, *Lost Youth in the Global City: Class, Culture and the Urban Imaginary.* New York: Routledge, 2010.

DiSessa, A. "Meta-representation: Native Competence and Targets for Instruction." *Cognition and Instruction* 22, no 3 (2004): 293–331.

DiSessa, A., and B. Sherin. "What Changes in Conceptual Change?" *International Journal of Science Education* 20, no 10 (1998): 1155–91.

Duncan, Simon. "What's the Problem with Teenage Parents? And What's the Problem with Policy?" *Critical Social Policy* 27 (2007): 307–334.

Eisenberg, Nancy, Tracy L. Spinrad, and Adrienne Sadovsky. "Empathy-Related Responding in Children." In *Handbook of Moral Development*, edited by

Lin Melanie Killen and Judith G. Smetana, 517–49. Mahwah/London: Erlbaum, 2006.

Falconer, Rachel. *The Crossover Novel*. New York: Routledge, 2009.

Farley, Paul, and Symmons Roberts, Michael. *Edgelands: Journeys into England's True Wilderness*. London: Jonathan Cape, 2011.

Feinstein, S.G. *Secrets of the Teenage Brain*. Thousand Oaks, Calif.: Corwin. 2009.

Flaker, Aleksander. *Modelle der Jeans Prosa*. Kronberg: Scriptor, 1975.

Flanagan, Victoria. *Into the Closet: Cross-Dressing and the Gendered Body in Children's Literature and Film*. New York: Routledge, 2008.

French, Marilyn. *Beyond Power: On Women, Men, and Morals*. New York: Summit, 1985.

Frith, Simon. *The Sociology of Rock*. London: Constable, 1978.

Frith, Simon. "Toward an Aesthetic of Popular Music." In *Music and Society: The Politics of Composition, Performance, and Reception*, edited by Richard Leppert and Susan McClary. Cambridge: Cambridge University Press, 1987.

Frodsham, John, trans. "The Ballad of Mulan." In *Classical Chinese Literature*, vol. 1, *From Antiquity to the Tang Dynasty*, edited by John Minford and Joseph S.M. Lau, p. 411, lines 60–63. New York: Columbia University Press / Hong Kong: The Chinese University Press, 2002.

Garber, Marjorie. *Vested Interests: Cross-dressing and Cultural Anxiety*. New York: Routledge, 1997.

Gergen, Kenneth. *The Saturated Self: Dilemmas of Identity in Contemporary Life*. New York: Basic Books, 2000.

Gregory, Lucille H. "Children of the Diaspora: Four Novels About the African-Caribbean Journey." *African-American Voices in Young Adult Literature: Tradition, Transition, Transformation*, edited by Karen Patricia Smith. Metuchen, N.J.: Scarecrow Press, 1994.

Griswold, Jerry. *The Classic American Children's Story. Novels of the Golden Age*. New York: Penguin, 1996.

Gore, Ariel, and Bee Lavender. *Breeder: Real-Life Stories from the New Generation of Mothers*. Seattle, Wash.: Seal Press, 2001.

Greenway, Betty. *Aidan Chambers: Master Literary Choreographer*. Lanham, Md.: Scarecrow, 2006.

Grosz, Elizabeth. "The Body of Signification." In *Abjection, Melancholia and Love: The work of Julia Kristeva*, edited by John Fletcher John and Andrew Benjamin. London: Routledge, 1990.

Grosz, Elizabeth. *Volatile Bodies: Toward a Corporeal Feminism*. Bloomington: Indiana University Press, 1994.

Grosz, Elizabeth. "Animal Sex: Libido as Desire and Death." In *Sexy Bodies: The Strange Carnalities of Feminism*, edited by Elizabeth Grosz and Elspeth Probyn, 278–99. London: Routledge, 1995.

Gutnick, A. L., M. Robb, L. Takenchi, and J. Kotler. *Always Connected: The New Media Habits of Young Children*. New York: Joan Ganz Cooney Center and Sesame Street, 2010.

Haggerty, Richard. *Dominican Republic and Haiti: Country Studies*, 28. Washington D.C.: Library of Congress, 1989.

Hajdu, David. *The Ten-¢ent Plague: The Great Comic Book Scare and How it Changed America*. New York: Farrar, Straus and Giroux, 2008.

Hall, Granville Stanley. *Adolescence: Its Psychology and its Relations to Physiology, Anthropology, Sociology, Sex, Crime, Religion and Education*. 2 vols. New York: Appleton, 1904.

Happé, F.G.E. "The Role of Age and Verbal Ability in the Theory of Mind Task Performance of Subjects with Autism." *Child Development* 66 (1995): 843–55.

Hastings, Paul D., Carolyn Zahn-Waxler, and Keely McShane. "We Are, by Nature, Moral Creatures: Biological Bases of Concern for Others." In *Handbook of Moral Development*, edited by Lin Melanie Killen and Judith G. Smetana. Mahwah/London: Erlbaum, 2006.

Heath, Shirley Brice. *Words at Work and Play: Three Decades in Family and Community Life*. Cambridge: Cambridge University Press, 2011.

Hendershot Parkin, Rachel. "Breaking Faith: Disrupted Expectations and Ownership in Stephenie Meyer's Twilight Saga." *Jeunesse: Young People, Texts, Cultures* 2, no 2 (2010): 61–85.

Highberg, Nels P. "The (Missing) Faces of African American Girls with AIDS." *Feminist Formations* 22, no 1 (2010): 1–20.

Higonnet, Anne. *Pictures of Innocence: The History and Crisis of Ideal Childhood*. London: Thames & Hudson. 1998.

Hoffman, M.L. "Empathy, its Development and Prosocial-implications." In *Nebraska Symposium on Motivation Social Cognitive Development*, edited by H.E. Howe and C.B. Keasy, 169–217. Lincoln: University of Nebraska Press, 1977.

Hornigk, Therese, and Alexander Stephan, eds. *The New Sufferings of Young W. and Other Stories from the German Democratic Republic*. New York: Continuum, 1997.

Howell, Amanda. "'If we hear any inspirational power chords ... ': Rock Music, Rock Culture on *Buffy the Vampire Slayer*." *Continuum: Journal of Media & Cultural Studies* 18, no 3 (2004): 406–422.

Hruby, George. C., and Usha Goswami. "Neuroscience and Reading: A Review for Reading Education Researchers." *Reading Research Quarterly* 46, no 2 (2011): 156–72.

Hunt, Caroline C. "Counterparts: Identity Exchange and the Young Adult Audience." *Children's Literature Association Quarterly* 11, no. 3 (1986).

Hunt, Peter. *Children's Literature*. Oxford: Blackwell, 2001.

Ingvar, D. "Memory of the Future: An Essay on the Temporal Organization of Conscious Awareness." *Human Neurology* 4/3 (1998): 127–36.

Intons-Peterson, M.J. "Imaginal Priming." *Journal of Experimental Psychology: Learning, Memory and Cognition* 19, no 1(1993): 223–35.

James, Kathryn. *Death, Gender and Sexuality in Contemporary Adolescent Literature*. New York: Routledge, 2009.

Jenkins, Elwyn, and Elizabeth Muther, "Cross-Cultural Misreadings: MacCann and Maddy's *Apartheid and Racism* Revisited." *The Lion and The Unicorn* 32, no 3 (2008).

Johnson, Kelli Lyon. "Both Sides of the Massacre: Collective Memory and Narrative on Hispaniola." *Mosaic: A Journal for the Interdisciplinary Study of Literature* 36, no 2 (2003): 75–92.

Kapchan, Deborah, and Pauline Turner Strong. "Theorising the Hybrid." *The Journal of American Folklore* 112, no 445 (1999): 239–53.

Kaywell, Joan F., et al. "Growing Up Female Around the Globe with Young Adult Literature." *The ALAN Review* (Summer 2006): 62–69.

Kingsley Kent, Susan. *Aftershocks: Politics and Trauma in Britain, 1918–1914.* Basingstoke: Palgrave Macmillan, 2009.

Kokkola, Lydia. "Sapphire's 'Palpable Designs': Is *Push* too Pushy?" In *Literary Community-Making: The Dialogicality of English Texts from the Seventeenth Century to the Present edited by Roger D. Sell.* Amsterdam: John Benjamin, 2011.

Kokkola, Lydia. "Virtuous Vampires and Voluptuous Vamps: Romance Conventions Reconsidered in Stephenie Meyer's 'Twilight' Series." *Children's Literature in Education* 42, no 2 (2011): 165–79.

Kosslyn, S.M., W.L. Thompson, and G. Ganis. *The Case for Mental Imagery.* Oxford: Oxford University Press, 2006.

Kristeva, Julia. *The Powers of Horror: An Essay on Abjection.* New York: Columbia University Press, 1982.

Kristeva, Julia. "The Adolescent Novel." In her *Abjection, Melancholia and Love,* 8–23. London: Routledge, 1990.

Larson, Reed. "Secrets in the Bedroom: Adolescents' Private Use of Media." *Journal of Youth and Adolescence* 24, no 5 (1995): 535–50.

Latham, Don. *David Almond: Memory and Magic.* Lanham, Md.: Scarecrow, 2006.

Latour, B. "Visualization and Cognition: Thinking with Eyes and Hands." *Knowledge and Society* 6 (1986): 1–40.

Laz, Cheryl. "Act Your Age." *Sociological Forum* 13, no 1 (1998).

Le Guin, Ursula. *Essays on Fantasy and Science Fiction.* New York: Putnam, 1979.

Lévi-Strauss, Claude. *Tristes Tropiques.* Translated from the French by John and Doreen Weightman. London: Jonathan Cape, 1974.

Levitin, David J. *This is Your Brain on Music: The Science of a Human Obsession.* New York: Dutton, 2006.

Lieber, T.M. "Ralph Ellison and the Metaphor of Invisibility in the Black Literary Tradition." *American Quarterly* 24, no 1 (1972): 86–100.

Lüthi, Max. "The Fairy-Tale Hero: The Image of Man in the Fairy Tale." In *Folk & Fairy Tales,* edited by Martin Hallett and Barbara Karasek. 2nd ed. Peterborough, ON: Broadview Press, 1996.

Marx. Leo. *The Machine in the Garden: Technology and the Pastoral Ideal in America.* New York: Oxford University Press, 1964.

MacCann, Donnerae, and Yulisa Amadu Maddy. *Apartheid and Racism in South Africa Children's Literature, 1985–1995*. London: Routledge, 2001.

McBratney, John. *Imperial Subjects, Imperial Space: Rudyard Kipling's Fiction of the Native-Born*. Columbus: Ohio State University Press, 2002.

McClintock, Anne. *Imperial Leather. Race, Gender and Sexuality in the Colonial Context*. London: Routledge, 1995.

McCallum, Robyn. *Ideologies of Identity in Adolescent Fiction: The Dialogic Construction of Subjectivity*. New York: Garland, 1999.

McGillis, Roderick. *Voices of the Other. Children's Literature and the Postcolonial Context*. New York: Garland, 2000.

McKibbin, Ross. *Classes and Cultures: England 1918–1951*. Oxford: Oxford University Press, 1998.

McLeod, Anne Scott. "The Journey Inward: Adolescent Literature in America, 1945–1995." In *Considering Children's Literature: A Reader*, edited by Andrea Schwenke Wyile and Teya Rosenberg. Peterborough, ON: Broadview Press, 2008.

McRobbie, Angela, and Jenny Garber. "Girls and Subcultures: An Exploration." In *Resistance Through Rituals: Youth Culture in Postwar Britain*, edited by Stuart Hall and Tony Jefferson. New York: Routledge, 2003.

Meek, Margaret, and Watson, Victor. *Coming of Age in Children's Literature; Growth and Maturity in the Work of Philippa Pearce, Cynthia Voigt and Jan Mark*. London: Continuum, 2003.

Melman, Billie. *Women and the Popular Imagination in the Twenties: Flappers and Nymphs*. Basingstoke: Macmillan, 1988.

Meltzoff, A., P.K. Kuhl, J. Movellan, and T.J. Sejnowski. "Foundations for a New Science of Learning." *Science* 325 (2009): 284–89.

Merriman, W.E., and J.M. Marazita. "Young Children's Awareness of their own Lexical Ignorance: Relations to Word Mapping, Memory Processes, and Beliefs about Change." In *Thinking and Seeing: Visual Metacognition in Adults and Children*, edited by D.T. Levin, 57–74. Cambridge, Mass: MIT Press, 2004.

Morton, Timothy. *Ecology Without Nature*. Cambridge, Mass.: Harvard University Press, 2007.

Naidoo, Beverley. *Through Whose Eyes? Exploring Racism: Reader, Text and Context*. London: Trentham Books, 1992.

Nalbantian, Suzanne. *Memory in Literature from Rousseau to Neuroscience*. Basingstoke: Palgrave Macmillan, 2003.

Natov, Roni. *The Poetics of Childhood*. New York: Routledge, 2006.

Newton, Pauline T. *Transcultural Women of Late-Twentieth-Century U.S. American Literature: First-Generation Migrants from Islands and Peninsulas*. Aldershot: Ashgate, 2005.

Nikolajeva, Maria. *From Mythic to Linear: Time in Children's Literature*. Lanham, Md.: Scarecrow, 2000.

Nikolajeva, Maria. *Power, Voice and Subjectivity in Literature for Young People*. New York: Routledge, 2010.

Nilsen, Alleen Pace, and Kenneth Donelson. *Literature for Today's Young Adults*, 6th ed. New York: Longman, 2001.

Nodelman, Perry. "The Other: Orientalism, Colonialism, and Children's Literature." *Children's Literature Association Quarterly* 17, no 1 (1992): 29–35.

Nodelman, Perry. "Males Performing in Female Space: Music and Gender in Young Adult Novels." *The Lion & the Unicorn* 16, no 2 (1992).

Nodelman, Perry. *The Hidden Adult. Defining Children's Literature*. Baltimore: The John Hopkins University Press, 2008.

Parnafes, O. "Self-generated Representations for Promoting Conceptual Understanding." In *Proceedings of the Chais Conference on Instructional Technologies Research 2009*. Raanana: The Open University of Israel, 2009.

Pattee, Amy S. *Reading the Adolescent Romance: Sweet Valley and the popular Young Adult Romance Novel*. New York: Routledge, 2011.

Paus, T. "Mapping Brain Maturation and Cognitive Development During Adolescence." *Trends in Cognitive Sciences* 9, no 2 (2005): 60–68.

Paus. T, M. Keshavan, and J.N. Giedd. "Why Do So Many Psychiatric Disorders Emerge During Adolescence?" *Nature Reviews* (2008): 947–57.

Perfetti, C.A., and G.A. Frishkoff. "The Several Bases of Text and Discourse Processing." In *Handbook of the Neuroscience of Language*, edited by B. Stemmer and H.A. Whitaker, 165–74. Burlington, Mass.: Academic Press, 2008.

Pinsent, Pat. "Language, Genres and Issues: The Socially Committed Novel." *Modern Children's Literature: An Introduction*, edited by Kimberley Reynolds, 191–208. New York: Macmillan, 2005.

Plotz, Judith A. "The Empire of Youth: Crossing and Double-Crossing Cultural Barriers in Kipling's *Kim*." *Children's Literature* 20 (1992).

Plumwood, Val. *Environmental Culture: The Ecological Crisis of Reason*. London: Routledge, 2002.

Pope, Mary. "'I am NOT just like one of the family ... ': The Black Domestic Servant and White Family Dynamics in 20th Century American and South African Literature." *Safundi: The Journal of South African and American Comparative Studies* 7 (2001).

Pratt, Annis (with Barbara White, Andrea Loewenstein and Mary Wyer). *Archetypal Patterns in Women's Fiction*. Bloomington: Indiana University Press, 1981.

Pugh, Martin. *We Danced All Night: A Social History of Britain Between the Wars*. London: Vintage Books, 2009.

Quayson, Ato. *Postcolonialism. Theory, Practice or Politics?* Cambridge: Polity Press, 2000.

Radway, Janice. *Reading the Romance: Women, Patriarchy & Popular Literature*. Durham: University of North Carolina Press, 1984.

Ramachandran, V.S., and E.M. Hubbard, "Synaesthesia: A Window into Perception, Thought and Language." *Journal of Consciousness Studies* 12 (2001): 3–24.

Ramadas, J. "Visual and Spatial Modes in Science Learning." *International Journal of Science Education* 31, no 3 (2009): 301–318.

Regis, Pamela. *A Natural History of the Romance Novel*. Philadelphia: University of Pennsylvania Press, 2003.

Reynolds, Kimberley. *Radical Children's Literature. Future Visions and Aesthetic Transformations in Juvenile Fiction*. Basingstoke: Palgrave, 2007.

Roberts, Donald F., and Ulla G. Foehr. *Kids and Media in America*. Cambridge: Cambridge University Press, 2004.

Rose, Jacqueline. *The Case of Peter Pan or The Impossibility of Children's Fiction*. Philadelphia: University of Pennsylvania Press, 1993.

Rosenblum, Gianine, and Michael Lewis. "Emotional Development in Adolescence." In *Blackwell Handbook of Adolescence*, edited by Gerald R. Adams and Michael D. Berzonsky. London: Blackwell, 2003.

Russell, D.A. "The Common Experience of Adolescence: A Requisite for the Development of Young Adult Literature." *Journal of Youth Services in Libraries* 2 (1988).

Savage, Jon. *Teenage: The Creation of Youth Culture*. London: Chatto and Windus, 2007.

Scherz, R., and S. Oren. "How to Change Students' Images of Science and Technology." *Science Education* 90 (2008): 965–85.

Silver, Anna. "Twilight is Not Good for Maidens: Gender, Sexuality and the Family in Stephenie Meyer's Twilight Series." *Studies in the Novel* 42, nos 1&2 (2010): 121–38.

Smith, Katherine Capshaw. "Trauma and National Identity in Haitian-American Young Adult Literature." In *Ethnic Literary Traditions in American Children's Literature*, edited by Michelle Pagni Stewart and Yvonne Atkinson. New York: Palgrave Macmillan, 2009.

Speer, N.K., J.R. Reynolds, K.M. Swallow, and J.M. Zacks. "Reading Stories Activates Neural Representations of Visual and Motor Experiences." *Psychological Sciences* 20, no 8 (2009): 989–99.

Spivak, Gayatri. *A Critique of Postcolonial Reason: Towards a History of the Vanishing Present*. Cambridge, Mass.: Harvard University Press, 1999.

Stahl, J.D. "American Myth in European Disguise: Fathers and Sons in The Prince and the Pauper." *American Literature* 58, no 2 (1986).

Stewart, Susan Louise. "In the Ellison Tradition: In/Visible Bodies of Adolescent and YA Fiction." *Children's Literature in Education* 40 (2009): 180–96.

Steyn, Melissa. *"Whiteness Just Isn't What It Used To Be": White Identity in a Changing South Africa*. Albany: State University of New York Press, 2001.

Strickland, Charles. *Victorian Domesticity. Families in the Life and Art of Louisa May Alcott*. Tuscaloosa: University of Alabama Press, 1985.

Suwa, M., and B. Tversky. "What Architects and Students Perceive in their Sketches: A Protocol Analysis." *Design Studies* 18 (1997): 385–403.

Tagg, Philip. "An Anthropology of Stereotypes in TV Music?" *Swedish Musicological Journal* (1989): 19–42.

Thompson, Mary. "Third Wave Feminism and the Politics of Motherhood." *Genders OnLine Journal*. (2006)

Tooby, John, and Leda Cosmides. "Does Beauty Build Adapted Minds? Towards an Evolutionary Theory of Aesthetics, Fiction, and the Art." *SubStance. A Review of Theory and Literary Criticism* 30, nos 1 & 2 (2001): 6–27.

Trites, Roberta Seelinger. *Disturbing the Universe: Power and Repression in Adolescent Literature*. Iowa City: University of Iowa Press, 2000.

Trites, Roberta Seelinger. "The Harry Potter Novels as a Test Case for Adolescent Literature." *Style* 35, no 3 (2001): 472–85.

Trites, Roberta Seelinger. *Twain, Alcott, and the Birth of the Adolescent Reform Novel*. Iowa City: University of Iowa Press, 2007.

Uttal, D.H., and K. O'Doherty, "Comprehending and Learning from 'Visualization': A Developmental Perspective." In *Visualization: Theory and Practice in Science Education*, edited by J.K. Gilbert, M. Reiner, and M. Nakhleh, 53–72. London: Springer, 2008.

Vázquez, Ana María B., and Rosa E. Casas. *Cuba*. Chicago: Children's Press, 1994.

Vidal, África. "Resisting Through Hyphenation: The Ethics of Translating (Im)pure Texts." In *Border Transits: Literature and Culture Across the Line*, edited by Ana Maria Manzanas. Amsterdam: Rodopi, 2007.

Voss, Christiane: *Narrative Emotionen. Eine Untersuchung über Möglichkeiten und Grenzen philosophischer Emotionstheorien*. Berlin: de Gruyter, 2003.

Wall, Barbara. *The Narrator's Voice: The Dilemma of Children's Fiction*. London: Macmillan, 1992.

Waller, Alison. *Constructing Adolescence in Fantastic Realism*. New York: Routledge, 2009.

Wallis, Claudia. *The Impacts of Media Multitasking on Children's Learning and Development: Report from a Research Seminar*. New York: The Joan Ganz Cooney Center at Sesame Workshop, 2010.

Webb, Caroline. "'Change the Story, Change the World': Witches/Crones as Heroes in Novels by Terry Pratchett and Diana Wynne Jones." *Papers: Explorations into Children's Literature* 16, no 2 (2006).

Wilkie-Stibbs, Christine. *The Feminine Subject in Children's Literature*. New York: Routledge, 2002.

Wilkie-Stibbs, Christine. "The 'Other' Country: Memory, Voices, and Experiences of Colonized Childhoods." *Children's Literature Association Quarterly* 31, no 3 (2006): 237–59.

Williams, Raymond. *The Country and the City*. London: Chatto and Windus, 1973.

Young, Robert J.C. *The Colonial Desire*. London: Routledge, 1995.

Index